WOMEN IN THE ENGLISH NOVEL, 1800-1900

WOMEN IN THE ENGLISH NOVEL, 1800–1900

Merryn Williams

St. Martin's Press   New York

All rights reserved. For information, write:
St. Martin's Press, Inc., 175 Fifth Avenue, New York, NY 10010
Printed in Hong Kong
Published in the United Kingdom by The Macmillan Press Ltd.
First published in the United States of America in 1984

ISBN 0-312-88741-8

Library of Congress Cataloging in Publication Data
Williams, Merryn.
Women in the English novel, 1800-1900.
Bibliography: p.
Includes index.
1. English fiction—19th century—History and
criticism. 2. Women in literature. 3. English fiction—
Women authors—History and criticism. I. Title.
PR830.W6W54 1983   823'.8'09352042   83-16087
ISBN 0-312-88741-8

PR
830
.W6
W54
1984

To David and Rosalind

Contents

Introduction

The nineteenth century was a time when a very high number of great novels were written and the English novel came of age. It was also a time when more and more people were asking basic questions about women. Feminism was not invented in the twentieth century; it entered English literature with the work of Mary Wollstonecraft in the 1790s, disappeared for fifty years and then became an important strand of opinion in the second half of the nineteenth century. During the same period enormous changes were taking place in women's daily lives and they were steadily gaining more power and freedom. Novelists, like other people, were forced to define or redefine their attitudes.

'Now all the most important characters seem to be women,' wrote the critic E. S. Dallas in 1866. 'Our novelists have suddenly discovered that the feminine character is an unworked mine of wealth. . . . This is all the more natural, seeing that most of our novelists just now seem to belong to the fair sex. But their masculine rivals follow in the same track.' Around this time women novelists, of whom there had always been large numbers, established their right to be taken seriously, and the titles of many novels by men – *The Bride of Lammermoor, Little Dorrit, Portrait of a Lady, Diana of the Crossways, Tess of the d'Urbervilles, The Odd Women, Esther Waters* – reveal their serious interest in the role of women.

The aim of this book is to trace attitudes to women in the English novel between 1800 and 1900. Some of these attitudes seem outdated; others are still very much alive. It will be helpful, I hope, not only to students of the novels but also to those interested in the problems of women then and now.

Readers will notice that I have given a good deal of space to women novelists who are usually called minor. This is because I believe their work has been neglected for too long, and ought to be more widely known.

Chronology

1801   Maria Edgeworth, *Belinda*.
1802   Harriet Martineau born.
1803   Methodist conference banned women from preaching.
1805   Maria Edgeworth, *The Modern Griselda*.
1806   Maria Edgeworth, *Leonora*. J. S. Mill born.
1810   Elizabeth Gaskell born.
1811   Jane Austen, *Sense and Sensibility*. W. M. Thackeray born.
1812   Maria Edgeworth, *The Absentee*. Charles Dickens born.
1813   Jane Austen, *Pride and Prejudice*.
1814   Jane Austen, *Mansfield Park*. Walter Scott, *Waverley*.
1815   Scott, *Guy Mannering*. Anthony Trollope born.
1816   Jane Austen, *Emma*. Charlotte Brontë born.
1817   Scott, *Rob Roy*. Jane Austen died.
1818   Jane Austen, *Northanger Abbey* and *Persuasion*. Susan Ferrier, *Marriage*. Scott, *The Heart of Midlothian*. Shelley, *The Revolt of Islam*. Mary Shelley, *Frankenstein*. Emily Brontë born.
1819   Scott, *The Bride of Lammermoor* and *Ivanhoe*. George Eliot born.
1820   Florence Nightingale and Anne Brontë born.
1821   Scott, *Kenilworth* and *The Pirate*.
1822   Shelley died.
1823   Charlotte Yonge born.
1824   Susan Ferrier, *The Inheritance*. Wilkie Collins born.
1828   Josephine Butler, George Meredith and Margaret Oliphant born.
1831   Susan Ferrier, *Destiny*. Catherine Gore, *Mothers and Daughters*.
1832   Scott died.
1834   Bulwer Lytton, *The Last Days of Pompeii*. Maria Edgeworth, *Helen*.
1836   Catherine Gore, *Mrs. Armytage*.
1837   Accession of Queen Victoria.
1838   Dickens, *Oliver Twist*.

1839   Dickens, *Nicholas Nickleby*. Harriet Martineau, *Deerbrook*.
        Infants' Custody Act.
1840   Frances Trollope, *Michael Armstrong*. Thomas Hardy
        born.
1841   Governesses' Benevolent Institution founded.
1842   Mrs Ellis, *Daughters of England*. Mines Act.
1843   Mrs Hugo Reid, *A Plea for Women*. Association for the Aid
        of Milliners and Dressmakers. Henry James born.
1844   Factory Act.
1847   Anne Brontë, *Agnes Grey*. Charlotte Brontë, *Jane Eyre*.
        Emily Brontë, *Wuthering Heights*. Chloroform first used in
        childbirth.
1848   Anne Brontë, *The Tenant of Wildfell Hall*. Dickens,
        Dombey and Son. Mrs Gaskell, *Mary Barton*. Thackeray,
        Vanity Fair. Womens' Rights Association founded in US.
        Queen's College, London, founded. Emily Brontë died.
1849   Charlotte Brontë, *Shirley*. Bedford College founded. Anne
        Brontë and Maria Edgeworth died.
1850   Dickens, *David Copperfield*. Thackeray, *Pendennis*.
1851   *Westminster Review* published 'The Enfranchisement of
        Women'. Women's Suffrage Petition presented to House
        of Lords.
1852   Thackeray, *Henry Esmond*. George Moore born.
1853   Charlotte Brontë, *Villette*. Dickens, *Bleak House*. Mrs
        Gaskell, *Ruth* and *Cranford*. Charles Kingsley, *Hypatia*.
        Dinah Mulock (Craik), *Agatha's Husband*. Charlotte
        Yonge, *The Heir of Redclyffe*.
1854   Dickens, *Hard Times*. Charlotte Yonge, *Heartsease*.
        Florence Nightingale in the Crimea. Susan Ferrier died.
1855   Mrs Gaskell, *North and South*. Thackeray, *The Newcomes*.
        Trollope, *The Warden*. Charlotte Brontë died.
1856   Dinah Mulock (Craik), *John Halifax, Gentleman*. Charlotte
        Yonge, *The Daisy Chain*. Petition for a Married Woman's
        Property Act.
1857   Dickens, *Little Dorrit*. Mrs Gaskell, *The Life of Charlotte
        Brontë*. Trollope, *Barchester Towers*. *Englishwoman's Journal*
        and Women's Employment Bureau founded.
        Matrimonial Causes Act. George Gissing born.
1858   George Eliot, *Scenes of Clerical Life*.
1859   George Eliot, *Adam Bede*. George Meredith, *The Ordeal of
        Richard Feverel*.

1860   Wilkie Collins, *The Woman in White*. George Eliot, *The Mill on the Floss*.
1861   Dickens, *Great Expectations*. George Eliot, *Silas Marner*. Trollope, *Framley Parsonage*. Mrs Henry Wood, *East Lynne*. Catherine Gore died.
1862   M. E. Braddon, *Lady Audley's Secret*. Collins, *No Name*.
1863   George Eliot, *Romola*. Mrs Gaskell, *Sylvia's Lovers*. Margaret Oliphant, *The Doctor's Family*. Frances Trollope and Thackeray died.
1864   Trollope, *The Small House at Allington*.
1865   Ruskin, *Sesame and Lilies*. Trollope, *Can you Forgive Her?* Charlotte Yonge, *The Clever Woman of the Family*. Mrs Gaskell died.
1866   Wilkie Collins, *Armadale*. George Eliot, *Felix Holt*. Mrs Gaskell, *Wives and Daughters*. Margaret Oliphant, *Agnes* and *Miss Marjoribanks*.
1867   Trollope, *Last Chronicle of Barset*. J. S. Mill moved vote in Parliament on women's suffrage.
1868   Wilkie Collins, *The Moonstone*.
1869   R. D. Blackmore, *Lorna Doone*. Mill, *The Subjection of Women*. Girton College founded. Women ratepayers got the municipal vote.
1870   Trollope, *The Vicar of Bullhampton*. First Married Women's Property Act. Ladies' National Association for the repeal of the Contagious Diseases Acts founded. Dickens died.
1872   George Eliot, *Middlemarch*.
1873   Collins, *The New Magdalen*. Hardy, *A Pair of Blue Eyes*. Trollope, *The Eustace Diamonds*. Charlotte Yonge, *Pillars of the House*. Girls' Public Day School Trust founded. Mill died.
1874   Hardy, *Far from the Madding Crowd*.
1875   Trollope, *The Way We Live Now*.
1876   George Eliot, *Daniel Deronda*. Margaret Oliphant, *The Curate in Charge*. Charlotte Yonge, *Womankind*. Flora Thompson born. Harriet Martineau died.
1877   James, *The American*. Harriet Martineau, *Autobiography*.
1878   Hardy, *The Return of the Native*.
1879   James, *Daisy Miller*. Meredith, *The Egoist*. Trollope, *John Caldigate*.
1880   George Eliot died.

1881   James, *Washington Square, Portrait of a Lady.*

1882   Second Married Women's Property Act. Trollope died.

1883   Mrs Lynn Linton, *The Girl of the Period.* Olive Schreiner,
       Story of an African Farm. Margaret Oliphant, *The Ladies
       Lindores.*

1885   Meredith, *Diana of the Crossways.* Age of consent raised to
       sixteen.

1886   Hardy, *The Mayor of Casterbridge.* James, *The Bostonians.*
       Moore, *A Drama in Muslin.* Contagious Diseases Act
       repealed.

1887   Hardy, *The Woodlanders.*

1888   Mrs Humphrey Ward, *Robert Elsmere.*

1889   M. E. Braddon, *The Day Will Come. Nineteenth Century*
       published 'An Appeal against Female Suffrage'. Collins
       died.

1890   Margaret Oliphant, *Kirsteen.*

1891   Gissing, *New Grub Street.* Hardy, *Tess of the d'Urbervilles.*

1892   Gissing, *Denzil Quarrier, Born in Exile.*

1893   Gissing, *The Odd Women.* Sarah Grand, *The Heavenly
       Twins.*

1894   Meredith, *Lord Ormont and his Aminta.* Moore, *Esther
       Waters.* Mrs Humphry Ward, *Marcella.*

1895   Grant Allen, *The Woman Who Did.* Hardy, *Jude the Obscure.*

1897   Sarah Grand, *The Beth Book.* Henry James, *The Spoils of
       Poynton.* Margaret Oliphant died.

1899   Margaret Oliphant, *Autobiography and Letters.*

1 Women in Society and in the Novel

In the year 1800 British women had few rights, few opportunities, and only a handful ever found an independent voice. Although the first feminist essay, Mary Wollstonecraft's *Vindication of the Rights of Woman*, had appeared as early as 1792, it was ridiculed at the time; and for many years afterwards, except in extreme radical circles, there was very little interest in feminist ideas. The history of women in the nineteenth century shows hardly any change before the reign of Queen Victoria but much progress during it. A series of Acts of Parliament, all passed after 1837, removed most of their legal disabilities, so that by 1900, although they still had no votes, they were very much freer than they had been. Good schools and colleges for girls had begun to open and many more jobs were available. Women had begun to form their own organisations and it was widely accepted that they should take an active part in the world outside the home. There was an intense public debate, often raising issues which have emerged again in the twentieth century, about how women ought to live. 'There can be no doubt,' wrote an observer in 1892, 'that the modes of thought and of life of women of all classes have altered considerably, for good or for evil, in the last hundred years.'[1]

But, before that, there had been a great deal of unhappiness and frustration among better-educated women. Much of it found expression in the novels which they were beginning to write. While women were kept out of most professions, literature had always been open to them. Some of the earliest English novelists were women – the *Monthly Review* noted in 1773 that novels were 'almost entirely engrossed by the ladies'[2] – and in 1800 the best known British novelist was a woman, Maria Edgeworth. Women were the chief readers, as well as the chief writers of fiction, and perhaps that was why novels were widely despised

1

in the days of Fanny Burney and Jane Austen. Over the next hundred years, as the novel steadily gained more prestige, women in ever greater numbers went on writing.

It was 'the age of female novelists',[3] as Margaret Oliphant, herself a very talented novelist, wrote in 1855. They included four really great writers – Jane Austen, Charlotte Brontë, Emily Brontë, and George Eliot. Other women novelists who still find readers today were Susan Ferrier, Frances Trollope, Mary Shelley, Harriet Martineau, Elizabeth Gaskell, Dinah Mulock (Craik), Anne Brontë, Charlotte Yonge, M. E. Braddon, Mrs Henry Wood, Mrs Humphry Ward and Olive Schreiner. While most people – including many of these writers – still believed in the inferiority of women, it had to be admitted that they could do at least one thing as well as men.

It was not only as novelists that women began to emerge from 'that great darkness which had hitherto enveloped the history of the female sex'.[4] 'Queen Victoria's reign,' writes one historian, 'was remarkable for the outstanding woman in almost every line of life.'[5] They included poets (Elizabeth Barrett Browning and Christina Rossetti), philanthropists and social reformers (Elizabeth Fry, Mary Carpenter, Florence Nightingale, Angela Burdett-Coutts, Josephine Butler and Octavia Hill), travellers (Lady Hester Stanhope, Mary Kingsley and Amelia B. Edwards), and one distinguished scientist, Mary Somerville. But women still had to face enormous legal, social and cultural difficulties, and it is likely that many others, almost as gifted as their more famous sisters, 'lived faithfully a hidden life, and rest in unvisited tombs'.[6]

We shall look more closely in Chapter 2 at the climate of opinion which shaped the lives of most women, outstanding and average alike. But it can be said briefly that almost everyone assumed that women were the inferior sex, and that marriage was their natural destiny. Given these assumptions, it followed that they had all kinds of disadvantages. In 1800 they could not vote (the idea was not even discussed for another fifty years), and if they married they could not own property and had no right to the custody of their children. Middle-class girls could not mix freely with men before marriage; they met only the people whom their parents allowed them to meet and they could neither live nor travel alone. If we look closely at their position, we shall find that many of the rights which we now take for granted did not exist.

MARRIAGE AND CELIBACY

Women were then, as now, the majority of the population. At the time of the 1801 census they outnumbered men by about 400 000, and the gap widened until in 1901 there was an excess of one million women. The figures can be explained by the growth of emigration (the healthy young men were naturally the first to go abroad and, as Dickens noted in *David Copperfield*, women could easily get married in Australia) and by the fact that female children have always been more likely to survive than males. It is less easy to measure the effect on women's self-respect when they were constantly being told that they ought to get married, and yet for large numbers of them this was impossible. W. R. Greg, in the middle of the century, concluded that there was something very wrong in British society because 'there is an enormous and increasing number of single women in the nation, a number quite disproportionate and quite abnormal. . . . After twenty years of age we may state broadly that about 106 women are to be found for every 100 men.'[7] The figures fluctuated, but approximately 11–14 per cent of women and 10 per cent of men never married. Late marriages were common, often after long engagements as middle-class couples had to wait until they could afford to set up house. The censuses show that during the second half of the century two-thirds of women between twenty and twenty-four – well past the usual age of a Victorian heroine – were still single. Most of them married over the next few years and several thousand when over thirty-five. It was late enough for them to have spent years worrying about their chances of ever finding husbands.

One of the worst aspects of the situation was that a middle-class woman was usually unable to support herself and was therefore a dead weight on a middle-class man. He would have to put off marriage until he could maintain a wife, a staff of servants and several children. Mr Irwine in *Adam Bede* 'would very likely have taken a comely wife in his youth, and . . . would have had tall sons and blooming daughters' if he had not had to keep his mother and 'two hopelessly-maiden sisters'.[8] Trollope wrote that many men 'literally cannot marry for love, because their earnings will do no more than support themselves'.[9] This is the basis for one of the great central themes in the nineteenth-century novel, that of marriage for money versus marriage for love. Jane Austen, Thackeray and Trollope all wrote at length about mothers scheming for their daughters, penniless young men who are expected to marry money, and girls who come labelled with the amount of their fortune or are penalised because they have not got one.

It is impossible to say how many marriages of convenience there were, but novelists give the impression that they were very common. 'Women sell themselves for what you call an establishment every day, to the applause of themselves, their parents, and the world,'[10] wrote Thackeray in *The Newcomes,* a novel which is a long attack on the upper-class marriage market. Wilkie Collins agreed; hundreds of women 'marry men without being greatly attracted to them or greatly repelled by them', and 'learn to love them (when they don't learn to hate!) after marriage, instead of before'.[11] Non-literary evidence is harder to find, but we may note Charlotte Brontë's comments in a letter of 1848 on the Robinson girls, former pupils of her sister Anne. 'Not one spark of love does either of them profess for her future husband, one of them openly declares that interest alone guides her, and the other, poor thing! is acting according to her mother's wish, and is utterly indifferent herself to the man chosen for her'.[12] Whatever the average person may have thought of these marriages, novelists were unanimously against them.

Major Dobbin, in *Vanity Fair,* asserts that 'an honest woman . . . never is separated from her family',[13] and except in drastic circumstances this was almost always true for a middle-class girl. Failing marriage, she remained with her parents all their lives and perhaps spent her closing years with a brother or sister. One woman who suffered cruelly from spending her young adulthood cooped up at home, Florence Nightingale, wrote in 1852 that sons escaped from the 'sacred hearth' as soon as possible and daughters day-dreamed endlessly about getting away. 'Marriage is the only chance . . . offered to women for escape from this death; and how eagerly and how ignorantly it is embraced'.[14] Middle-class girls read a great many bad novels and derived false and sentimental ideas from them. 'It is only the made-up stories that end nicely,' says Lyndall in *The Story of an African Farm.*[15]

Women dreaded remaining single. 'In spite of shining examples of single life in every station, the unmarried woman, or old maid, was looked down upon with mixed pity and contempt.'[16] Around

Population of England and Wales (by sex), 1801–1901 (in thousands)

	Males	Females	Females per 1000 males
1801	4 255	4 638	1 057
1811	4 874	5 291	1 054
1821	5 850	6 150	1 036
1831	6 771	7 126	1 040
1841	7 778	8 137	1 046
1851	8 781	9 146	1 042
1861	9 776	10 290	1 053
1871	11 059	11 653	1 054
1881	12 640	13 335	1 055
1891	14 060	14 942	1 063
1901	15 729	16 799	1 068

the turn of the century Mary Clive met several kindly and interesting older women who had, inexplicably as it seemed, never married:

> The answer generally was that when she was young the fence round her had been too high . . . They were dragged home early from dances, made to refuse exciting invitations, and chaperoned as closely as though they were escapers from a reformatory. As a result the countryside was dotted with despairing Marianas in moated granges waiting for suitors who did not even know they existed, helplessly feeling their youth and prettiness slipping away and eventually turning from anxious captive maidens into resigned old maids . . .
>
> A further injustice was that it was assumed by almost everyone that until a girl was rescued by marriage she was her parents' chattel, and however brilliant or earnest she might be, it was her duty to grow grey at home, unpaid companion to a selfish, able-bodied pair who could do without her perfectly well if she had the excuse of a husband.[17]

Yet women might have grasped less eagerly at marriage if they had fully understood what it meant. An 'old maid' could not vote, but at least she had the right to her own earnings and property and was a reasonably free agent. But 'by marriage the very being or legal existence of a woman is suspended, or at least it is incorporated or consolidated into that of the husband'.[18] A wife was classed with lunatics, criminals and minors. It was very difficult for her to leave her husband, however badly he might treat her; in 1840 a judge upheld a man's right to lock up his wife, and even to beat her in moderation. Anne Brontë's Helen Huntingdon, fleeing from her husband in the 1820s, had to leave him in great secrecy and lived in fear of being brought back. Another judge, in 1852, ruled that a man might not force his wife to live with him, but for many years after that the position remained unclear. Gwendolen Grandcourt thought, perhaps mistakenly, that 'her husband would have power to compel her to return',[19] and Trollope's Lady Laura Kennedy had to live on the continent to be out of her husband's reach. In 1884, though, the Matrimonial Causes Act decreed that men did not have this right, and a judgement in 1891 protected women from being kidnapped by their husbands.

John Stuart Mill said in 1867 that men could use their wives as they liked – 'I should like to have a return laid before this House of the number of women who are annually beaten to death, kicked to death or trampled to death by their male protectors; and, in an opposite column, the amount of the sentences passed'.[20] It was generally thought that only working-class men could be so brutal, but modern experience suggests that wife-battering happens in all classes, and George Eliot showed a violent middle-class marriage in *Janet's Repentance*.

Married women owned nothing, although the rich usually made marriage settlements for their daughters so that the children could inherit the money. As soon as a woman became engaged – and engagements were a very serious commitment in the nineteenth century – she lost her right to dispose of her property without her future husband's consent. Even her own earnings did not belong to her; her husband, even if he no longer lived with her, could take them all. In 1857 the Matrimonial Causes Act gave a legally separated wife the right to keep what she earned, and in 1870, after many years of campaigning, the first Married Women's Property Act became law. A later Act in 1882 gave them complete control of their incomes.

Throughout the nineteenth century the father was considered the natural guardian of a legitimate child. Before 1839 he could take his children from their mother (giving them to his mistress, if he liked) and she would not necessarily be allowed to see them. Caroline Norton (1808–77) found herself in this position when her estranged husband kept her three children away from her for several years. But she was a determined and articulate woman, though no feminist, and her pamphlet, 'The Natural Claims of a Mother to the Custody of her Child' (1837), helped to change the climate of opinion and led to the Infants' Custody Act of 1839. This made it possible for a mother to be given custody of her children under seven, and to visit the older ones, and in 1873 the courts were empowered to grant her custody of children under sixteen. But she had no automatic right to see them, particularly not if she was even suspected of adultery. 'When a married woman has followers and the husband don't go to the wrong side of the post too, or it ain't proved again him that he do, they'll never let her have nothing to do with the children',[21] says a character in Trollope's *He Knew He Was Right*. This novel shows how a man can take a child away from his mother (who has *not* had followers, in fact) and how she is absolutely helpless.

Divorce was impossible before 1857 except by a private Act of Parliament, which only the very rich could afford. Thus a Mr Rushworth or a Barnes Newcome could obtain a divorce without difficulty but it was out of the question for an ordinary person (e.g. Stephen Blackpool in *Hard Times*). The Matrimonial Causes Act of 1857 enabled any man to divorce his wife for adultery, but a woman had to prove adultery aggravated by other circumstances, such as cruelty or desertion. It is unusual for nineteenth-century novelists to show a wife obtaining a divorce. In *The Woodlanders*, Grace Fitzpiers tries to use the 'new law' to divorce her husband for adultery, but is told 'He has not done you *enough* harm! You are still subject to his beck and call.'[22]

The law only reflected the state of public opinion. A respectable woman was totally damned if she was known to have had a lover, but men were expected to do as they liked, and while middle-class girls were carefully protected a working-class woman was fair game. Novels (e.g. *Mary Barton*) constantly warn working girls not to trust 'gentlemen'. Edgar Tryan in *Janet's Repentance* confesses, 'At college I had an attachment to a lovely girl of seventeen; she was very much below my station in life, and I never contemplated marrying her; but I induced her to leave her father's house'.[23] (Predictably for a novel, the girl becomes a prostitute and dies.) According to Emerson, Dickens said in 1848 that 'chastity in the male sex was as good as gone in our times', and that 'if his own son were particularly chaste, he should be alarmed'.[24] This points to a deep split between public and private attitudes, as virtually all novels, including Dickens' own, took the view that loss of chastity was the worst thing that could happen to a woman and that the man had behaved despicably. There were very large numbers of prostitutes, especially in London, partly because the middle-class custom of late marriage encouraged irregular relationships and partly because women workers often could not earn a living wage. Incidentally, between 1880 and 1900, fifteen hundred babies died every year of venereal disease.

Even the happiest marriages brought their own perils for women. Childbirth was not only very painful (one of the first women to have chloroform in labour was Queen Victoria, in 1853, despite hostility from people who thought that the Bible commanded women to suffer) but was also dangerous. Thousands of women died around the time of birth, and there were other pregnancy-related diseases. Charlotte Brontë died in 1855 of hyperemesis gravidarum, a severe form of morning sickness which made it impossible for her to carry her baby to term.[25] Thackeray's wife Isabella became insane after the birth of their third child and spent the rest of her life in care. Almost certainly she was suffering from what we would now call post-natal depression, which the Victorians scarcely understood and could not treat.[26]

Contraception was practised throughout the century (Mill was jailed in 1823 for distributing pamphlets on birth control) but not widely. From the 1870s onwards the middle classes began to have distinctly fewer children – while working-class families remained large – and in 1889 Grant Allen noted the existence of small groups of 'advanced' women who did not want children at all.[27]

A great many children died, and there was not much improvement before the twentieth century. (In 1839, the first year for which we have statistics, 151 of every thousand babies born alive in England and Wales died before their first birthday, and in 1900 the figure was 154.) Since married women had on average five or six children the chances that they would lose at least one were very high.[28] This was so much taken for granted that Charlotte Brontë could write in *Villette* that the Brettons have an unusually happy life and 'no excessive suffering' although one of their children dies.[29] It appeared a minor sorrow, but perhaps only to the childless. Mrs Gaskell, Mrs Oliphant and Josephine Butler, who all lost children, all left written records of their grief.

WORK AND EDUCATION

The typical heroine of a nineteenth-century novel is a girl without a job. She may do charitable work, or nurse and educate the older and younger members of her family, but it is fairly unusual for her to be in the labour market. The middle classes saw women's work as 'a misfortune and a disgrace'.[30] Tom Tulliver will not let Maggie take in plain sewing to help the family pay its debts because 'I don't like *my* sister to do such things. . . . *I'll* take care that the debts are paid, without your lowering yourself in that way.'[31]

The life of the average girl at home was restricted and trivial. Around the beginning of the century the women in better-off families had given up doing housework and had been left with a good deal of time on their hands. Girls might study at home, in an unsystematic way, or they might be sent away to schools which often did no more than groom them for marriage. When they came out in mixed company they were expected to be 'accomplished', that is to sing and play the piano, draw, speak French and fill their time with a host of useless activities. 'They all paint tables, cover screens and net purses,'[32] says Bingley in *Pride and Prejudice* of the typical 'accomplished' young girl. In 1868 the report of the Schools Enquiry Commission found that there had been little real change since the days of Jane Austen:

> The picture brought before us of the state of the middle-class female education is, on the whole, unfavourable . . . We have had much evidence showing the general indifference of parents to girls' education, both in itself and as compared to that of boys . . . There is a long-established and inveterate prejudice . . . that girls are less capable of mental cultivation, and less in need of it than boys; that accomplishments and what is showy and superficially attractive are what is really essential for them; and in particular that, as regards their relations to the other sex, and the probabilities of marriage, more solid attainments are actually disadvantageous.

'I have been astonished in my association with young ladies,' wrote Sarah Ellis, who published several popular books of advice for women in the 1840s, 'at the very few things they appear to have to think about . . . The consequence too frequently is, that they grow weary of themselves, then weary of others, and lastly

weary of life.'[33] Although they had no real work there were
constant small distractions which led Florence Nightingale to
complain that women 'never have an half-hour in all their lives
. . . that they can call their own . . . Women are never supposed
to have any occupation of sufficient importance *not* to be
interrupted . . . They have accustomed themselves to consider
intellectual occupation as merely selfish amusement, which it is
their ''duty'' to give up for every trifler more selfish than
themselves.'[34] She herself managed to find a vocation and a few
other exceptional women who could write, act, paint or sing
sometimes made a career. But the vast majority were taught and
believed that this was not in their power, nor was it even
desirable. Man is 'the doer, the creator, the discoverer', said
Ruskin, while a woman's intellect 'is not for invention or
creation, but for sweet ordering, arrangement and decision',[35] –
meaning that it was a woman's job to keep a nice home for a man.
Dickens' good housekeepers, Agnes Wickfield and Esther
Summerson, are contrasted with Dora Copperfield who is too
feather-headed to run David's home efficiently. This was thought
to be appropriate work for women whether they got married or
not; they might be expected to keep house for a widowed father or
an unmarried brother because there was nothing more valuable
they could do.

There were many attacks on women working outside the home.
It was said that they neglected their children, were debauched by
the male workers and never learned to run a house. The great
majority of these workers were herded into the least satisfying
jobs. The 1841 population returns show them falling into five
main categories – servants (this was by far the largest group),
factory workers, needlewomen, agricultural labourers and
workers in the domestic industries. Harriet Taylor, who later
married Mill and had an enormous influence on him, wrote in
1848 that women were enslaved 'to modes of earning their living
which (with the sole exception of artists) consist only of poorly
paid and hardly worked occupations, all the professions,
mercantile clerical legal and medical, as well as all government
posts being monopolised by men'.[36]

'Of all wage-earning heroines in early nineteenth-century
literature the governess occupied by far the most conspicuous
place.'[37] An educated girl forced to earn her living had virtually
no other options, and she attracted a great deal of sympathy. Jane

Austen, who is famous for her silence on most public issues, spoke out with extraordinary violence in *Emma* where Jane Fairfax compares the hiring of governesses to the slave trade. In the middle of the century there were well over twenty thousand governesses, the supply exceeding the demand. They were usually ill-paid – sometimes getting only their board – and the novels of Anne and Charlotte Brontë vividly show their loneliness and their bad treatment. Elizabeth Rigby, in her famous review of *Jane Eyre* and *Vanity Fair* (both novels about governesses), quoted several sad examples of how they struggled to fulfil their responsibilities to their families – 'Obliged to maintain an aged sister, who has no one else to depend upon'; 'Entirely impoverished by endeavouring to uphold her father's efforts in business'; 'Supported both her aged parents, and three orphans of a widowed sister'; 'Has helped to bring up seven younger brothers and sisters'.[38] Many of them were left destitute when they grew too old to work and an unusually high proportion became insane.

At the beginning of the century unskilled women worked side by side with unskilled men. Until women and children were excluded from the mines in 1842 they worked, and sometimes gave birth, underground. Disraeli described the wretched conditions of these women and was shocked by the coarseness he heard 'from lips born to breathe words of sweetness'.[39] The Factory Acts of 1847 and 1850 restricted them to a ten-and-a-half hour day. For many years after that they continued to work on the land in all weathers, as portrayed by Hardy in *Tess of the d'Urbervilles,* although by the end of the century women land workers had almost disappeared.

'The root of women's manual employments,' wrote Dinah Mulock in 1857, 'is undoubtedly the use of the needle.'[40] Countless women did sewing at home for money, or worked outside the home like Little Dorrit who 'let herself out to do needlework'.[41] Then there were the slop-workers or makers of cheap clothes – 'You may see the poor creatures clustering about the doors of the slop-shops, with their sharp eager faces waiting for their supply of wretched work, as though their very lives depended upon the issue,'[42] wrote one observer – and the girls who worked for eighteen hours a day in the London season to make ball dresses for their better-off sisters. Women were still exploiting women in this way in 1894, when Blatchford wrote, 'I believe it is a literal fact that many of the artificial flowers worn at court, are actually stained with the tears of the famished and exhausted girls who make them'.[43]

Writers showed the greatest sympathy for all these women. Thomas Hood's poem, 'The Song of the Shirt', about slop-workers, caused a sensation when it appeared in 1843. Among novelists, Mrs Gaskell wrote the most realistically and thoroughly about women workers, particularly in the clothing and textile trades. Bessy Higgins, in *North and South*, is killed by the conditions in the cotton mill where she works:

> 'Fluff,' repeated Bessy. 'Little bits, as fly off fro' the cotton, when they're carding it, and fill the air till it looks all fine white dust. They say it winds round the lungs, and tightens them up. Anyhow, there's many a one as works in a carding-room, that falls into a waste, coughing and spitting blood, because they're just poisoned by the fluff.'[44]

In the early, perhaps the most interesting chapters of *Ruth*, Mrs Gaskell shows a group of dressmaker's apprentices working until 2 a.m. – 'stay up as late as they might, the work-hours of the next day must begin at eight'– and then being turned out of the house on Sundays. She argues that Ruth would not have been seduced if her employer had looked after her properly, and this theme recurs in much of the writing about dressmakers. The fact was that many of them could not live on their wages and turned to part-time prostitution. Some had to come home late at night and were thus exposed to risks never faced by a middle-class girl.

Very few novelists showed any sympathy for, or interest in, servants. Yet it is worth remembering that, except where factories offered alternative work, the majority of working-class women (13 per cent of all women in 1851) were servants of some sort for at least a few years of their lives. 'The home', a woman's natural place, could only be preserved by having other women leave their homes as soon as they were old enough to work. Flora Thompson, growing up in an Oxfordshire village in the 1880s, describes how girls of eleven or twelve were pushed out of their overcrowded homes to 'go into service'. 'The unselfish generosity of these poor girls was astonishing',[45] for they sent back large slices of their wages to their parents. Novelists could hardly help mentioning servants, as no middle-class family was without them, but they are usually there only to open doors and bring tea. Dickens, whose grandparents had been servants, wrote very sympathetically in *The Old Curiosity Shop* about the Marchioness, a little drudge who 'must have been at work from her cradle'.[46] He even made her marry a gentleman in the end, but he did not expect his readers to weep over her as they did over the more refined Little Nell. This convention, like so many others, only began to change towards the end of the century, when Moore, in *Esther Waters*, was able to see that an illiterate servant girl could be a heroic woman.

WOMEN WRITERS

One group of women workers deserving special attention are writers, for we have already seen that they were important. 'Women writers' usually means women poets or novelists; they did not often write textbooks except on distinctively feminine subjects, like Isabella Beeton's famous and popular *Book of Household Management* (1861). 'The number of youthful novelists, and of young lady novelists, extant at this moment passes calculation, and was unparalleled at any former epoch,' W. R. Greg noted in 1859. 'Indeed, the supply of the fiction market has mainly fallen into their hands.'[47] Mrs Lynn Linton wrote some years later that women were 'almost the monopolists of the whole section of light literature and fiction'.[48]

It has been calculated that women wrote about 20 per cent of all books published in the nineteenth century, but about half of published novelists were women, and so were two-thirds of writers whose novels were not accepted.[49] This suggests that writing fitted in fairly easily with a middle-class woman's way of life. She did not have to go out to work, and above a certain income bracket she had a husband or father to pay her bills and a staff of servants to look after her children and house. George Eliot, who disapproved of most women novelists, thought that for each one who wrote because she needed the money there were three who wrote to please themselves. Some of them, such as Frances Trollope and Margaret Oliphant, supported husbands, children and other relations on their earnings. If they were lucky enough to become established authors they could earn a steady income, even if they did not write a best-seller like *Adam Bede* or, on a lower level, *East Lynne*. Literature was one of the few professions which granted equality to women, and female novelists and journalists were always paid on the same terms as men.

But although there were great opportunities for a woman writer there were also great problems. Novels known to be by a woman were unlikely to be taken seriously, and for this reason many of them felt it wise to adopt a male pseudonym, like George Eliot or Currer Bell. Critics often speculated about the sex of a novelist and felt free to rebuke her for being unfeminine. Charlotte Brontë, who suffered more than most women from this accusation, wrote to one of her critics, G. H. Lewes,

> I wish all reviewers believed 'Currer Bell' to be a man; they would be more just to him. You will, I know, keep measuring me by some standard of what you deem becoming to my sex; where I am not what you consider graceful you will condemn me . . . Come what will, I cannot, when I write, think always of myself and of what is elegant and charming in femininity; it is not on those terms, and with such ideas, I ever took pen in hand: and if it is only on such terms my writing will be tolerated, I shall pass away from the public and trouble it no more.[50]

'Literature cannot be the business of a woman's life, and it ought not to be,' Southey had told Charlotte when she sent him some of her early poems. 'The more she is engaged in her proper duties, the less leisure will she have for it, even as an accomplishment and a recreation.'[51] Although a woman writer might be physically and emotionally supported by her family, it could also get in her way. Relations felt free to meddle with her work; Charlotte Yonge's grandmother tried to stop her publishing her first novel and only yielded on condition that she gave any profits to charity, and Maria Edgeworth's father constantly tried to 'improve' her books. Miss Edgeworth was the eldest daughter in a family of twenty and had to write in the sitting-room as well as caring for little brothers and sisters. Frances Trollope got up at four to write when she was nursing her dying husband and children. Mrs Gaskell, one of the few who managed to be both a serious novelist and a mother, described the conflict which most women writers faced:

When a man becomes an author, it is probably merely a change of employment to him . . . another merchant or lawyer, or doctor, steps into his vacant place, and probably does as well as he. But no other can take up the quiet, regular duties of the daughter, the wife and the mother, as well as she whom God has appointed to fill that particular place; a woman's principal work in life is hardly left to her own choice; nor can she drop the domestic charges devolving on her as an individual, for the exercise of the most splendid talents that were ever bestowed. And yet she must not shrink from the extra responsibility implied by the very fact of her possessing such talents. She must not hide her gift in a napkin; it was meant for the use and service of others. In a humble and faithful spirit must she labour to do what is not impossible, or God would not have set her to do it.[52]

Mrs Gaskell herself found her double life a strain; her biographer suggests that 'this sense of being frequently drawn in opposite directions was in large measure responsible for her untimely death'.[53] 'One thing is pretty clear', she wrote, '*women must give up living an artist's life, if home duties are to be paramount*',[54] and she explained in a long and kind letter to an unknown female scribbler that she had found it impossible to write when her children were little and believed that her family must always come first.[55] The quality of a woman writer's work could suffer when she tried to do too much. Margaret Oliphant was already writing one or two books a year to support her children when her brother's family was ruined and appealed to her for help:

I remember making a kind of pretence to myself that I had to think it over, to make a great decision, to give up what hopes I might have had of doing now my very best, and to set myself steadily to make as much money as I could . . . I don't think, however, that there was any reality in it. I never did nor could, of course, hesitate for a moment as to what had to be done.[56]

Perhaps it is significant that the four really great women novelists of the nineteenth century – Jane Austen, the two Brontës and George Eliot – were all childless and married late or not at all. But all of them felt responsible as daughters for helping in the family home. 'Composition seems to me impossible with a head full of joints of mutton and doses of rhubarb,' Jane Austen wrote at a time of stress.[57] Emily Brontë baked bread and did a good deal of heavy housework. Charlotte, at the height of her fame, spent weeks nursing the old servant Tabby and her father, 'all her care was to discharge her household and filial duties, so as to obtain leisure to sit down and write'.[58] George Eliot began her career when she was over thirty, having stayed at home and looked after her father (she is said to have been a devoted nurse and housekeeper) till he died. As in their novels, so in their personal lives we find the conviction that a woman cannot think first of herself.

NEW OPENINGS

During the 1840s people concerned with the plight of single women began to talk seriously about training them for a career. By this time there was great sympathy for governesses, and it was recognised that they were badly paid because they were not properly trained. Queen's College, intended for girls who hoped to teach, was opened in 1848, and Bedford College in the following year. In 1857 a group of feminists founded their own employment bureau, which developed into the Association for the Promotion of the Employment of Women. In the same year a thoughtful article in the *North British Review* said:

> This is the great cardinal error of our system. High and low, it is all the same. Instead of educating every girl as though she were born to be an independent, self-supporting member of society, we educate her to become a mere dependant, a hanger-on, or, as the law delicately phrases it, a *chattel*. We bring up our women to be dependent, and then leave them without anyone to depend on.[59]

Even in the workhouse, pauper boys were taught a trade while the girls only learned to read, write, sew and scrub floors. But when women tried, as they increasingly did in the second half of the century, to do jobs which had always been reserved for men there was bitter opposition. They were excluded from the Trades Union Congress for many years and we find such diverse groups as watchmakers, Post Office workers and schoolmasters all objecting to the employment of women on equal terms with themselves. Women were not able to qualify as doctors in Britain until the late 1870s, after a long struggle, and the Church and legal profession continued to bar them from men's work. On the other hand, the numbers of women teachers and trained nurses grew rapidly. The last forty years of the century saw a great increase of women shop assistants, telegraphists, clerks and secretaries, most of them unmarried girls living at home. In 1876 it was noted that 'there is much less every year of the fear of losing caste by absolute labour',[60] and this went on being true.

Ruskin in 1865 had said that of course a woman should be educated, but 'only so far as may enable her to sympathise in her husband's pleasures, and in those of his best friends'.[61] However, more and more people were beginning to realise that a girl needed a thorough education rather than a string of 'accomplishments'. The pioneers in this field were Frances Mary Buss (1827–94), who founded the North London Collegiate School in 1850, and Dorothea Beale (1831–1906) who became the principal of Cheltenham Ladies' College in 1858. The Girls' Public Day School Trust, founded in 1873, started several good and cheap schools. Meanwhile Emily Davies (1830–1921), a feminist who was particularly interested in education, founded what was later called Girton College in 1869. It was followed in the 1870s by Newnham, Somerville and Lady Margaret Hall. Although women students were not recognised as full members of Oxford and Cambridge universities, they were allowed to take the same examinations as the men and did extremely well.

Although many who supported higher education for women did not support the suffrage, the movement undoubtedly helped women to become more independent. By the end of the century more and more girls were leaving their homes and travelling alone to study or attend classes. Some novelists who disliked this new trend complained that girl students were working themselves into nervous breakdowns, and would not be fit to be wives and mothers.[62]

THE BEGINNINGS OF CHANGE

The question of women's rights was discussed in public for a few

women's rights

years after the death of Mary Wollstonecraft, in 1797, and then it
lapsed. One of the few writers to take it seriously was Shelley,
who was married to Mary Wollstonecraft's daughter. 'Can Man
be free if Woman be a slave?' he asked in *The Revolt of Islam*
(1818). In the 1830s some Chartists supported the principle of
votes for women, and in 1843 *A Plea for Women*, by Mrs Hugo
Reid, aroused some interest, although it is significant that the
author, like many women writers, preferred to sink her own
identity in her husband's name. But the issue still remained
outside the mainstream of political and intellectual life.

In July 1851, the *Westminster Review* published an article, 'The
Enfranchisement of Women', which called for full equality
between the sexes. Written by Harriet Taylor, it pointed out that
people would find it difficult to accept this idea because they had
never heard of it before, and the 'strongest of prejudices' was 'the
prejudice against what is new and unknown'. By this time there
was a flourishing women's rights movement in the United States.
Two women who read the article and were impressed by some of
its arguments were Elizabeth Gaskell and her friend Charlotte
Brontë. But neither of them could completely accept it; Charlotte
felt that the author must be 'a woman who longed for power, and
had never felt affection', and who 'forgets there is such a thing as
self-sacrificing love and disinterested devotion'.[63] In the years to
come the argument that women would become less good and
loving if they agitated for their rights would be heard over and
over again.

The movement is mentioned in the last chapter of *Bleak House*
(1853), where Mrs Jellyby, who neglects her husband and
children for various 'causes' of doubtful value, 'has taken up with
the rights of women to sit in parliament'. There is no doubt that
Dickens expected his readers, male and female, to find this
supremely ridiculous. But the cause made steady progress over
the next few decades until educated people, including novelists,
were forced to take it seriously. In 1867 Lady Frederick
Cavendish noted, disapprovingly, that female suffrage was
'beginning to be spoken of without laughter'.[64] Trollope's later
novels contain several references to women who are suspected of
'going in for' or 'taking up' women's rights, a position which still
seems extreme, but no longer absurd. Alice in *Can You Forgive Her*
(1865) is one of these discontented women, although 'she was not
so far advanced as to think that women should be lawyers or

doctors, or to wish that she might have the privilege of the franchise for herself'. But she cannot accept that her destiny is to be merely the wife of a country gentleman, and she is haunted by the question, 'What should a woman do with her life?'.[65]

'From England, Scotland, Sweden, America and other parts of the civilised world' (said the 1857 article in the *North British Review*) 'come utterances, more or less articulate and intelligible . . . all starting with a general recognition of the fact, that there is "something wanting", and tending to the common assurance that "something must be done" to supply the want.' The first organised campaign by women, for a Married Women's Property Act, began in the mid-1850s and was finally won in 1882. Another very important campaign, which did not succeed until the twentieth century, was the agitation for the vote. The feminists had the influential backing of J. S. Mill, who in 1867 raised the question for the first time in Parliament and examined the philosophical arguments in *The Subjection of Women* (1869). By this time a London National Society for Women's Suffrage had been founded and over the next thirty years, while women in practice got more and more freedom, the cause steadily gathered support.

Inevitably, not all women agreed. Queen Victoria wrote privately in 1870:

The Queen is most anxious to enlist everyone who can speak or write to join in checking this mad, wicked folly of 'Women's Rights', with all its attendant horrors, on which her poor feeble sex is bent, forgetting every sense of womanly feeling and propriety . . . God created men and women different – then let them remain each in their own position . . . Woman would become the most hateful, heartless and disgusting of human beings were she allowed to unsex herself, and where would be the protection which man was intended to give the weaker sex?[66]

In 1889 more than a hundred well-known women published an 'Appeal against Female Suffrage'. Two of their arguments are particularly interesting; that there was a danger that women 'leading an immoral life' might get the vote and that women's true sphere was 'the care of the sick and the insane; the treatment of the poor; the education of children'.[67] Other kinds of work, particularly warfare, belonged to men, and if they led an immoral life that did not much matter.

Feminists were split over another campaign which marked the entry of women in great numbers into the nation's political life. The Ladies' National Association for the Repeal of the Contagious Diseases Acts was founded in 1870 by Josephine Butler (1828–1906). These Acts, passed during the 1860s, made women living in certain garrison towns liable to be declared common prostitutes and forcibly examined for venereal disease. Many women felt that this not only attacked their personal freedom but also legalised the double standard, because the Acts assumed that soldiers and sailors would go to prostitutes but punished only the women, not the men. The campaign went on until the Acts were repealed in 1886. To the Victorians, unaccustomed to hearing women speak in public at all, it was doubly shocking for them to speak about 'a subject on which all respectable and decent women must of necessity be totally ignorant',[68] and for this reason many feminists kept away from Mrs Butler's campaign. It is important to realise that the women campaigners of this generation tended to be puritanical and wanted men to accept the sexual standard which had long been compulsory for middle-class women. Pressure from Mrs Butler and others against the prostitution of young girls led in 1885 to the Criminal Law Amendment Act, which raised the age of consent from twelve to sixteen.

Less spectacular changes were happening at about the same time. In 1869 women ratepayers got the municipal vote and gradually they won the right to become Poor Law Guardians and to sit on school boards. The two main parties started their own organisations for Liberal and Conservative women and the Women's Protective and Provident League, for organised workers, was founded by Emma Patterson in 1875. It became increasingly difficult to argue that women's place was in the home when they were visibly involved in civic life.

It is interesting to read the views of a conservative critic, Charlotte Yonge, on the situation in the 1870s. She thought that girls by this time had 'a much freer, bolder life . . . travelling alone is hardly doubted about'. There were many aspects of this new freedom which she thoroughly disliked – the custom of girls 'enjoying cigarettes', for instance, or reading novels which tampered with 'dilemmas about the marriage vow', or even 'openly taking up causes of which their parents are known to disapprove'. Insubordination seemed to her the most serious problem – 'Some clergymen say that they find brides trying to slur over the word obey; and the advanced school are said to prefer a civil marriage because it can thus be avoided'.[69] Yet she was not opposed to all the new things which were happening; in her novel *Pillars of the House* (1873) Robina, though not 'going in for women's rights', prefers to continue working as a governess and saving up to get married rather than let her brother support her. By 1889 a man was 'no longer expected, even in well-to-do middle-class society, to support his adult sisters and daughters as well as his wife and infant children'.[70] Smaller changes also helped women to become emancipated. Bicycles, widely used in the 1890s, enabled them to travel alone. The incredibly restrictive and time-consuming outfits which women had had to wear for decades were gradually adapted so that they could walk freely, and it was argued that 'a woman should have the full use of her limbs, lungs, heart and every other organ and muscle, so that life might be a pleasure to her and not a continual exertion'.[71] An observer said of the girl of the 1890s that 'her mind and character are strung up to a firmness of which a sentimental heroine of fifty years ago would have been ashamed'.[72]

In the 1880s and 1890s the fact that 'the woman question' was being debated everywhere meant that many things could be discussed in fiction which had once been taboo. More and more writers attacked the double standard and occasionally marriage itself. The emphasis shifted away from the girl living at home with her family and towards the girl as an independent citizen. As the century closed an increasing number of people were asking the question, 'What should a woman do with her life?' and there was no longer a single obvious answer.

2 Ideology and the Novel

Practically everyone born in the nineteenth century believed that men were the superior sex. This was accepted even by women like Mrs Norton who fought very hard to improve the condition of their own sex; she wrote in 1855 that she had 'never pretended to the wild and ridiculous doctrine of equality'.[1] Anna Jameson, one of the first people to argue for women's right to do meaningful work, wrote 'The intellect of woman bears the same relation to that of man as her physical organisation; it is inferior in power, and different in kind'.[2] Of course this attitude existed long before 1800 – it would be difficult to say exactly how old it is – and can be found in the earliest English novels. Sophia, the lovely and virtuous heroine of *Tom Jones* (1749), is a good starting-point, for she sets the pattern for generations of later heroines. She is chaste, unlike the man she marries; with one important exception she does everything her father wishes, and best of all she has no strong opinions of her own but 'always shewed the highest deference to the understanding of men; a quality absolutely essential to the making of a good wife'.[3] This is certainly a man's version of the perfect woman, but it is important to realise that most women did not disagree.

Women were considered not only inferior to men, but also very different. The purpose of their lives was marriage, and their proper sphere was the home, while men had all the rest of the world to exercise their talents. One of the few challenges to this assumption before the 1850s came in Bulwer Lytton's novel, *The Last Days of Pompeii* (1834). The heroine, Ione, pleads:

> Alas! – is it only to be among *men* that freedom and virtue are to be deemed united? Why should the slavery that destroys you be considered the only method to preserve us? Ah! believe me, it has been the great error of men – and one that has worked bitterly on their destinies – to imagine that the nature of

woman is (I will not say inferior, that may be so, but) so different from their own, in making laws unfavourable to the intellectual advancement of women. Have they not, in so doing, made laws against their children, whom women are to rear?[4]

It is interesting that Lytton, Jane Austen, Scott and other writers in the first third of the century had distinctly more liberal ideas about women than the typical mid-Victorian (Ruskin, Patmore, Dickens). This does not mean that they seriously challenged prevailing ideas about the roles of the sexes, only that they did not make the impossible demands on women which later became fashionable. Cobbett's *Advice to Young Men* (1830) takes the superiority of men for granted but urges husbands to treat their wives more kindly, to help them in the house, not to go out drinking, and to show them 'respect and honour by personal attention and acts of affection'. His ideal woman seems to have been a cheerful hard-working girl, who could 'cook and wash, and mend and make, and clean the house and make the bed' (he had little time for 'accomplishments'), and he particularly warned young lovers to check that their sweethearts had no 'grime behind the ears'.[5] In Cobbett's letters a woman is at least a normal human being, but in Ruskin's lecture 'Of Queens' Gardens', published in 1865, she has been transformed into an Angel in the House:

The man, in his rough work in the open world, must encounter all peril and trial . . . often he must be wounded, or subdued; often misled; and *always* hardened. But he guards the woman from all this; within his house, as ruled by her, unless she herself has sought it, need enter no danger, no temptation, no cause of error or offence. This is the true nature of home – it is the place of Peace; the shelter not only from all injury, but from all terror, doubt, and division. . . .This, then, I believe to be – will you not admit it to be? – the woman's true place and power. But do not you see that, to fulfil this, she must – as far as one can use such terms of a human creature – be incapable of error? So far as she rules, all must be right, or nothing is. She must be enduringly, incorruptibly good; instinctively, infallibly wise – wise, not for self-development, but for self-renunciation: wise, not that she may set herself above her husband, but that she may never fail from his side.[6]

Between these dates a number of books and articles had appeared telling women how to behave. One of the earliest of these books was Mrs John Sandford's *Woman in her Social and Domestic Character* (1831), followed in the 1840s by Mrs Ellis's *Daughters of England, Wives of England* and *Mothers of England* (all dedicated to the Queen). Ruskin was only saying, more poetically, what almost all writers now believed – a woman's work was to make a man's home happy; she was purer and better than men, and, above all, she must willingly lead a life of self-renunciation.

SACRIFICE AND THE FAMILY

At the beginning of the century, and for a long time afterwards, novelists assumed that an 'honest woman' was 'never separated from her family'. Besides this she owed a duty to her family, particularly the men in it, which meant that she deserved no respect if she put her own wishes before theirs. In one of the first great nineteenth-century novels, *Waverley*, Rose Bradwardine is described approvingly like this:

> Her very soul is in home, and in the discharge of all those quiet virtues of which home is the centre. Her husband will be to her what her father now is, the object of all her care, solicitude and affection. She will see nothing and connect herself with nothing, but by him and through him.[7]

Fathers have the first claim on the heroine of a novel, which rarely follows her past marriage. They are much more important in fiction than mothers who, as Florence Nightingale noted, are usually dead. From *Tom Jones* onwards, it is common for the heroine to be unable to marry before the last chapter because of her family responsibilities. Even Jane Austen accepted this; Emma feels that she cannot leave Mr Woodhouse to get married, although she would only be moving a mile or two away, and that even to have considered it was 'a sin of thought'. And if this sounds far-fetched, consider what a real woman, Charlotte Brontë, is believed to have said to her father, for whom she made sacrifices all her life:

She said, 'Father I am not a young girl, not a young woman even – I never was pretty. I now am ugly. At your death I shall have £300 besides the little I have earned myself – do you think there are many men who would serve seven years for me?' And again when he renewed the conversation and asked her if she would marry a curate? – 'Yes I must marry a curate if I marry at all; not merely a curate but *your* curate; not merely *your* curate but he must live in the house with you, for I cannot leave you.'[8]

One of the most striking examples of daughterly devotion in literature is Madeline Bray in *Nicholas Nickleby*. Her father has squandered all his money, so 'this young girl had struggled alone and unassisted to maintain him by the labour of her hands . . . for two long years, toiling by day and often too by night, working at the needle, the pencil and the pen, and . . . as a daily governess',[9] although her friends offer her a home if she will give him up. Dickens is, of course, disgusted at the unnatural phenomenon of a man who lets a woman support him, but he still sees Madeline's conduct as saintly, not perverse. She even agrees to marry a repellent old miser so her father can have an income, and only fails to do so because Bray dies suddenly just before the wedding. This was necessary because Dickens wanted a happy ending but could not allow so good a woman as Madeline to set herself free. Many novelists twisted probability in much the same way.

Other male members of the family could command a heroine's first loyalty. Looking no further than Dickens, we find Little Nell sacrificing herself for her half-witted grandfather and Harriet Carker, in *Dombey*, cheerfully turning her back on the world to look after her disgraced brother. Charlotte Yonge in *The Daisy Chain* (1856) developed the doctrine of self-renunciation to its logical extreme. Ethel May meets an attractive man who likes her but runs away as soon as she realises that she is beginning to prefer his company to her father's. She accuses herself of being 'unkind, ungrateful, undutiful towards her father',[10] who never even knows what she has given up for his sake. Unlike most sacrifices in novels, this is not a symbolic one, for Norman marries someone else and Ethel remains single.

The conventional view was that parents had the right to forbid a daughter's marriage, but not to make her marry a man she disliked. Sophia in *Tom Jones* says of her father it hath always been a fixed principle with me, never to have marry'd without his consent. This is, I think, the duty of a child to a parent; and this, I hope, nothing could ever have prevailed with me to swerve from. I do not indeed conceive, that the authority of any parent can oblige us to marry, in direct opposition to our inclinations.[11]

More than a hundred years later, this still seemed a moderate and reasonable point of view. Bell in *The Small House at Allington* (1864) says, 'I would accept no man in opposition to mamma's wishes; but not even for her could I accept any man in opposition to my own'.[12] 'It is not because of the reasonableness of our parents' commands that we are required to obey them,' says Mary in Susan Ferrier's *Marriage*, 'but because it is the will of God.'[13] Thackeray queried this in *The Newcomes* – 'nor can there be a wholesomer task for the elders, as our young subjects grow up, naturally demanding liberty and citizens' rights, than for us gracefully to abdicate our sovereign pretensions and claims of absolute control'.[14] But the situation of the heroine turning down the man she loves because of her family persists in novel after novel and only becomes less acceptable towards the end of the century, when so many other conventions were under attack. It is almost parodied in *Robert Elsmere* (1888), where Catherine refuses to desert her mother and sisters and then finds that they are anxious to get rid of her, especially her younger sister who wants to be 'free to live my own life a bit'.[15] But as late as 1892 Sidwell, in Gissing's *Born in Exile*, decides to send away the man she wants to marry because her family dislike him:

You see, I cannot think and act simply as a woman, as a human being. I am bound to a certain sphere of life. The fact that I have outgrown it, counts for nothing. I cannot free myself without injury to people whom I love.[16]

When a woman married in church she promised to obey her husband and from then on her first duty was to him. 'I think a wife is bound to the very last to obey in all things, not absolutely wrong, her husband's will,'[17] says the ideal Christian hero of *John Halifax, Gentleman*. In contrast, feminists stressed a wife's duty *not* to obey if her husband outraged her conscience. Mrs Hugo Reid said of Chaucer's patient Griselda, 'A woman is thought perfect if she is represented as continuing to love, with the most ardent and constant affection, a monster who first gained her love by guile, and then treated her in so brutal a manner as to merit the contempt of the whole world'. She argued that 'the old prejudices regarding women convert the noble duty of self-renunciation into a most criminal self-extinction . . . the inflexible rule of duty into a very flexible principle of submission to, and connivance at, all the weaknesses and wickednesses of man'.[18]

In the middle years of the century a rash of novels depicted heroines, and sometimes heroes, sacrificing themselves for no particular reason. W. R. Greg, in 'The False Morality of Lady Novelists' (1859), commented on the 'fantastic and flatulent morality' which made so many characters in these novels sacrifice their own reasonable needs; for instance, in one book, the heroine gives up marriage to support her worthless brother instead of forcing him to make an effort. He argued that self-sacrifice was sometimes necessary, but 'to make this sacrifice to family pride, to the world's breath, to the wrong passions or the shallow prejudices of others, is a spurious and histrionic counterfeit'.[19] Over the next forty years, more and more people came to agree.

DOUBLE STANDARDS

We have already seen that the nineteenth century demanded very different sexual standards from women and from men. Few defended male unchastity in public; the hero of a nineteenth-century novel could not very well have behaved like Tom Jones. Nevertheless a double standard was quietly taken for granted; as a famous article on prostitution pointed out, public opinion regarded 'a whole life of indulgence on the part of one sex as venial and natural, and a single false step on the part of the other as irretrievable and unpardonable'.[20] 'In regard to a sin common to the two sexes,' wrote Trollope, 'almost all the punishment and all the disgrace is heaped upon the one who in nine cases out of ten has been the least sinful. . . . Life without a hope . . . is the life to which we doom our erring daughters . . . But for our erring sons we find pardon easily enough!'[21]

The cruelty of the middle classes to 'fallen' women, who were made to suffer with their children while the men went on being respected members of society, was obvious to most novelists. They showed a great deal of sympathy for the young girl who had

been seduced, and even for the prostitute – 'that unhappy being
. . . who is scorned and insulted as the vilest of her sex, and
doomed for the most part to disease and abject wretchedness and
an early death'.[22] Jane Austen is perhaps an exception, although
she was well aware that the double standard was unjust, noting in
the last chapter of *Mansfield Park* that 'the penalty is less equal
than could be wished'. Lydia Bennet is treated unsympathetically
because she can see nothing more important than her own
gratification and is too stupid to realise that she could have ruined
her life. There are traces of the same attitude in George Eliot, who
depicts Hetty in *Adam Bede* as a selfish girl. Ultimately, though,
when the 'poor sinner' is 'forsaken of all', it is the one really pure
woman in the novel, Dinah, who is prepared to help.[23]

By the middle of the century there was a consensus, at least
among novelists, that erring women could be saved and that their
sisters ought not to shrink from them. *The Heart of Midlothian*,
David Copperfield and *Adam Bede* were all popular, even at the times
of greatest public squeamishness, because they contrasted a weak
and sinning heroine with a strong and good one. But the response
to Mrs Gaskell's *Ruth* (1853) was much more mixed. This novel
provoked much the same kind of controversy as *Tess of the
d'Urbervilles* nearly forty years later, because it tried to show that a
'fallen' woman could herself be strong and good. A great many
people criticised Mrs Gaskell:

> A moral lapse in a woman was spoken of as an immensely
> worse thing than in a man; there was no comparison to be
> formed between them. A pure woman, it was reiterated, should
> be absolutely ignorant of a certain class of evils in the world,
> albeit those evils bore with murderous cruelty on other
> women.[24]

This was written by Josephine Butler, whose campaign against
the C. D. Acts helped to turn opinion against the double
standard. When *Tess* was reviewed in the 1890s, most critics
condemned Angel Clare for rejecting his wife, although he had
been no more chaste than she had. But Hardy remarked that 'I
have had many letters from men who say they would have done
exactly as he did'.[25]

Originally most writers seem to have felt that a fallen woman,
even if she repented, could never be truly happy again. Hetty

Sorrel, Ruth and Esther in *Mary Barton* all die. Little Em'ly goes to Australia and remains single for life. But in the latter part of the century some novelists suggested that women should not go on being punished for ever. In *The New Magdalen* (1873) Wilkie Collins made his heroine a reformed prostitute who after much suffering marries a saintly man, but there is so much prejudice against them that they have to emigrate.

While the novelists were certainly ahead of public opinion on this issue most of them felt that there should be a double standard within marriage. The *Westminster Review* summed up the general climate of opinion in October 1864:

> No man, it is urged, in whom remains any sense of honour, could receive back to his embraces the violator of his marital confidence, but there are few cases in which an injured wife might not gracefully pardon an erring husband.

The Lord Chancellor, in the debate on the Matrimonial Causes Act of 1857, defended this distinction on the grounds that 'the adultery of the wife might be the means of palming spurious offspring upon the husband, while the adultery of the husband could have no such effect with regard to the wife'.[26] Cobbett used the same argument, though he observed that most women disagreed with it, 'They say that adultery is adultery, in men as well as in them; and that, therefore, the offence is as great in the one case as in the other'.[27] The usual advice to women was to put up with their husbands' infidelity – 'oh! how infinitely preferable is the feeling of having borne unfaithfulness, than of having been unfaithful ourselves!'[28]

'I have broken my marriage oath,' Richard admits to Lucy in *The Ordeal of Richard Feverel* (1859). She replies 'Darling! kiss me!'[29] A woman who made the same confession to her husband could expect a very different response. Novelists treated the adulterous wife with particular horror, whatever her provocation. Lady Clara Newcome leads a miserable life after she has left her husband, although she had been forced to marry him and he had been extremely brutal. Lady Isabel Carlyle in *East Lynne* (1861), divorced after having eloped in a moment of madness, loses husband, home and children to a second wife (her children are told she is dead and forbidden to mention her), and finally dies of a broken heart. Trollope's Lady Glencora and Dickens'

Louisa Gradgrind only just escape from an equally awful fate.

Yet it was increasingly recognised that people did make the wrong marriage and many novelists in the second half of the century were concerned with this problem. Books which 'tampered with dilemmas about the marriage vow' do not seem to have appeared in large numbers before the 1870s. One of the earliest was *Jane Eyre* (1847), but although Rochester is trapped in an arranged marriage to a mad wife Jane decides to 'keep the law given by God; sanctioned by man'.[30] She has her reward when Rochester's wife dies, and many other novels (*The Tenant of Wildfell Hall, David Copperfield, The Woman in White, Far from the Madding Crowd, The Prime Minister*) allow the hero or heroine to escape from a bad marriage by killing off their wife or husband. While the Victorians were certainly much more familiar with death than we are, the number of convenience deaths in their novels is still unnaturally high.

Later Victorian novelists began to explore what happened when a marriage broke down, but neither partner died. Although divorce was legal by this time, in some circumstances, it remained unusual and rather scandalous, and novelists were reluctant to use it as a solution. *Middlemarch* is a study of two couples who marry with false expectations, and although Dorothea is released by her husband's death, Lydgate has to accept his 'narrowed lot with sad resignation'.[31] Wilkie Collins' *No Name* (1862) goes so far as to show a faithful common-law marriage, though cautiously and in a sub-plot. Andrew Vanstone has unsuspiciously married a woman with a past, whom he cannot divorce. He is saved from a life of dissipation by a good woman who becomes his 'wife in the sight of heaven'.[32] This was exactly the kind of hard case which was most likely to win the Victorians' sympathy, as a man was not expected either to be celibate or to tolerate an impure wife. There was much sympathy, too, for George Eliot, who considered herself married to G. H. Lewes although they could not go through the ceremony. By the 1890s it was widely accepted, in some circles, that people whose marriages had failed should be allowed a fresh start, and novels by Meredith (*One of our Conquerors, Lord Ormont and his Aminta*), Gissing (*Denzil Quarrier*) and Hardy (*The Woodlanders, Jude the Obscure*), explore this situation. A different kind of attack on conventional·morality came from a smaller group of writers who criticised marriage itself.

There were two main arguments for 'free unions' versus marriage, first that on marriage the woman became the man's property, and second that lifelong commitments made no sense. 'Love withers under constraint; its very essence is liberty . . . to promise for ever to love the same woman is not less absurd than to promise to believe the same creed'.[33] This was written by Shelley in 1813, but there had been little discussion of his ideas for the best part of a century. They resurfaced in several late Victorian novels, few of which, though, showed a free union that worked. Lyndall in *The Story of an African Farm* (1883) dies after having an illegitimate baby and the heroine of William Barry's *New Antigone* (1887) becomes a nun. The most famous anti-marriage novel was Grant Allen's *The Woman Who Did* (1895), which presents the heroine, driven to suicide, as a martyr in the cause of progress. There are traces of the same idea in Hardy's *Jude the Obscure*, published later that year. Its message is that the unsanctified union between Jude and Sue cannot last because other people's prejudices are too strong.

Interestingly enough, the best-known of these novels were written by men and some of the strongest attacks on them came from women. *The Woman Who Did* was unfavourably reviewed by Millicent Garrett Fawcett, the suffragist leader, and also by Margaret Oliphant, who coupled it with *Jude* in a review called 'The Anti-Marriage League'. She was worried by a tendency 'to place what is called the Sex-Question above all others as the theme of fiction',[34] and it is probable that she spoke for most women in rejecting the idealisation of free love. The benefits to men were obvious but fallen women in the 1890s still faced a great deal of public hostility.

A journalist who interviewed Hardy in 1892 referred to 'the idea much put forward of late by certain very earnest people that purity is as binding on men as on women'.[35] Among these 'very earnest people' were several feminists; 'Votes for Women and Purity for Men', said a suffragette banner just before the Great War. Although things did not work out quite like that, the double standard was intellectually discredited by 1900.

WOMEN AND RELIGION

The nineteenth century was a very much more religious age than our own, and although agnosticism grew steadily among

intellectuals, novelists like George Eliot and Hardy who had lost
faith in Christianity continued to be strongly influenced by it.
Upper- and middle-class ladies tended to be extremely pious;
church work was one of their few legitimate activities outside the
home and many writers commented on their fondness for the
clergy. According to the majority view among critics and
novelists, women had a simple faith, often complacent, and while
they could put men to shame by their goodness they could easily
become narrow and dogmatic. Ruskin in 'Of Queens' Gardens'
said:

> There *is* one dangerous science for women – one which they
> must indeed beware how they profanely touch – that of
> theology . . . they will plunge headlong, and without thought
> of incompetency, into that science in which the greatest men
> have trembled, and the wisest erred . . . they dare to turn the
> Household Gods of Christianity into ugly idols of their own.[36]

George Eliot complained in 1856 that there were an enormous
number of bad religious novels by women, each pushing the
virtues of her own particular sect.[37] In most novels by men, the
female enthusiast is both comic and hateful. Miss Clack in *The
Moonstone*, who forces tracts on everyone she meets, is an
example, as is Mrs Bolton in Trollope's *John Caldigate* and
Dickens' Mrs Pardiggle, who marches into a wretched working-
class home, where a baby is dying, and takes the whole family
'into religious custody'. She is contrasted with Esther and Ada,
who are genuinely compassionate – 'We tried to comfort the
mother, and we whispered to her what Our Saviour said of
children' – and therefore genuinely Christian.[38] There seems to
have been a feeling that if a woman was too religious she would
become a nuisance and might even dominate men.

In *Adam Bede*, which begins in 1799, George Eliot shows a
Methodist girl, Dinah Morris, preaching in public and bringing
ordinary people closer to an understanding of God. But by the
time the novel ends, in 1807, the Methodists had driven out
women preachers and throughout the nineteenth century they
were not recognised by any major Church. Broadly speaking, the
more 'Protestant' a sect was the more likely it was to sympathise
with women. Quakers, Unitarians and the Salvation Army were
all fairly liberal; on the other hand Catholics and some Anglicans
felt the clergy should be not only male but celibate too.

There was certainly a Christian tradition which saw women as corrupt and corrupting, on the grounds that it was Eve who tempted Adam.[39] Women are 'the first fruits of the devil, the authors of all evil, the subtlest of all Satan's snares . . . accursed for ever, for the deceit of their first mother, by whom sin entered into the world',[40] says the abbot in Kingsley's *Hypatia* (1853). This is a particularly interesting novel because it is about a woman intellectual, a character whom Kingsley could hardly have imagined if she had not really lived (Hypatia was a philosopher who was torn to pieces by militant Christians in the fifth century). In Kingsley's book she lectures in public to male students, does not want to be married, and has a more powerful mind than most men. But she is morally inferior to the Christian heroine, Victoria, because her intellectual eminence makes her arrogant and unsympathetic to humble people. Victoria is a much more traditional woman in that she lives and is prepared to die for others. 'If weak woman can endure this, how much more a Son of God.'[41] Kingsley, who was strongly opposed to celibacy, argued that women could have a thoroughly good influence on men. This doctrine was obviously much more welcome to his readers – most of whom were women, after all – than old-fashioned direct attacks on the sex.

Religion could be, and often was, used to keep women in their place. ('The head of every man is Christ; and the head of the woman is the man,' said St Paul.) Yet it was also recognised as the one thing which could legitimately matter to a woman even more than her family. Lady Jane Grey in Ainsworth's popular historical romance *The Tower of London* (1840) refuses to convert to Catholicism, even to save her husband's life. In *The Heart of Midlothian*, Jeanie will not give false evidence to save her sister because to her this would be disobeying God. Like Dinah in *Adam Bede*, she is better and stronger than the other girl because her life revolves around God, not a man. It is clear that some women, including feminists, felt that religion could be a liberating force because it gave them an independent standard of behaviour. Frances Power Cobbe spoke of man's 'monstrous claim to be the reason of an immortal creature's existence',[42] and Florence Nightingale and Josephine Butler both found that their personal belief in God gave them the strength to bear unpopularity.

While religion had begun to come under attack by the end of the century, it remained true that women were more devout than men. Gissing in *Born in Exile*, Hardy in *Jude the Obscure* and even Mrs Humphry Ward in *Robert Elsmere* all saw the Church as a repressive force, trapping the woman after the man has liberated himself.

IMAGES OF WOMEN IN THE NOVEL

The most striking fact about women in the nineteenth-century novel is that they are overwhelmingly upper or upper-middle class. We have noted that, while they may be quite poor, few heroines actually work; a novel like *Mary Barton* which is set among working-class people is very much an exception. Just as limited as the social range is the range of female characters which most novelists present. They can be divided into a very few, easily identifiable groups – on the one side heroines, and on the other fallen women, heartless fine ladies, shrews, and, towards the end of the century, 'new' or 'strong-minded' women. Novelists were often sympathetic to fallen women, as we have seen, but towards the other deviant groups they showed no mercy. Their ideal woman is summed up thus – 'Young and lovely, religious, submissive and dependent, confiding and sensitive and chaste, accepting without question the destiny of marriage, the heroine emerges from the pages of the popular novels and periodicals as a well understood and consistent type'.[43]

Heroines

The heroines of Jane Austen and (sometimes) Scott play a real role in the novels in which they appear. Elizabeth Bennet, who thinks nothing of a three-mile walk in the mud – 'jumping over stiles and springing over puddles' – and Jeanie Deans, walking alone from Edinburgh to London, are obviously not just fine ladies who sit in a drawing-room waiting to be married. Jane Austen was not afraid to show that her heroines had faults – sometimes unfeminine faults, like the desire to dominate – and, most unusual of all, in *Persuasion* she focuses on a woman of twenty-seven who only just escapes being an old maid. The heroines of Scott are usually strong women, not afraid to take sides in politics and religion, and capable of looking after themselves and others; a Scott heroine who is weak and clinging is unlikely to survive in his tough world. But the later, Victorian heroine is too often a shrunken human being who takes no part in events and exists only to uplift and inspire. Often she is no more than a crock of gold at the rainbow's end, part of the hero's reward for succeeding. This is particularly true in many novels by Dickens – *Nicholas Nickleby, Martin Chuzzlewit, David Copperfield* – which are basically about a man's struggle, and Dickens' concept of women was enormously influential. In *Oliver Twist* he describes Rose Maylie:

> She was not past seventeen. Cast in so slight and exquisite a mould; so mild and gentle; so pure and beautiful; that earth seemed not her element, nor its rough creatures her fit companions. The very intelligence that shone in her deep blue eyes, and was stamped upon her noble head, seemed scarcely of her age, or of the world; and yet the changing expression of sweetness and good humour, the thousand lights that played about the face, and left no shadow there; above all, the smile, the cheerful, happy smile, were made for Home, and fireside peace and happiness.[44]

The lively heroines of Jane Austen are well in the past and here is a typical man's woman – pure and beautiful, home-loving (in the next sentence she is 'busily engaged in the little offices of the table'), and as young as possible. 'A heroine past the age of twenty-three is a rarity, past the age of thirty is an impossibility.'[45] Beauty was so much taken for granted that even Emily and Anne Brontë thought 'that it was impossible to make a heroine interesting on any other terms'.[46] Finally Rose (who will not marry her lover because it might harm his career) is a typical heroine because of the 'perfect sacrifice of self which, in all matters, great or trifling, has always been her characteristic'.[47]

Although marriage was assumed to be a young woman's destiny, she was supposed to behave as if she was unaware of it. Mrs Ellis advised girls in 1842 that 'the first restriction to a woman of delicacy, of course, will be, never to entertain this sentiment (love) towards one by whom it has not been sought or solicited'.[48] Of course the novelists knew this was not always the case – there were many jokes about husband-hunting girls and matchmaking mothers – but a true heroine, like Amy in *The Heir of Redclyffe*, does not allow herself to speculate about marriage. 'I don't like it, and mamma would not wish me to talk of such things.'[49] With a few exceptions, notably Miss Yonge, women novelists showed much more sympathy than men for the feelings of a girl who, after all, had little to do but fall in love.

The mid-Victorian heroine is a very passive creature. If, like Laura Fairlie, she is in physical danger, she usually has to be saved by someone else. Heroines constantly faint or become seriously ill and it was assumed that an emotional crisis could destroy them. The tragic heroine, if she does not die, may suffer a total breakdown. A woman's mind was supposed to be more delicately balanced than a man's and therefore more likely to give way. Catherine in *Wuthering Heights* develops brain fever and dies, as do Lucy in *The Bride of Lammermoor* and her namesake in *Richard Feverel*. Laura Fairlie does not die, but the mere fact of having been locked up in a mental home causes her to show genuine symptoms of mental disease.

This conviction of woman's fragility was linked with the feeling that she could and should love only one man. In *Belinda* (1801) the heroine makes no progress with the man she likes best and briefly gets engaged to someone else. Some critics objected, saying that her first love should have been 'an almost sacred bond' and Miss Edgeworth changed the novel accordingly when it was reissued.[50] Again we find that Jane Austen was less sentimental than the Victorians, for Elizabeth Bennet takes her disappointments fairly calmly. But Caterina, in *Mr. Gilfil's Love Story*, is almost driven mad when a man plays with her feelings and her subsequent death in childbirth is linked to this – 'the delicate plant had been too deeply bruised, and in the struggle to put forth a blossom it died'.[51] Trollope's Lily Dale, and Mrs Gaskell's Cousin Phillis, never recover from being abandoned. One reason why some critics disliked *Villette* was because Lucy gets over a hopeless attachment, turning from John Bretton to the Professor because there is more likely to be a future in the second relationship. 'I don't make my *good* women ready to fall in love with two men at once,'[52] complained Thackeray. The heroine's spotless purity was certain to be soiled if she made more than one choice.

Old Maids

Trollope's Lily Dale decides to remain a spinster, and Scott showed some noble women, like Rebecca in *Ivanhoe* or Minna in

The Pirate, who had been 'disappointed' and chose to live for
others. But only a few novelists were sympathetic to old maids,
who, Mrs Ellis thought, were often 'the most admirable of their
sex'.[53] Generally these unlucky women, unless they happened to
be rich, were despised by everyone. 'A single woman with a very
narrow income must be a ridiculous, disagreeable old maid! the
proper sport of boys and girls,' Jane Austen noted in *Emma*,[54]
where Miss Bates has no husband and therefore no one to protect
her from Emma's rudeness. Dickens obsessively attacks ugly
women who lie about their conquests and hate anyone younger
and better looking than themselves. Other novelists, particularly
women, showed more sympathy. Thackeray in *Vanity Fair*
describes the 'awful existence' of Jane Osborne, whose father has
chased away the only man who liked her – 'as he wanted a woman
to keep his house, he did not choose that she should marry.'[55]
Miss Matty in *Cranford* has also had to give up her marriage to
please her family, but this does not embitter her. Although she is
elderly, single and slightly ridiculous, she is the purest character
in the book. Possibly Mrs Gaskell had been influenced by
a chapter in *Shirley* called 'Old Maids'.[56] Caroline, certain that
she will never marry or have children, reflects that she may
have to live alone for another half-century – 'What am I to do
to fill the interval of time which spreads between me and the
grave?'

She goes to see two old maids, both middle-aged, ugly and
much laughed at by 'lively young gentlemen'. Caroline has
laughed at them herself in the past but when she gets to know
them she finds that one 'had been a most devoted daughter and
sister, an unwearied watcher by lingering deathbeds; that to
prolonged and unrelaxing attendances on the sick the malady that
now poisoned her own life owed its origin'. The other is a Christ-
like woman who devotes herself to the poor – 'for this goodness
she got but little reward in this life'. Although she learns to
respect them deeply Caroline is aware that their kind of life would
not satisfy her and suspects the motives of those who tell single
women to sacrifice their own needs. Charlotte Yonge's Ethel, in
the last chapter of *The Daisy Chain*, accepts 'that the unmarried
woman must not seek undivided return of affection, and must not
set her love, with exclusive eagerness, on aught below, but must
be ready to cease in turn to be first with any'. But Charlotte
Brontë comments through Caroline, 'I perceive that certain sets

of human beings are very apt to maintain that other sets should give up their lives to them and their service, and then they requite them by praise: they call them devoted and virtuous. Is this enough? Is it to live?'

By the end of the century the fact that women outnumbered men had become so notorious that there was widespread discussion about what was to be done with old maids. Gissing's *The Odd Women* (1893) looks closely at their problems – 'odd' in this context meaning not eccentric but surplus. At the centre of the novel is a group of sisters in dead-end and soul-destroying jobs. One rushes into a bad marriage to escape, another becomes an alcoholic, and all are more or less unhappy. Gissing reaches what some would call a feminist solution; women must stop being afraid of single life and get a training so that they have a better choice of jobs.

Shrews

Writers had always been aware that not all women fitted the feminine stereotype. Throughout the centuries there had been stories of women who beat their husbands or told them what to do, and this was funny precisely because it was so outrageous. The nineteenth-century novel is full of shrews but few of them are taken very seriously. The young shrew is usually a woman in search of a husband who does not care how absurd she becomes in the process. She may even grow violent when thwarted, like Fanny Squeers who 'beat Nicholas to her heart's content, animating herself at every blow with the recollection of his having refused her proffered love',[57] or Trollope's Camilla French who hides a carving knife in her bed. These are both comic episodes (there are almost no serious studies of feminine jealousy) and derive their humour from the unnatural – but not unheard-of – phenomenon of a woman pursuing a man.

The older shrew is likely to be a married woman who bullies her husband and anyone else within her power. An early example, who is treated seriously and even tragically, is Lady Ashton in Scott's *Bride of Lammermoor,* an evil woman who destroys her daughter under the influence of revenge and ambition. But a more typical married shrew is Mrs Bumble, who begins her reign over her husband by beating him and then forces him into crime.[58] Dickens presented several other shrews (Miggs,

Miss Knag, Mrs Gargery, Mrs Snagsby, and the symbolically-
named Mrs MacStinger in *Dombey*). In *The Newcomes* there is Mrs
Mackenzie, whose conduct is particularly shocking because she
torments a virtuous old gentleman. Trollope's Mrs Proudie, the
'Lady Bishop', is another well-known bossy woman.

'There is nothing so odious to man as a virago', Trollope wrote
elsewhere.[59] Male novelists, as we have seen, could be tender to
the fallen woman, who would not have fallen if she had not had at
least some of the feminine virtues. But a woman who challenged
male supremacy was very much more dangerous.

Adventuresses

A 'female adventurer', means an unscrupulous woman whose
aim is to use sex, her only real weapon, to get money and power.
Mrs Clay in *Persuasion* is such a woman (she ends up as a kept
mistress) and the type is quite common in the late nineteenth-
century novel. Adventuresses are generally past their first youth,
do not live at home, and carefully conceal their backgrounds.
When an infatuated man (usually very young or very old) wants
to marry them, his friends are entitled to take extreme measures
to keep them apart.

Thackeray, whose novels are full of scheming women, created
the finest English adventuress since Moll Flanders in *Vanity Fair*.
Becky Sharp, by the artful use of her charms, and a shrewd sense
of money values, does better in every way than the virtuous and
conventional Amelia. Since her success is based on being female
she is able to invert the normal husband–wife relationship; she
treats her husband as her 'upper servant', tolerated only because
she *must* be a married woman to move freely about in society. It is
possible that many women would have liked to behave like this
and that many men had always thought women were schemers.
At any rate, we can believe in Becky's end. Her relationships
break down, because no one can love her when they get close to
her, but she continues to live comfortably and never feels any
remorse.

Thackeray makes the point that Becky is alone in the world and
therefore must look after herself while more privileged young
women can let their parents do it for them. He does, in the long
run, condemn her, but he does not suggest how she could have
been a better woman, given her situation. Other novelists who

treat such women sympathetically point out the special circumstances – poverty, absence of a mother, and so on – which have made them what they are. 'Society has used me cruelly', says the ex-prostitute in *The New Magdalen*, 'I owe nothing to society. I have a right to take any advantage of it I can.'[60]

One of the most interesting of these novelists is M. E. Braddon, who in *Lady Audley's Secret* (1862) shows an apparently sweet, pure, youthful heroine who bigamously marries an old man for security and then pushes her first husband, when he reappears, down a well. Unlike Becky, though, she is unmasked and dies in a lunatic asylum. Trollope attempted the Becky Sharp type in Lizzie Eustace, but not very successfully. Meredith's Diana Warwick, living on the fringes of society because she is separated from her husband and has to support herself by writing, realises near the end that an adventuress is what she is. Wilkie Collins drew several women who battle alone against the world – Magdalen Vanstone in *No Name*, Lydia Gwilt in *Armadale*, and Mercy Merrick in *The New Magdalen*. But all of them have some redeeming qualities, and all are saved eventually through loving a man. The consistent adventuress, like Becky, cares for neither men nor children, and is unlikely ever to repent.

New Women

We have seen that the last quarter of the nineteenth century was a time when women's roles were being widely discussed. Higher education, the growth of the female labour market, the campaign for the vote and (to a limited extent) birth control, all produced a feeling that the world was changing rapidly. 'Ours is a time of transition, and all our ideas, political, social and even religious, are being tested anew as with fire,' wrote one woman in 1894. 'Our sons . . . are the pioneers of the new life, how should our daughters escape their share of the burden?'[61]

Women who studied rather than flirted had long been called 'blue' or 'blue-stockings'. In the middle of the century women who were interested in public life were laughingly called 'strong-minded'. *The Clever Woman of the Family* (1865), by Charlotte Yonge, shows one of these 'strong-minded women', a rash girl who gets involved in foolish schemes because she has no father or brother to control her and becomes 'that object of general scorn and aversion, a woman who had stepped out of her place'.[62]

In 1868 Mrs Lynn Linton invented the name 'girl of the period' for young women who lived only for pleasure and did not accept their parents' authority. Feminists were sometimes called 'wild women' or 'the shrieking sisterhood', but the most common name, during the 1890s, was 'new women'. Flora Thompson describes how ordinary women saw them:

> The New Woman, of course, they knew by repute for she was a familiar figure to all newspaper readers, usually depicted as hideous, in semi-masculine garb, with hands extended to grab male privileges, while a balloon of print issuing from her mouth demanded 'Votes for Women!' . . . Mothers and elder sisters described the new women, not one of whom they had seen, as 'a lot of great, coarse, ugly creatures who can't get themselves husbands'. 'I'd rather see you in your coffin', parents told their daughters, 'than wearing them bloomers and bawling for votes.'[63]

A small group of late nineteenth-century novelists, some of them very distinguished, tried to study the new woman seriously. They were often hostile to what they saw as her neurotic tendencies. Henry James' *The Bostonians* (1886) is dominated by an American feminist, Olive Chancellor, who instinctively dislikes and distrusts men. Cecilia Cullen, in George Moore's *Drama in Muslin* (1886), is another woman who hates men and marriage. She is 'deformed', and eventually becomes a nun. Gissing's Mrs Wade in *Denzil Quarrier* (1892) is a hard, cold woman who wants the vote and destroys the sweet, feminine Lilian, who does not. All these novels suggest that new women are the enemies of 'real' women and are doing their best to destroy happy relationships between the sexes.

On the other hand Meredith in *Diana of the Crossways* (1885) drew an attractive picture of an emancipated woman who is said to have been based on Mrs Norton. Gissing, whose views seem to have changed fairly rapidly between novels, was also sympathetic, in *The Odd Women*, to the central figure, Rhoda Nunn. Her life is devoted to improving the status of single women, for whom she runs a training school, and although she considers both marriage and a free union she finally decides, without too much unhappiness, to stay as she is. Seeing what happens to married women and also to unskilled 'old maids' in this novel one might conclude that the independent, self-respecting spinster was the type most likely to survive.

Towards the end of the century the 'new woman' theme became entangled with the theme of 'free unions', although it is worth noting that most feminists strongly disapproved. Possibly the first new woman in English fiction is Georgiana, a character in a long-forgotten novel by Richard Jefferies, *Restless Human Hearts* (1875). 'It was in the interest of her whole sex that she hesitated to enter into matrimony,'[64] we are told. She and her lover, who thinks she is being unwise, sign a contract to live together for three years, but the experiment fails and they get married when Georgiana realises that 'after all the true sphere of woman was her home'.[65]

The same pattern– the woman rejecting marriage in favour of a high-minded free union, the man unconvinced – recurs in several novels of the eighties and nineties. In *The Woman Who Did* Herminia, a former Girton student and a 'free woman', decides to have a child outside marriage and to bring her up 'to free half the human race from aeons of slavery'.[66] Her lover dies and she supports herself and her child by journalism. But her daughter grows up into a conventional girl who angrily rejects her mother, so Herminia commits suicide to be out of her way. The author's message is that such women are destined for martyrdom because of course society will punish them cruelly, but 'from their graves shall spring glorious the church of the future'.[67]

These heroines called marriage 'an assertion of man's supremacy over women'[68] although by this time most of the laws discriminating against married women had been removed. But when Hardy wrote *Jude the Obscure* (1895), after a rash of 'new woman' novels had appeared, he made Sue's reasons for distrusting the marriage tie more individual and interesting.

> The social moulds civilisation fits us into have no more relation to our actual shapes than the conventional shapes of the constellations have to the real star-patterns. I am called Mrs Richard Phillotson, living a calm wedded life with my counterpart of that name. But I am not really Mrs Richard Phillotson, but a woman tossed about, all alone, with aberrant passions, and unaccountable antipathies . . . [69]

A woman can no longer be seen as the other half of a man but is driven, sometimes against her will, to take her decisions alone.

The most disappointing thing about the New Woman novels is that few of them were, in fact, written by women and this meant that the heroines were seen primarily in terms of their effect on men. 'The sex question' tended to dominate these novels, rather than the work which the feminists had done to improve women's legal position, their education, and their right to be involved in the community.

To summarise, there had been definite changes between 1800 and 1900 in novelists' images of women. By the 1890s there was an emphasis on self-fulfilment rather than self-sacrifice. Chastity was still highly valued but was no longer thought to be absolutely essential. The Jane Austen heroine, who could never get away for very long from her elders, had given place to a fairly independent woman, often isolated from her family, or working for a living, or both. The novel did not always faithfully reflect what was happening in society, but nobody tracing its development through the nineteenth century could doubt that there had been some sort of revolution.

3 Jane Austen

Northanger Abbey, although not published until 1818, is actually one of the first nineteenth-century novels. Jane Austen completed it in 1803, having begun work some years earlier, and it had a particular point for the young women of her generation who were unable to read it at the time. Her aim was to parody a sister novelist, Mrs Ann Radcliffe (1764–1823), whose tales of terror were enormously popular and widely imitated around the turn of the century. We get the impression that such novels were written by and for women and that most men claimed to despise them. Catherine assumes that Henry does not read novels 'because they are not clever enough for you; gentlemen read better books'. The fact that her cultural life consists of reading 'horrid mysteries' with her man-hunting friend Isabella naturally makes Henry laugh at her, just as Mr Bennet laughs at his daughters for being 'silly and ignorant like other girls'. As Jane Austen noted (*Persuasion*, Chapter 23), women had been largely deprived of education, and if some of them were very silly this was hardly surprising. Indeed, she said in *Northanger Abbey* that men preferred a good-looking girl to be ignorant, and that 'a woman, especially if she have the misfortune of knowing anything, should conceal it as well as she can' (Chapter 14). But Catherine, partly through native common sense and with some help from Henry, finally accepts that life is very different from a Gothic novel. As well as commenting on the preoccupations of young girls at that time, Jane Austen is hinting that the novel can do something more serious than tell a thrilling story.

As all her critics point out, she covers a very small range of experience; she could hardly help it. Her work makes it clear that middle-class women in the early nineteenth century were not allowed to experience very much. Emma is the only Jane Austen heroine who is the mistress of her own household, but even she has never been far from home and has to plan her life around her father. All the others – the Dashwood and Bennet girls, Fanny Price and Anne Elliot – are completely dependent on their parents or guardians and cannot move around the country unescorted. Everything they do is watched by 'a neighbourhood of voluntary spies' (*Northanger Abbey,* Chapter 24) who do not hesitate to criticise them severely; Jane Fairfax cannot even walk to the post office without it being solemnly talked over. The only powerful, independent women in the novels are the rich middle-aged wives or widows like Mrs Ferrars, Mrs Churchill and Lady Catherine de Bourgh. They are not only free to do what they wish but can even make other people, including men, dance to their tune.

Most nineteenth-century readers felt that Scott, whose canvas was extremely wide, was a truly great novelist, whereas Jane Austen was not fully appreciated for some time. Perhaps this reflects the assumption that women's concerns are not really important. Jane Austen wrote primarily about other women; her novels end, like more conventional works, with the heroine getting married, and they consist of 'all those little matters on which the daily happiness of private life depends' *(Emma*, Chapter 14). 'We live at home, quiet, confined, and our feelings prey upon us', says Anne Elliot (*Persuasion*, Chapter 23). Jane Austen studies, brilliantly and realistically, the feelings of women living at home and what happens to them.

Her society judged each woman by whether or not she married, and after that by whether or not she had married 'well'. Jane Austen's women aspire to a 'good' match as her clerical heroes do to a 'good' living, and their prospects in the marriage market are ruthlessly assessed. Their claims rest partly on fortune, partly on beauty and accomplishments, and partly on what was called 'birth'. The Bennets in *Pride and Prejudice* have hardly any money and some embarrassing relations, so their chances are not good.

'If they had uncles enough to fill *all* Cheapside,' cried Bingley, 'it would not make them one jot less agreeable.'

'But it must very materially lessen their chance of marrying men of any consideration in the world,' replied Darcy. (Volume 1, Chapter 8)

The same realism is shown in the musings of an intelligent, worldly girl, Mary Crawford, who is pretty enough and rich enough to have a fairly wide choice. Near the beginning of

Mansfield Park she considers marrying Tom Bertram, as he is highly eligible.

> Miss Crawford soon felt that he and his situation might do. She looked about her with due consideration, and found almost everything in his favour – a park, a real park, five miles round, a spacious modern-built house . . . pleasant sisters, a quiet mother, and an agreeable man himself . . . It might do very well; she believed she should accept him. (Chapter 5)

Miss Crawford is certainly one of her more calculating characters, but Jane Austen did not even pay lip-service to the notion that a proper young lady ought never to allow herself to think about men. She made light fun of it in *Northanger Abbey* – 'If it be true, as a celebrated writer has maintained, that no young lady can be justified in falling in love before the gentleman's love is declared, it must be very improper that a young lady should dream of a gentleman before the gentleman is first known to have dreamed of her' (Chapter 3) – and at all times she took it for granted that a normal girl would feel a warm interest in the opposite sex. She disapproved only when it became an obsession and the woman was interested in nothing else.

In her first published novel she demonstrated that 'sense' was a more valuable quality than 'sensibility'. (Other women writers of her generation, like Maria Edgeworth and Susan Ferrier, agreed.) She did not believe that a girl who had been 'disappointed' would die or be damaged for life. Marianne Dashwood blames herself severely for having fretted herself into a dangerous illness; Elinor, who does not forget the claims of others when she is unhappy, is a finer character. It is unwise, and also morally wrong, to be besotted with any man.

Mrs Bennet is not as romantic as Marianne, but she too is obsessed with men and marriage and has very little 'sense'. She marks down Bingley as a son-in-law before she has even seen him and looks on the other matrons as her natural enemies because they too have daughters and nieces to place. Kitty and Lydia have picked up their mother's attitudes and are so obsessed with officers that no one respects them. The form of marriage – not its moral or emotional significance – is all that matters to Mrs Bennet, so she and Lydia congratulate themselves when Lydia finally marries Wickham, although he is 'one of the most worthless young men in Great Britain'. While accepting that people could not 'afford to marry without some attention to money' (Volume 2, Chapter 10), Jane Austen felt very seriously that marriage was not worth having unless it was a real marriage, based on love and respect. Emma Watson expresses her own views on husband hunting:

> To be so bent on marriage – to pursue a man merely for the sake of situation – is a sort of thing that shocks me: I cannot understand it. Poverty is a great evil, but to a woman of education and feeling it ought not, it cannot be the greatest. I would rather be a teacher at a school (and I can think of nothing worse) than marry a man I did not like.

Yet it is quite possible for a reasonable woman to think differently. Emma's sister retorts, 'I would rather do anything than be a teacher at a school . . . *I* have been at school, Emma, and know what a life they lead you; *you* never have . . . I think I could like any good humoured man with a comfortable income.'[1] Charlotte Lucas, though sensible and intelligent, accepts Mr Collins because she is twenty-seven and wants a home of her own. Nothing terrible happens to her but she can only enjoy her new 'establishment' (the word is often used in place of 'marriage') by having as little to do with her husband as possible. In the same novel we see the results of another flawed marriage; Mr Bennet has married a pretty but stupid woman and now takes no real part in family life. His daughters suffer from their mother's folly and he does not care enough to protect them.

Elizabeth's quality is shown by the fact that she rejects two proposals, while other women are working and scheming to get them. She turns down Mr Collins because she cannot possibly respect him, although he points out that she may never get another chance. Darcy's offer is a much better one (he knows himself to be extremely eligible, which is why he can afford to be rude to women), but his arrogant manners and the fact that he has hurt her sister make him unacceptable to Elizabeth. He has to learn that not every woman is 'wishing, expecting my addresses' before he and she can meet on equal terms.

But a Jane Austen heroine has a great deal to overcome before she reaches her eventual goal of a happy marriage. Like Victorian heroines, she must be prepared to give it up rather than lower her standards. If she marries she must reconcile it with her duty to the older members of her family; Anne Elliot feels she was right to break off her engagement because Lady Russell, who was in the place of her mother, advised it, and Emma thinks that to leave her father would actually be a sin. Parent-figures in Jane Austen are usually a great nuisance to the heroine; indeed two of them, Lady Bertram and Mr Woodhouse, have to be cared for like babies and must never be left alone in the house. The one exception is Mrs Dashwood, who is not only happy to let her daughters leave home but also respects their privacy and will not ask them embarrassing questions. But Elinor thinks this 'romantic delicacy' is 'overstrained'. (*Sense and Sensibility*, Chapter 16)

By the same token, a heroine must not snatch crudely at the man she wants but must at all times preserve her integrity. A short conversation between Elizabeth and Lady Catherine de Bourgh illustrates what is meant by this. Lady Catherine says that younger sisters should be kept at home until the older ones are married, to prevent them from competing. Elizabeth replies that this would not only be hard on them but 'would not be very likely to promote sisterly affection or delicacy of mind'. (Volume 2, Chapter 6)

'Sisterly affection' and 'delicacy of mind' – these are touchstones for Jane Austen. It always seemed to her particularly shocking when two sisters quarrelled over a man, and when this happens in her novels – *The Watsons, Mansfield Park*, and *Persuasion* – neither of them gets him. Indeed the idea of a woman competing with any other woman was distasteful to her; the cattiness of Miss Bingley in *Pride and Prejudice* is treated severely and does her no good. Elinor knows that she should not try to separate Lucy from Edward ('She was firmly resolved to act by her as every principle of honour and honesty directed') and Emma is aware that she has 'transgressed the duty of woman by woman' when she gossips about Jane Fairfax to a man. The idea of solidarity between women can be found in her private letters too; writing about the Prince Regent's wife Caroline she observed, 'Poor woman; I shall support her as long as I can, because she *is* a woman, and because I hate her husband'.[2] And in *Persuasion* Anne remarks that 'we each begin, probably with a little bias towards our own sex' (Chapter 23), which was by no means obvious to everyone in an age so heavily biassed towards men.

'Delicacy of mind' is more difficult to define and indeed the whole concept is not simple. Jane Austen demanded high standards from herself and others and her moral scrutiny often makes the reader uncomfortable. It includes not being spiteful, for instance, even in one's thoughts; when Lydia describes Elizabeth's rival, Miss King, as 'a nasty little freckled thing' Elizabeth is 'shocked to think that, however incapable of such coarseness of *expression* herself, the coarseness of the *sentiment* was little other than her own breast had formerly harboured and fancied liberal'. (Volume 2, Chapter 16) Other qualities which seemed important to her were consideration for everyone, compassion for the weak and helpless, loyalty to one's family (which did not mean being unaware of their faults) and being guided in one's personal life by reason and morality rather than caprice and self-interest. Miss Bates, though ridiculous and an old maid, is a finer character than many more intelligent people because she is free from this kind of coarseness.

Mansfield Park resembles *Pride and Prejudice* in that the heroine refuses a 'good' offer while the anti-heroine breaks all the rules by running away with a man. Fanny's marriage prospects are discussed in the first chapter when the Bertram family are making up their minds to take her into their home. Sir Thomas points out at the time that they will have to give her 'the provision of a gentlewoman' if she does not marry, and when she rejects Henry Crawford he tells her that this may well be her last chance. 'You . . . are, in a wild fit of folly, throwing away from you such an opportunity of being settled in life, eligibly, honourably, nobly settled, as will, probably, never occur to you again.' And, like Lady Catherine,[3] he feels strongly that a young woman should not have opinions:

I had thought you peculiarly free from wilfulness of temper, self-conceit, and every tendency to that independence of spirit which prevails so much in modern days, even in young women, and which in young women is offensive and disgusting beyond all common offence. But you have now shown me that you can be wilful and perverse; that you can and will decide for yourself, without any consideration or deference, for those who have surely some right to guide you, without even asking their advice. (Chapter 32)

This seems a grotesque description of Fanny, the most meek and dutiful of all Austen heroines, but as well as insisting on her right to choose her own husband the author is backing her judgement, for Fanny has good reason to distrust Crawford anyway. 'I cannot think well of a man who sports with any woman's feelings,' she says (Chapter 36). Sir Thomas, in spite of some qualms, has allowed his daughter Maria to marry a stupid man whom she despises because the alliance 'would bring him such an addition of respectability and influence' (Chapter 21). The misery which she brings down on herself and her parents (like all adulterous wives, she is banished for ever from society) proves that Fanny acted sensibly. Emma Woodhouse is another heroine who would rather be single than marry the wrong person. She is in a much stronger position than most of Jane Austen's women – she has thirty thousand pounds and 'a most affectionate, indulgent father' – and so has 'none of the usual inducements of women to marry'. To Harriet, who is a little shocked by her attitude, she explains:

> a single woman of good fortune is always respectable, and may be as sensible and pleasant as anybody else! . . . Mine is an active, busy mind, with a great many independent resources; and I do not perceive why I should be more in want of employment at forty or fifty than one and twenty. (Chapter 10)

Emma is contrasted favourably with the mindless Harriet, but she is far from being a perfect character. Because she herself is flattered by almost everybody, she cannot see how little real power women have. (And in fact her 'active, busy mind' does more harm than good; she dabbles in human relationships, as she dabbles in painting, because she has no serious work to do.) Mr Elton's 'charade' on courtship is just the kind of sentiment she is used to hearing:

> My first displays the wealth and pomp of kings,
> Lords of the earth! their luxury and ease.
> Another view of man, my second brings,
> Behold him there, the monarch of the seas!
>
> But ah! united, what reverse we have!
> Man's boasted power and freedom, all are flown:

> Lord of the earth and sea, he bends a slave,
> And woman, lovely woman, reigns alone.

This offers a thoroughly conventional view of the roles of the sexes. The public world belongs to men – lords of the earth and sea, who have the power and the freedom – while in private life women are supreme. But the very existence of her friend Harriet, for whom she imagines the poem has been written, is a proof that men may treat women in other ways than this. When she has persuaded Harriet to refuse the best offer she is likely to get, Mr Knightley tries to explain to her how little an illegitimate girl can expect:

> Miss Harriet Smith may not find offers of marriage flow in so fast, though she is a very pretty girl. Men of sense, whatever you may choose to say, do not want silly wives. Men of family would not be very fond of connecting themselves with a girl of such obscurity – and most prudent men would be afraid of the inconvenience and disgrace they might be involved in, when the mystery of her parentage came to be revealed.

At the same time he is thoroughly annoyed with Emma for saying, predictably enough, that men fall in love with 'handsome faces' rather than 'well-informed minds'. 'Better be without sense than misapply it as you do.' (Chapter 8)

The moral – and it is implicit in all Jane Austen's fiction – is that a woman can expect deference only if she has something which men want, and that she will not get it if she is illegitimate, poor or an old maid. Mr Knightley is, of course, right about Elton, who has made it clear when alone with other men that he will only marry a woman with money. Later he is seen in his true colours when he snubs Harriet by refusing to dance with her, and this pinpoints the difference between him and Mr Knightley, who gives up his own inclinations to get her out of an unpleasant position.[4] However bluntly he may speak in private about Harriet's empty mind and her poor chances in the marriage market, he will not tolerate open nastiness to Harriet herself. Mr Knightley is above all a genuine, direct man, who 'cannot make speeches', but whose real kindness contrasts very favourably with the polished phrases of a Mr Elton. Here, as in her other novels, the man who treats women as his equals – even if he is sometimes rude – can be trusted more than the man who flatters them.

The Victorians liked heroines to resemble Fanny Price, with her headaches, her shrinking-violet nature and her willingness to let other people form her mind. But the typical Jane Austen heroine is very different, and has fewer successors. I have pointed out that she is often seen refusing a proposal, an act which to many women would have seemed like madness. She is just as likely to be found having a lively discussion, if not an actual argument, with a man (Elizabeth and Darcy, Emma and Mr Knightley, Anne and Captain Harville). For Jane Austen, in spite of the limited world which she had no choice but to live in, was a free spirit. She was a woman who delighted in using her mind, and she could not endure any relationship between two people who were not mentally equal. The word 'rational', like the word 'delicacy', is always used by her as a term of high praise. When we appreciate the author's scheme of values, there is an added resonance in Elizabeth's plea to Mr Collins, 'Do not consider me now as an elegant female attempting to plague you, but as a rational creature speaking the truth from her heart'.

4 Scott

Scott has been so neglected in the twentieth century that we can easily forget how very important he was to the Victorians. Throughout the nineteenth century he remained enormously popular, the reading public revered him, and he had a strong influence on some of the great Victorian novelists, notably the Brontës and George Eliot. Novels written much later in the century very often echo his work.

Whereas Jane Austen's novels are written entirely from a woman's point of view, in Scott's the viewpoint is masculine, and the women in his novels are only part of a much wider picture. One of his greatest works, *Old Mortality*, has a painfully ladylike heroine who blushes at her own impropriety when she visits the hero in his cell and who speaks standard English although everyone around her speaks Scots. This does not particularly matter, though, because in this novel the love interest is not important. Scott's women, whether or not they have loyalties and opinions of their own, are dragged along in the wake of the rebellions, wars and conspiracies which are his real subject matter. 'Freedom is for man alone,' says Isabelle in *Quentin Durward*, 'woman must ever seek a protector, since nature made her incapable to defend herself.' (Chapter 23) Some of the most interesting things he wrote are about how individual women cope with their defenceless situation.

Scott realised that women were extremely vulnerable. He wrote about violent societies and had also had some personal experience of violence, and this gave him a warm and deep sympathy with women, who were so often the victims. His attitude to them was, in the best sense of the word, chivalrous. He was quite aware that they could be ruthlessly married off or imprisoned in convents, violated, killed, or see their children slaughtered by the opposing army. Even in a civilised society they were often treated as pawns in a power game. Lucy, in *The Bride of Lammermoor*, is cruelly manipulated by her parents, who expect her to fall in love and get married according to their political plans. Scott comments on 'the

53

strict domestic discipline, which, at this period' (the early eighteenth century) 'was exercised over the females of a Scottish family'. (Chapter 30) In *Rob Roy*, which is set at about the same time, he says that in most upper-class marriages 'the feelings of the principal parties interested were no more regarded than if they had been a part of the live stock upon the lands'. (Chapter 37)

Another victim of society was the unmarried mother, whom Scott always treated sympathetically. Henry Warden, in *The Monastery*, voices the author's own opinion on the duties of men to women. Here we see a violent man, Julian Avenel, whose mistress Catherine, heavily pregnant, frightened and despised, is living with him in a state of 'handfasting' or trial marriage. Warden denounces this as a damnable system:

> It binds thee to the frailer being while she is the object of desire – it relieves thee when she is most the subject of pity – it gives all to brutal sense and nothing to generous and gentle affection . . . I say it is contrary to the pure Christian doctrine, which assigns woman to man as the partner of his labour, the soother of his evil, his helpmate in peril, his friend in affliction; not as the toy of his looser hours, or as a flower, which, once cropped, he may throw aside at pleasure. (Chapter 25)

As this indicates, Scott believed that woman, though 'the frailer being', should be an equal 'partner' and 'helpmate' to man. The difference between strong and weak women ('weak' not necessarily meaning 'fallen') is very important in his novels. Some (*The Bride of Lammermoor*) are built around a woman's weakness; others (*The Heart of Midlothian*) around a woman's strength. Ruskin paid a special tribute to Scott's heroines:

> In his imaginations of women . . . with endless varieties of grace, tenderness, and intellectual power, we find in all a quite infallible sense of dignity and justice; a fearless, instant, and untiring self-sacrifice, to even the appearance of duty, much more to its real claims; and, finally, a patient wisdom of deeply-restrained affection, which . . . gradually forms, animates and exalts the characters of the unworthy lovers . . . so that, in all cases, with Scott as with Shakespeare, it is the woman who watches over, teaches, and guides the youth.[1]

This suggests some of the reasons why Scott's women were thoroughly acceptable to the Victorians. They are – usually – morally stronger than men, but they do not defy them, and their self-sacrifice 'to even the appearance of duty' has no limits. Loyalty to family, nation, church or clan is seen by Scott as an important virtue, particularly in a woman. His heroines will not desert their group; 'I may not change the faith of my fathers like a garment,' says Rebecca (*Ivanhoe*, Chapter 44). Diana Vernon (*Rob Roy*, Chapter 9) gives much the same reason for refusing to abandon Catholicism. Most heroines have a father or brother to whom they are dutiful and devoted, even when they know he does not deserve it. A true heroine will not marry against her parents' wishes. Amy Robsart, in *Kenilworth*, breaks her father's heart by running away to get married and then allowing him to think she is a kept woman. Scott implies that a stronger heroine would have said no, but Amy, a 'lively, indulged and idle girl', whose father 'contradicted her in nothing', thinks only of herself. Her undutiful behaviour leads to her death, and although this is sad, it is not entirely undeserved.

At the same time Scott recognised that submission to a husband's or parent's wishes could go too far. He did not believe that a woman should, like Chaucer's Griselda, patiently put up with anything. When Lucy, in *The Bride of Lammermoor*, allows her parents to marry her to the wrong man, Scott says bluntly (in the introduction) that she acted weakly. Amy, a partly weak and partly strong character, refuses to obey her husband when he wants her to deny their own marriage. To his 'I command you', she replies: 'I cannot put your commands, my lord . . . in balance with those of honour and conscience. I will NOT, in this instance, obey you'. (Chapter 35) A woman can reasonably be asked to sacrifice her personal wishes, but not her honour or her conscience.

Another important quality of Scott's women is that they are the peacemakers. Those of them who live in violent times are more enlightened than the men around them because they are opposed in principle to revenge and pointless killing. Catherine, the Fair Maid of Perth, Bessie Maclure in *Old Mortality* and Rebecca in *Ivanhoe* all embody the 'feminine' qualities of endurance, caring and compassion. Rebecca is, significantly, a healer, a pupil of the woman doctor Miriam who has fallen 'a sacrifice to the fanaticism of the times', and she too is nearly burned as a witch for practising medicine. Although she will sacrifice her life if necessary she cannot see the point of the chivalrous code which assumes that men exist only to fight.

A feminist critic, in 1898, praised Scott because there was 'less of the accepted cant about women in his novels than in the works of some who are supposed to know better'.[2] Some cant there certainly is; many of his heroines are genteel nonentities and the great majority are young, beautiful, conventional and upper-class. But Scott was also interested in the kind of woman whose devotion to a cause was stronger than her devotion to a man, and he did not think it was absolutely necessary for a woman to get married.

The hero of his first novel, *Waverley*, is strongly attracted to two different women and two incompatible ways of life. The theme of the book is romantic heroism versus normality, and while Flora inspires Waverley to fight for a noble, but doomed cause, Rose offers him a conventional marriage and a quiet life. Flora understands that Waverley is not her natural mate because 'the woman whom you marry ought to have affections and opinions moulded upon yours. Her studies ought to be your studies, her wishes, her feelings, her hopes, her fears, should all mingle with yours.' Rose is this kind of woman and certainly will not blame Waverley for quietly detaching himself from the Jacobites. But Flora is probably the first heroine in fiction whose political loyalties are more important to her than anything else.

> I dare hardly . . . tell you the situation of my feelings, they are so different from those usually ascribed to young women at my period of life . . . From my infancy till this day, I have had but one wish – the restoration of my royal benefactors to their rightful throne. It is impossible to express to you the devotion of my feelings to this single subject, and I will frankly confess, that it has so occupied my mind as to exclude every thought respecting what is called my own settlement in life. (Chapter 27)

Flora and Rose are the first of many pairs of what Maggie Tulliver called dark and fair heroines. Like Rebecca and Rowena in *Ivanhoe*, and Minna and Brenda in *The Pirate*, they have very different destinies, because the 'fair' girls with no spiritual depths 'carry away all the happiness' while the author's real sympathy remains with 'the dark unhappy ones'.[3] Because they are committed to a losing cause or a doomed love affair, these women remain single. Flora goes into a convent and Minna and Rebecca dedicate their lives to helping others, and Scott insists that this is not as sad as it appears:

> But Minna – the high-minded and imaginative Minna – she, gifted with such depth of feeling and enthusiasm, yet doomed to see both blighted in early youth . . . was she, could she be happy? Reader, she *was* happy; for . . . to each duty performed there is assigned a degree of mental peace and high consciousness of honourable exertion, corresponding to the difficulty of the task accomplished. (*The Pirate*, Chapter 42)

This may sound smug, but in fact Scott is saying something very important – and something which the Victorians almost forgot – that an unmarried woman can lead a worthwhile life. At the same time he sees Minna's duties as very traditional (looking after her father and sister) and he endorses the convention that a woman can love only one man.

In *Ivanhoe* the contrast between the 'fair' and 'dark' heroine is explored in detail when Rowena and Rebecca are imprisoned by the Norman war lords who desire them. As a Saxon and a Jewess, both of them belong to a subject race and can expect no mercy. Scott tells us (Chapter 23) that the times were so violent that women were safe only in convents, and in the character of Ulrica, or Urfried, he shows us the common fate of Saxon women. Her father and brothers have been killed by the Normans, but although she is now too old to rouse any feelings but contempt, she has been allowed to live on as 'the paramour of their murderer'. Everyone agrees that she is a polluted creature who ought to have committed suicide rather than let this happen. She has lost what Scott considered the most precious virtues in a woman – loyalty to her family group, and chastity – and Rebecca and Rowena now face the same fate. Their reactions, though, are extremely different.

Rowena has been accustomed to get everything she wants and when she realises that she is in the power of a violent man she is terrified and breaks down. Scott had too much consideration for his readers to let her be raped, but he leaves us in no doubt that, if this had happened, she would have become another Ulrica. In more than one novel he says that women should not be pampered because then they will not know how to defend themselves in a crisis. Amy Robsart and Effie Deans are other examples of women who have been spoiled, and are therefore helpless. Amy had 'only been accustomed to form and to express her wishes, leaving to others the task of fulfilling them; and thus, at the most momentous period of her life, she was alike destitute of presence of mind, and of ability to form for herself any reasonable or prudent plan of conduct'. (*Kenilworth*, Chapter 25)

Rebecca, on the other hand, has always known that she is liable to be attacked and is 'better prepared by habits of thought, and by natural strength of mind to encounter the dangers to which she was exposed'. (Chapter 24) She is able to reason calmly with Bois-Guilbert and is prepared to jump off the tower rather than submit to him. 'God made women weak', as she says, but women can still choose whether to sacrifice their integrity or to suffer with courage:

> I tell thee, proud Templar, that not in thy fiercest battles hast thou displayed more of thy vaunted courage than has been shown by women when called upon to suffer by affection or duty. I am myself a woman, tenderly nurtured, naturally fearful of danger, and impatient of pain – yet, when we enter those fatal lists, thou to fight and I to suffer, I feel the strong assurance within me that my courage shall mount higher than thine. (Chapter 39)

The weak women in Scott, though, usually do the maximum amount of damage to themselves and others. Lucy Ashton, a 'fair' heroine – 'in the last degree gentle, soft, timid and feminine' – destroys herself and Ravenswood because she gives in meekly to her parents. The 'softness' of her mind, Scott suggests, amounts 'almost to feebleness'. (Chapter 20) Berengaria in *The Talisman* is another ultra-feminine woman who thinks she can do what she likes with men. She and her ladies play a childish trick on Kenneth, which nearly causes his death. Edith, the only sensible woman in the court, is unpopular with them because she has 'a more noble cast of thoughts and sentiments' and is less preoccupied with dress. At the beginning of the novel Kenneth and Saladin have an interesting argument about the status of women. The Moslem believes that they only exist to please men; the Crusader argues that devotion to one woman ennobles a man and that women in harems are 'poor sensual slaves'. Scott emphatically agrees with the Christian/chivalric view of women, but he shows us, too, that a good many western women are not worth a man's worship. Only the exceptional woman, like Edith, deserves devotion.

Edith is interesting mainly as a symbol, because basically she is exactly like many other Scott heroines, who are all pure and noble and talk unconvincing high-flown English. Only two of his strong heroines, Diana Vernon and Jeanie Deans, are not quite like this. Diana is a lively girl whom the Scottish characters call 'daft' (mad or frolicsome), and who makes an attractive first impression. She has a 'powerful mind', is 'accustomed to mind nobody's opinion but my own', and has free-and-easy manners, 'I belong, in habits of thinking and acting, rather to your sex, with which I have always been brought up, than to my own' (Chapter 13). She is, in fact, an ancestress of Shirley Keeldar, Diana of the Crossways and Sue Bridehead – all heroines who seem much more bold and unconventional than they really are. Actually Diana has no strong opinions; her Catholicism is little more than family tradition and, unlike Flora, she is quite prepared to marry someone who is not a Jacobite. At the end of the novel she is revealed as a completely traditional woman when we find that she is acting under her father's orders. He has given her the choice between marrying one of her boorish cousins or going into a convent, and although Scott clearly perceives the cruelty of this treatment, Diana does not – ' ''And she will never leave her dear father!'' exclaimed Miss Vernon, clinging fondly to his arm.' (Chapter 38) We are told in the last chapter that 'so dutiful a daughter cannot but prove a good wife'.

Scott was usually more successful with lower-class women than with 'young ladies'. His ladies' maids are often more sensible and resourceful than their mistresses (e.g. Janet in *Kenilworth* and Jenny in *Old Mortality*). His greatest heroine, Jeanie Deans, is infinitely more convincing than his Ediths and Isabellas because she is a working woman, who speaks in dialect and relies only on herself.

The Heart of Midlothian, though connected with the Porteous riots of 1737, is more directly concerned with women's problems than any other novel Scott wrote. George Staunton ruins two women, Madge Wildfire and Effie, and then stays in the background while they, and the innocent Jeanie, bear the suffering, guilt and shame. Jeanie, as the 1898 reviewer said, 'has 'few of the stock attractions of her sex'. She is nearly thirty, plain and has an awkward conscience which will not allow her, even for the best of reasons, to tell a conventional lie. It is a measure of Scott's genius that he makes us sympathise with her decision, although few readers would do the same. Effie, who is young, beautiful and pathetic, has all the stock attractions of her sex (she would probably have been the heroine if the novel had been written seventy years later), but Scott makes it clear, in spite of his great sympathy for her, that she is a much weaker person than her sister.

Jeanie, who has a 'depth of thought and force of character superior to the frivolous part of her sex' (Chapter 14), feels that she can be responsible only to her sense of right and wrong. When Staunton, like Rochester in *Jane Eyre*, tries to bully her out of her convictions he gets nowhere. The discipline of her church encourages her to seek advice directly from God, which means, in effect, that she has to think long and deeply about the principles on which her conduct is based. She is devoted to her father and later to her husband, but thinks it wise to keep certain things concealed from them (an action which Charlotte Yonge, in the mid-nineteenth century, considered a serious sin). Her father cannot help her with her terrible problem, and Butler, who has a much more nervous and 'feminine' temperament than she has, is little more use. When he asks her, 'Would you undertake such a journey without a man to protect you?' she replies, 'Alas! who will protect and take care of you?'. (Chapter 27) (Scott's ladylike heroines do have to be protected on journeys and it is only Jeanie's good sense which enables her to survive.) Scott does not rely on the power of virtue to overcome all obstacles but shows that Jeanie is successful in most things she undertakes because, as well as being good, she is resourceful, hard-working and shrewd.

Yet goodness, in the end, is what matters most. Jeanie's respect for life (and here she is contrasted with Staunton, who makes Effie's situation worse by the killing of Porteous) is what eventually saves her sister; when the Queen asks her about Porteous she is able to say honestly that she would have 'gone to the end of the earth' to save him, and this tips the scale. An important theme of this novel is that taking the easy way out is fatal; Margaret Murdockson tries to save her daughter's reputation by killing her baby, but all this does is drive her mad.

Jeanie refuses to do evil in the name of good, and is triumphant.

Margaret Murdockson is one of the few violent women in Scott; another is Rob Roy's wife, Helen MacGregor, who is much more bloodthirsty than her husband. There is some excuse for her, though, because she has been raped and lives on, like Ulrica, with a deep sense of shame. Another woman outlaw – this time a fairly friendly one – is the gypsy Meg in *Guy Mannering*, 'the wild chieftainess of the lawless people amongst whom she was born'. (Chapter 55) An Amazon six feet high, who bullies timid men like the Dominie and easily overshadows the two nominal heroines, she boasts:

I can do what good women canna, and daurna do. I can do what would freeze the blood of those bred in biggit wa's [builded walls] for naething but to bind bairns' heads, and to hap them in the cradle. (Chapter 47)

But in spite of being a fighting woman, Meg has kindly qualities (she is attached to her benefactors and likes children) which make her, in the long run, a force for good, and she completely dominates the novel in which she appears. Scott's 'ladies' are failures, but women living outside polite society had a liberating effect on his imagination.

5 Women Novelists of the Early Nineteenth Century

'The literary class of women,' wrote Harriet Taylor, 'especially in England, are ostentatious in disclaiming the desire for equality of citizenship, and proclaiming their complete satisfaction with the place which society assigns to them.'[1] Broadly speaking, this was true when she wrote it in 1851 and went on being true throughout the century. Most women novelists accepted things as they found them and several insisted in public that women were the inferior sex. Others, including Mrs Gaskell and George Eliot, stated their support for a Married Women's Property Act in 1856. Towards the end of the century a few feminist novelists appeared, most of them now forgotten. Almost all talented women writers – of whom there were many – gave a much more lively and realistic picture of women than most male novelists did.

The first feminist writer was Mary Wollstonecraft (1759–97) whose unfinished novel *The Wrongs of Woman* was published posthumously in 1798. At the time her views caused a certain amount of sensation. Maria Edgeworth, in her early novels, attempted to discredit extreme feminism, after which the theme disappears from the English novel for half a century.

MARIA EDGEWORTH

Maria Edgeworth (1768–1849)[2] was a minor writer who influenced several major writers. Her *Castle Rackrent* (1800) was the first important regional novel, and she is best remembered for this and her other Irish stories, *Ormond* and *The Absentee*. Scott paid tribute to this part of her work in the Postscript to *Waverley*. She also wrote 'English' novels, mostly about fashionable life, of which the earliest, *Belinda*, was warmly praised by Jane Austen.[3]

She had an unusually wide range of interests for a woman writer; her moral stories for children were famous in their day and her pictures of Irish life are superb. It is only possible to look at one aspect of her work here.

In an early work, 'Letter from a Gentleman to his friend upon the birth of a daughter', she expressed the belief that women were standing on the threshold of a new age. 'Till of late women were kept in Turkish ignorance'. Now some were being educated and, far from despising domestic duties, they were likely to make the best wives. However, she disliked 'that daring spirit which despises the common forms of society, and which breaks through the delicacy and reserve of female manners'.[4]

Belinda (1801) explores the question of how a woman ought to live. The heroine is launched on to the marriage market by an aunt who believes 'that a young lady's chief business is to please in society'. (Chapter 1) She is chaperoned by Lady Delacour, who is secretly dying from a wound received in a duel with another woman. Belinda becomes 'convinced that the life of a fine lady would never make me happy' (Chapter 10), and refuses to marry for money, as her aunt wishes – 'she judges and acts for herself'. (Chapter 9)

Contrasted to the world of fashion is the world of 'domestic happiness'. The Percivals are a devoted couple who help all their children, boys and girls, to develop their talents. (Children are important in Miss Edgeworth's scheme of things; Lady Delacour is redeemed through learning to love her small daughter, who had been rejected by her father for not being a son.) The wife has 'much accurate knowledge, and a taste for literature, which made her the chosen companion of her husband's understanding, as well as of his heart. He was not obliged to reserve his conversation for friends of his own sex.' (Chapter 16) Mr Percival argues against those who advocate 'the rights of women', but he also asks:

Without diminishing their grace, softness or delicacy, might not they cultivate their minds? Do you think ignorance . . . an amiable defect, essential to the female character?

The main plot almost certainly had some influence on the Elinor plot in *Sense and Sensibility*. Belinda is attracted to Clarence, who seems to love her, but she finds that he is committed to a younger girl. Belinda assumes she is his mistress and, like Elinor, feels she has no right to come between them. The truth is that

Clarence has read Rousseau's *Emile* and is educating an inexperienced girl to be his wife. He soon realises, though, that she compares badly with Belinda:

> The one he found was his equal,, the other his inferior; the one he saw could be a companion, a friend to him for life, the other would merely be his pupil, or his plaything. Belinda had cultivated taste, ·an active understanding, a knowledge of literature, the power and the habit of conducting herself; Virginia was ignorant and indolent, she had few ideas, and no wish to extend her knowledge. (Chapter 26)

Belinda's virtues spring 'from reason'; like Jane Austen, Miss Edgeworth believed strongly that both sexes could and should be rational. She also made Belinda deny 'that a wife is a being whose actions are necessarily governed by a husband'. (Chapter 9) But feminists are ridiculed in this novel. Mrs Freke, 'a champion for the Rights of Woman' (Chapter 17), is one of a band of 'female outlaws', who roams round at night in men's clothes and, like Dickens' Miss Wade, persuades a young girl to run away from home and live with her. She scoffs at marriage and wants to abolish 'female delicacy' – 'Why, when a woman likes a man, does she not go and tell him so honestly?'. This kind of woman, Miss Edgeworth feels, is not only absurd but dangerous; it is she who provokes the duel between two women in which one of them nearly dies. She does not deserve to be taken seriously because she is merely an eccentric member of a circle where most people are rich, bored and useless. Husbands and wives dislike each other, girls marry for money and a constant round of parties leaves no time for reading or any constructive activity.

The Modern Griselda (1805) argues that a wife need be neither a slave or a tyrant. The heroine is a woman who bullies her husband and eventually drives him away. Discussing Chaucer's Griselda, Emma, a happy wife, says she 'could never have loved or esteemed' a man who wanted abject obedience, but

> The situation and understandings of women have been so much improved since [Chaucer's] days. Women were then slaves, now they are free. (Chapter 4)

The theme of *Leonora* (1806) is that women must not forfeit their new freedom by wild behaviour. 'What a misfortune it is to be born a woman!' the novel begins. These are the words of Olivia, the villainess, and they echo those of Maria in *The Wrongs of Woman*, 'Why was I not born a man, or why was I born at all?'[5] Like Mary Wollstonecraft's heroine, Olivia is separated from her husband, loves another man, and wishes she could get divorced. The trusting Leonora protects her when she is in danger of being thrown out of society, and Olivia ungratefully goes off with Leonora's husband. She gets him back only after great suffering, which she bears uncomplainingly, and the predictable moral is that only a good woman can hold a man. As in *Sense and Sensibility*, the woman who controls her feelings is compared favourably with the woman who does not. Olivia claims that she 'dares to rise above the prejudices of her sex' (Letter 1), but in fact she is one of the weaker members of her sex because she is a slave to her own emotions and cannot live without men. Leonora's mother gives Miss Edgeworth's point of view:

> Of late years we have heard more of sentiment than of principles; more of the rights of woman than of her duties. If in this age of reason women make a bad use of that power which they have obtained by the cultivation of their understanding, they will degrade and enslave themselves beyond redemption. . . . If men find that the virtue of women diminishes in proportion as intellectual cultivation increases, they will connect, fatally for the freedom and happiness of our sex, the idea of female ignorance and female innocence . . . Opinion obtained freedom for women; by opinion they may be again enslaved. (Letter 4)

Maria Edgeworth shared some of the prejudices of her time, for instance on illegitimacy and the double standard. She did not defend unchastity in men, but she felt it was a much more serious fault in a woman. Leonora does not (like a Mary Wollstonecraft heroine) renounce her husband when he is unfaithful; she does everything possible to win him back. Ormond is a lovable rake, very like Tom Jones, but when he hears that the woman he admires has been 'imprudent' he drops her. In *The Absentee* (1812) we are expected to be shocked when a man introduces his mistress to respectable ladies. The hero of this novel, a thoroughly good young man, renounces Grace, the woman he wants to marry, because he has heard she is illegitimate – 'Lord Colambre had the greatest dread of marrying any woman whose mother had conducted herself ill'. (Chapter 7) The story turns out to be false but, although Grace is hurt, she 'sighed, and acknowledged that, in prudence, it ought to have been an *invincible* obstacle – she admired the firmness of his decision.' (Chapter 17)

Helen (1834) was highly praised by Mrs Gaskell, who borrowed the central situation for the 'letters plot' in *Wives and Daughters*. Although it begins slowly, and the first half is less good than the second, it is an impressive novel which deserves reprinting. In the background is a 'female politician', Lady Davenant, who has some interesting comments on the role of her sex:

> Let me observe to you that the position of women in society is somewhat different from what it was . . . thirty years since. Women are now so highly cultivated, and political subjects are at present of so much importance . . . to all human creatures who live together in society, you can hardly expect, Helen, that you, as a rational being, can go through the world as it now is, without forming any opinion on points of public importance. You cannot, I conceive, satisfy yourself with the common namby-pamby little missy phrase, 'ladies have nothing to do with politics'. (Chapter 28)

We are meant to take this seriously. However, Lady Davenant blames herself because, 'engrossed with politics', she neglected the training of her daughter Cecilia, who has grown up weak and selfish. Before marriage she exchanged love letters with a man and has not told her husband, who has vowed 'never to marry a woman who had ever had any previous attachment'. (Chapter 32) When the letters turn up she persuades her friend Helen to take the blame, and this part of the novel is very much more powerful than the corresponding episode in Mrs Gaskell. Both girls are made to go through the extremes of terror and anguish, and in trying to save Cecilia's marriage Helen nearly forfeits her own. 'I am not fit to be your wife. Your wife should not be suspected,' she writes to her fiancé, Beauclerc, when she realises that society has condemned her. Beauclerc, though, is a finer character than Cecilia's husband, because he agrees to trust Helen although she cannot explain her behaviour. He even feels that he loves her better 'for the independence of mind she shows in thus braving my opinion', and is glad that she is not a 'discreet proper-behaved young lady' but 'a being able to stand alone, to think and feel, decide and act for herself'. (Chapter 34)

Even Cecilia's husband comes to feel that his demands on his wife were unreasonable. He does not blame her for having been in love before she knew him, but for having been dishonest. Although the novel's great theme is the importance of truthfulness, we are made to see that fashionable society encourages women to lie. When they are totally condemned for one small mistake, it is not surprising that some of them, like Cecilia, will sacrifice their friends to save themselves. Most Edgeworth novels end with weddings; like her contemporaries, she did not discuss the problems of the single woman in depth. Personally, though, she was 'not afraid of being an old maid'.[6] A character in *Helen* complains that 'every girl in these days is early impressed with the idea that she must be married, that she cannot be happy unmarried' (Chapter 19), although Helen herself feels that she could be. Olivia is despised for her over-dependence on men, 'What will become of Olivia when she ceases to love and be loved?'. (*Leonora*, Letter 79) The plain girl in *The Absentee*, Miss Broadhurst, refuses to flirt with the men who are after her money because she has 'a just sense of her own merit, and of what was becoming and due to the dignity of her sex'. (Chapter 4) Whatever her circumstances, Miss Edgeworth believed that a woman should hold on to her dignity.

SUSAN FERRIER

Susan Ferrier (1782–1854), sometimes called the Scottish Jane Austen, wrote only three novels, *Marriage* (1818), *The Inheritance* (1824) and *Destiny* (1831). But they were good enough to win the admiration of Scott and of Miss Edgeworth, who shared the younger writer's regional loyalties and her strong dislike of the fashionable world. She differs from the average woman novelist, not only in being more witty, but also in her attitude to her female characters. The most important problem for a Ferrier heroine is not whom she marries but how she lives; her outlook is strongly Christian. But she was more radical than many Christians, in that she did not believe that women had been created inferior to men.

Her first two novels, *Marriage* and *The Inheritance*, begin with the birth of the heroine, and in each case she makes fun of 'those sturdy sticklers for man's supremacy' *(Inheritance*, Chapter 1) who wanted a male baby. In *Destiny* the bigoted Highland chief Glenroy idolises his lazy son and despises his daughter. In all three books Miss Ferrier contrasts those who try to lead a decent and moral life, usually in Scotland, with worldly Londoners. *Marriage* and *Destiny* both follow the fortunes of two girls brought up in different households. In each case one girl is beautiful, selfish, and makes a fashionable marriage which breaks down. The other girl is less glamorous and more moral, and in the end her goodness brings its own reward. In *The Inheritance*, there is only one important woman character, and her good and evil impulses pull her two ways.

Gertrude is unusually interesting because her behaviour is 'contrary to all that was then considered correct in a heroine'.[7] She is 'ardent, enthusiastic and susceptible', but she has faults and makes mistakes which most novelists thought were perfectly normal for a young man but very dangerous for a woman.

Gertrude's uncle Lord Rossville, whose title she inherits halfway through the novel, and her mother (who is really not her mother) both want to push her into an unwelcome marriage. Lord Rossville, a stupid tyrant who thinks it unladylike to go for a walk before breakfast, complains – 'A young female to presume to judge for herself in opposition to the wishes of her parents, to the opinion of the world, to the general voice of mankind . . . it is lamentable, it is deplorable, it is monstrous!'. (Chapter 37) Gertrude, an independent girl, feels 'that, to be approved of, she must cease to act, cease to think, cease to feel, cease to love, but as directed by the will of her mother and uncle'. (Chapter 38) Understandably, she rebels, although she admits in theory that children should obey their parents. She tries to resolve this contradiction by saying she will give her mother 'the reverence of a child' but not 'the submission of a slave'. (Chapter 58) Miss Ferrier's judgement is that parents who bully and use emotional blackmail have only themselves to blame if there is friction. 'Had Mrs St.Clair ever been the *friend* of her daughter, Gertrude would not have acted thus.' (Chapter 32)

Gertrude is in love with Colonel Delmour, who is chiefly interested in her money, and who also wants to dominate her and make her indifferent to principle. 'Woman's heart,' he says, 'is indeed a royal palace if it admit but one guest', and she is to be 'mine, solely and exclusively mine.' (Chapter 72) All this time she is loved by her guardian Lyndsay, although he is well aware of her faults. These faults blaze out when Gertrude, now very rich, plunges into high society, wastes money and forgets her obligations to her friends. When she turns out not to be a countess after all the Colonel deserts her and she marries Lyndsay, leads 'a happy and useful life', and learns to 'bless the day that had deprived her of her earthly inheritance'. (Chapter 106)

It is unusual for a heroine to lose a fortune, instead of gaining it, at the end of a novel. Still more surprising are Lyndsay's and Gertrude's respective roles. It is the woman who falls in love rashly, overspends and makes mistakes which she bitterly regrets; the man who has no faults and waits patiently for her to reform. The implication is that women, as well as men, can go wrong and hopefully recover. *Destiny* is another novel where the heroine is jilted, but is allowed to marry a better man. Miss Ferrier, tongue in cheek, describes her as 'a quiet, inoffensive, temperate creature, which is all that can be expected of a female'. (Chapter 12) In fact Edith is a 'naturally strong' character, but her mind has been 'relaxed and enfeebled, from the constant habit of looking to Reginald as the ruler and arbiter of her very thought'. (Chapter 28) Both novels, like those of Charlotte and Anne Brontë, stress that a woman must not make an idol of the man she loves. Religion, on the whole, has a bracing effect, and women who lose their lovers are encouraged to exert themselves and think of other people.

As well as being original, Susan Ferrier's novels are extremely funny. There are satirical portraits of doting couples, selfish men, spoiled children, girls who cultivate the cant of sensibility and a spinster, Miss Becky Duguid, who 'as a single woman, had vainly expected to escape the cares and anxieties of the married state' but finds that everyone assumes 'that, as a single woman, she could have nothing to do but oblige her friends'. (*Inheritance*, Chapter 30) Admittedly, her plots can be conventional, but at her best she is not hurt by comparisons with Jane Austen.

CATHERINE GORE, HARRIET MARTINEAU AND FRANCES TROLLOPE

Some of the most popular novels written between 1825 and 1850 belonged to the 'silver-fork school', which dealt with the upper-class marriage market and fashionable life. Most of the authors are deservedly forgotten, but the best of them, Catherine Gore (1799–1861), has her place in literary history. Her most famous novel is *Mothers and Daughters* (1831). The central figure, Lady Maria Willingham, is a type very familiar in nineteenth-century fiction, a 'manoeuvring mamma'. In the early chapters she and her sister-in-law have a race to produce a male heir to the family property, and there is universal horror when they have only daughters. 'Thank God, I never cursed myself with any thing but *sons*' says Maria's father-in-law, while her husband defends her, 'I assure you she was deeply concerned by the birth of a second daughter'. (Volume 1, Chapter 2) When the wretched girls grow up she is 'desperately determined' to marry them off. Men sneer at them for failing to find husbands and their mother assures them 'that they had been a drawback upon her own comfort and happiness from the hour of their birth'. There is no happy ending for them because they have been corrupted by fashionable society and because the supply of young women exceeds the demand. The only girls who do get married are those who do it for the right reasons. Although the moral is very obvious, *Mothers and Daughters* gives a depressing picture of a society where women have no intrinsic value and have to strain every nerve to get an establishment.

A non-silver-fork novel, *Mrs. Armytage, or Female Domination* (1836) is about a masterful widow who keeps her son out of his inheritance and forbids her daughter to get married, so that she dies of a broken heart. Mrs Armytage is 'a squire in petticoats, a beardless justice of the peace'. (Volume 1, Chapter 10) In her way she is a great woman, but, as one character asks:

> What business has a woman with *great* qualities? Unless you could make a Lord Chancellor, an Archbishop of Canterbury, or a Commander-in-Chief of Mrs. Armytage, I don't see any use that her qualities could be put to! (Volume 3, Chapter 6)

Female domination is a wholly bad thing; Mrs Armytage repents and dies miserably, while her son manages the estate more efficiently than she did. A bossy Duchess, who is even worse than Mrs Armytage because she interferes in politics, is finally forced to give in to her husband and stop tormenting her children. Mrs

Gore feels that women should be domesticated, pure and loving, and then their femaleness can be respected. Mrs Armytage's 'masculine propensities' have so distorted her nature that she resents her own granddaughter because she wanted an heir. The author cannot understand how 'the birth of so fair and promising a creature could be a source of annoyance to any human being'. (Volume 2, Chapter 1)

Harriet Martineau's novel *Deerbrook* (1839) almost failed to get published because it was so different from the silver-fork variety. Miss Martineau (1802–76) was a self-supporting woman of letters, an influential writer on political economy, and a feminist.[8] *Deerbrook* was much admired by Charlotte Brontë, perhaps because it gives a sympathetic picture of a poor and plain governess, Maria Young. Maria is lame and knows she will not marry, but she is determined to be cheerful and useful. Women who are disappointed in love, she insists, can recover if they try. Margaret, the heroine, is a robust girl who is prepared to do a servant's work if necessary. But when she wants to earn money Maria tells her:

> 'For an educated woman . . . there is in all England no chance of subsistence but by teaching . . . or by being . . . the feminine gender of the tailor and the hatter.'
>
> 'The tutor, the tailor and the hatter? Is this all?'
>
> 'All, except that there are departments of art and literature from which it is impossible to shut women out. These are not, however, to be regarded as resources for bread.' (Chapter 39)

Original in some ways, the novel reveals a conventional view of women in others. Margaret's fiancé leaves her because he hears that she has been attracted to another man in the past and he wants 'a first, and an entire, and an exclusive love'. (Chapter 36) Though pure 'as the world esteems purity', she does not come up to his standard because she is 'no longer with virgin affections'. (Chapter 35) Of course he is mistaken; Margaret is too perfect a heroine to have fallen in love twice. But there is no suggestion that he behaved unreasonably, given the circumstances, or that he will be anything but a good husband.

Frances Trollope (1780–1863) is usually remembered only as the mother of Anthony and the first woman to write a book about America. But she was also a fine novelist; *The Vicar of Wrexhill*

(1837) – about a cleric who exploits the emotions of women – and *The Widow Barnaby* (1839) are both memorable works. *Michael Armstrong: The Factory Boy* (1840) was written to expose the dreadful conditions of child workers before the Ten Hours Act. The heroine is a young girl, Mary Brotherton, who is in the pleasant position of having a large fortune and no relatives to control her, but who is profoundly ignorant of where her money comes from. When she decides to stop being a conventional rich young lady and to find out what is happening Mrs Trollope shows us, through her eyes, exactly what child labour meant.

Mary, a strong woman who is quite prepared to go into dangerous places to save a child, feels that 'if I have not vigour enough both of mind and body to be in some degree useful, I should hardly think it worth while to live'. (Chapter 22) There is an important scene between her and Martha Dowling, a poor plain girl who feels that her highest duty is to her odious father, the factory owner, although she knows he is making other people suffer. Mary tells her that although her duty as a child is important, she has a higher duty 'to your own soul'. (Chapter 21) Mary, with her 'powerful, healthy, unprejudiced and unselfish mind' (Chapter 14), gets her own way most of the time by ignoring the codes of polite behaviour – 'I am not a gentlewoman – and why should I torment myself by affecting to be one?'. (Chapter 10) One of the few ways in which a woman could exercise power at this time was by having a lot of money, and Mary uses hers to help several people. She finally marries a working-class boy, younger than herself, whom she has sent to school; an ending so extraordinary that Mrs Trollope could only hint at it.

All these writers made a real contribution to the novel in the early nineteenth century. They were overshadowed by a greater group of women writers who appeared in the 1840s, but they remain worth reading, and it is sad that the twentieth century hardly knows them.

6 Dickens

In *Dombey and Son*, the first of his great novels and one which almost wholly turns on the differences between the sexes, Dickens says that women's nature

> is ever, in the mass, better, truer, higher, nobler, quicker to feel and much more constant to retain, all tenderness and pity, self-denial and devotion, than the nature of men. (Chapter 3)

This was his considered opinion. In his novels, as in Scott's, women are, broadly speaking, the better, kinder and purer sex. He was aware that there were many exceptions. He drew a whole gallery of murderous women, sordid old crones, husband-hunting girls who fight viciously for men and women who bully their husbands once they are caught, and his early novels are full of derisive comments about women who pretend to be younger and more attractive than they really are. In the *Pickwick Papers*, Jingle elopes with a rich, but ugly and foolish spinster. When her brother comes after them to get her back he protests:

> '. . . lady's free to act as she pleases, – more than one-and-twenty.'
> 'More than one-and-twenty!' ejaculated Wardle, contemptuously, 'More than one-and-forty!'
> 'I an't' said the spinster aunt, her indignation getting the better of her determination to faint.
> 'You are', replied Wardle, 'you're fifty if you're an hour.'
> Here the spinster aunt uttered a loud shriek, and became senseless. (Chapter 10)

The same brutal jokes about older women disfigure *Barnaby Rudge* and *Nicholas Nickleby*. Fanny Squeers, who is twenty-three and still unmarried, is ridiculed for her attempts to get a husband

and compared unfavourably with her engaged friend, 'Tilda, who is only eighteen. In the same novel, Miss Knag 'still aimed at youth, though she had shot beyond it years ago' (Chapter 17) and Mrs Nickleby is shown to be vain and silly because, at a time of life when she ought to know better, she is flattered by the attentions of the man next door. Similar types appear in the 'very decidedly grown-up daughter' in *Little Dorrit* and the 'mature young lady' in *Our Mutual Friend*. But Dickens' point was that these women are funny or repellent because they do not live up to the highest standards of their sex.

Like Scott, again, he was very conscious that women were often cruelly treated by men. He shows several violent husbands or husband-substitutes – Sikes, Quilp, Jonas Chuzzlewit, Jerry Cruncher and the brickmakers in *Bleak House*. Jonas is 'determined to conquer his wife, break her spirit, bind her temper, crush all her humours like so many nut-shells – kill her, for aught I know'. Dickens comments:

> Oh woman, God beloved in old Jerusalem! The best among us need deal lightly with thy faults, if only for the punishment thy nature will endure, in bearing heavy evidence against us on the Day of Judgement. (Chapter 28)

Cruelty to the fallen woman was another social fact which he often criticised. In *Oliver Twist*, the angelic Rose Maylie, poles apart from the prostitute Nancy, is the only person who is kind to her. 'If there was more like you,' Nancy sobs, 'there would be fewer like me.' (Chapter 40) Nancy finally decides that she wants to lead a better life and dies clasping Rose's handkerchief, the symbol that she is redeemed. The situation is repeated in three of his later novels (between Harriet Carker and Alice Marwood, Agnes and Little Em'ly, and Esther and her mother, Lady Dedlock), and, as we have seen, it became a popular theme in Victorian fiction.

However, what Dickens was most concerned with in his treatment of male/female relationships was psychological cruelty. Believing that the best women were always ready to sacrifice themselves, he was interested in how this could be exploited. He also had a great deal to say about the father–daughter relationship in Victorian England and the assumption that a woman should live for and through her family.

We may begin with Little Nell, whose great popularity with the public suggests that she embodied many of the age's ideals about women. At fourteen she takes on the enormous responsibility of caring for her grandfather and keeping him out of trouble, and in the end it kills her. Dickens shows her to be a pleasant little girl who could easily survive on her own because people give her work and want to help her. But her grandfather, a 'sacred charge' to her, is a distasteful nuisance to practically everyone else. Through the eyes of Mrs Jarley, by no means a hard-hearted woman, Dickens shows us how the relationship appears to other people:

> 'I can't leave her,' answered the old man, 'We can't separate. What would become of me without her?'
> 'I should have thought you were old enough to take care of yourself, if you ever will be,' retorted Mrs Jarley sharply.

Nell quickly assures her that they cannot bear to be parted from each other, at which

> Mrs Jarley looked at the old man, who tenderly took Nell's hand and detained it in his own, as if she could have very well dispensed with his company, or even his earthly existence. (*The Old Curiosity Shop*, Chapter 27)

This is not the only place where Dickens comments sharply, through a less ethereal woman, on a heroine's saintly self-sacrifice. Nell is, in effect, handcuffed to the crazy old man, and would not have died if he had left her alone. 'My love for my dear child was a diseased love,' as Mr Wickfield says of Agnes, for all the grandfather's troubles spring from his desire to make Nell rich, a theme taken up again in *Bleak House*. And her devotion achieves nothing, because he goes to pieces and dies as soon as she is gone. Again and again Dickens comes back to this situation. His typical heroine has a father, brother, or husband whom she unquestioningly loves and supports although he usually does not deserve it. These heroines run in an almost straight line from Madeline in *Nicholas Nickleby* to Lizzie in *Our Mutual Friend*. In the latter novel we find the crippled Jenny Wren, a sourer Little Nell, supporting an alcoholic father, whom she calls her child, and not attempting to hide her hostile feelings.

Nell is the only heroine who actually dies. More often the

father-figure dies or reforms, and she is set free. Some women in the dark novels of the 1850s (Ada, Louisa, Pet) have their entire lives blighted because of their love for an undeserving man. But in most of his novels the gentle self-sacrificing girl is triumphant. Dickens was interested in the effects of the environment on character; writing about prostitutes, the French Revolution and so on, he often said that people could not be blamed for behaving badly if they had never had a fair chance. However, he just as constantly shows a heroine remaining good in almost impossible circumstances. It is unlikely that Florence would really have gone on loving her father for as long as she does, or that Esther would have been the saintly person she is when she had had nothing but hostility for the first fourteen years of her life. But that is what Dickens says. He was convinced that feminine goodness could overcome evil, and that some spark of it survived in all but the worst women.

DICKENS' HEROINES AND THEIR MALE RELATIONS

Novel	Heroine	Relations	What happens
Nicholas Nickleby	Madeline Bray	Father	Dies
The Old Curiosity Shop	Little Nell	Grandfather	Nell dies
Barnaby Rudge	Emma Haredale	Uncle	Goes into a monastery
Martin Chuzzlewit	Mary Graham	Employer	Reforms
Dombey and Son	Florence Dombey	Father	Reforms
David Copperfield	Agnes Wickfield	Father	Reforms
Bleak House	Ada Clare	Husband	Dies
Hard Times	Sissy Jupe	Father	Runs away 'rather than pull her down with him'
	Louisa Gradgrind	Brother	Emigrates
Little Dorrit	Amy Dorrit	Father	Dies
	Pet Meagles	Husband	Nothing happens
A Tale of Two Cities	Lucie Manette	Father	Survives
Our Mutual Friend	Lizzie Hexam	Father	Dies

His attitude to the way in which selfish parents manipulated their children was ambiguous. In most cases he was on the children's side. 'Oh! don't talk of duty as a child, Miss Summerson,' exclaims Caddy in *Bleak House*, 'where's Ma's duty as a parent?' (Chapter 5) He considered it reasonable that Arthur

Clennam should choose his own job against his mother's wishes, and that Edward Chester and Joe Willet in *Barnaby Rudge* should leave home when life becomes intolerable. But he never suggested that it could be right for a young woman to leave home (the only heroine who does this is Florence, and she has no choice). A good daughter should be devoted to her father, even when she cannot help seeing his faults. 'The harder father is borne upon, the more he needs me to lean on,' says Lizzie (Volume 1, Chapter 6). He also felt that a woman should continue to love her husband in all circumstances, like Pet Gowan:

> She is so true and so devoted, and knows so completely that all her love and duty are his for ever, that you may be certain she will love him, admire him, praise him, and conceal all his faults, until she dies. (*Little Dorrit*, Volume 2, Chapter 11)

Ada has the same feelings for Richard – 'the more he needed love from one unchanging heart, the more love that unchanging heart would have to give him'. (*Bleak House*, Chapter 37) Yet Dickens fully sympathises with Stephen Blackpool, in *Hard Times*, who feels that he has to get rid of his impossible wife after he has done everything he reasonably can. Only women, in his novels, are expected to be endlessly loving and forgiving.

Dickens did not believe that women were stupid, and he respected a woman who worked when she had to, but neither did he expect them to achieve distinction in any sphere outside the home. Only three women in his novels can be said to have a profession – Miss La Creevy, Cornelia Blimber and Sally Brass. The first is a poor painter, the second torments schoolboys, and Sally, who works as an attorney, is a gruff and grim spinster with no taste for 'those gentler and softer arts in which women usually excel'. (Chapter 36) On the other hand Dickens liked women to be 'accomplished', and his heroines always make a house look pleasant:

> But how the graces and elegancies which she had dispersed about the poorly-furnished room, went to the heart of Nicholas! Flowers, plants, birds, the harp, the old piano . . . every slender ornament, the occupation of her leisure hours, replete with the graceful charm which lingers in every little tasteful work of woman's hands! (*Nicholas Nickleby*, Chapter 46)

For Dickens there was a close connection between a woman's moral influence and a woman's touch in the home. His description of Agnes keeping house for her father shows the same association of ideas:

> Agnes played the piano to him, sat by him, and worked and talked, and played some games at dominoes with me. In good time she made tea, and afterwards, when I brought down my books, looked into them, and showed me what she knew of them (which was no slight matter, though she said it was) . . . I feel that there are goodness, peace and truth, wherever Agnes is; and that the soft light of the coloured window in the church, seen long ago, falls on her always. (*David Copperfield*, Chapter 16)

This is Ruskin's ideal woman, who is educated but not obtrusively so, and who is transcendentally good but exists only through the tiny details of keeping house.

Dombey and Son deserves very close attention because in it Dickens explores male attitudes towards women in detail and also shows why he thought that men would fail if they tried to live without 'female' values. Dombey superficially resembles Jane Austen's Darcy – a stiff, proud man of money who expects all women to recognise his importance. The novel begins when he has at last got a son, and this is so important to him that the death of his wife seems a small price to pay. The first Mrs Dombey lacks the will to live because her marriage has been loveless, but she does love one person, her daughter Florence, who 'had been unwelcome to [Dombey] from the first'. (Chapter 20) 'Girls,' as he says later, 'have nothing to do with Dombey and Son.' (Chapter 10) Dombey is made uneasy by the deep relationship between the little girl and her mother because it excludes him, and because he cannot comprehend love for a child who can do nothing for the firm. Like the clergyman who is 'obviously afraid of the baby' (Chapter 5) Dombey prefers to keep women and children at a distance (this is why he gets on with the woman-hating Major). Paul, the son and heir, is important to him not as a child but as a grown man – the 'Son' of 'the Firm'. (Chapter 8)

The first quarter of the book demonstrates that Paul can survive only for as long as he is nurtured by women. He is ruthlessly separated first from his wet-nurse Polly, and then from his mother-substitute, Florence. Then he is handed over to Cornelia Blimber who has practically no 'female' qualities and who works him – literally – to death. There is a marked contrast between Cornelia and Florence, who works at Paul's books not because she is interested in them but in order to help him – 'taught by that most wonderful of masters, love'. (Chapter 12) Dickens felt that a woman, while she should certainly be educated if possible, should not concentrate her whole mind on academic subjects (the same point is made in *Hard Times*).

Dombey's precious son is killed, then, indirectly by Dombey's own system. He can give the child money and a name, but only Florence and other insignificant women (like the Blimber's servant 'Melia) can give him care. Paul does not remember his mother or his old nurse but he is quite aware of their importance for him. On the other hand he has no real feeling for his father, because at this stage his father can give him nothing he actually needs. Once Paul is gone, Dombey begins to hate his daughter because she is alive instead of his son. This is convincing; Dickens was unquestionably aware that girls were often born where they were not welcome, and that they were more robust than boys. But Dombey has another reason for resenting Florence, because he knows that Paul unaccountably loved her best.

At this point we shift to Florence's consciousness. She is aware that she is an unwanted child and that the children in the opposite house, although they are all girls, are loved. Accepting, like a good daughter, that Dombey can do no wrong, she decides that it is her own fault and that she will have to work to deserve his affection. This quickly becomes an obsession and causes her to turn away from life; she shuns anyone who wants to make friends with her and 'longed for the old dark door to close upon her, once again'. (Chapter 28) Her father's blow is the best thing that ever happens to her because it finally makes her realise that it is Dombey who is sick and not her. Thrust out into 'the unexpected glare and freedom of the morning', she is at last able to find a new life with people who accept her. Of course she could not conscientiously have married Walter without Dombey's consent if she had not been disowned.

Dickens contrasts Florence, who is always perfectly patient and loving, with a much tougher woman, Susan Nipper. Susan is not at all 'feminine', but she is 'womanly', because she is totally committed to the child she cares for. When she finally breaks out and tells Dombey that his treatment of Florence is cruel he is predictably outraged. 'A gentleman – in his own house – in his own room – assailed with the impertinence of women-servants!' (It would certainly have been unusually daring behaviour in Victorian England, when women-servants were the lowest of the low.) When, following her revolt, Susan is sacked by Mrs Pipchin, Dickens enjoys the comedy of the scene, but he also makes sure we know that they represent respectively good and evil. The same thing happens in his next book when Miss Trotwood and Miss Murdstone have a violent verbal fight over the body of the child David. This shows that Dickens was now able seriously to use a situation (two women quarrelling) which had simply been comic in an early work like *Nicholas Nickleby*. Significantly, Susan has only female babies, her husband saying proudly that 'the oftener we can repeat that most extraordinary woman . . . the better'. (Chapter 62)

Dombey gets married again, after Paul has died, presumably because he wants another son. Dickens was only following many other novelists when he attacked upper-class marriages in which love played no part, and Edith is not particularly convincing. There is no real reason for her to marry Dombey, except that she is tired of being paraded in front of men by Mrs Skewton. (Cleopatra is condemned both because she has been a bad mother to Edith and because, at seventy, she still pretends to be young and glamorous; Dickens felt that older women should accept a maternal role and not try to compete with the young.) What is interesting about their marriage is that it does not occur to Dombey that he need have any human relationship with his wife. When he realises that Edith is not a meek woman like Florence and Florence's mother, he informs her that 'I am to be deferred to and obeyed'. (The wife-murderer Rigaud says much the same thing in the first chapter of *Little Dorrit*, 'I can't submit; I must govern'.) This demand would have seemed perfectly reasonable to most people – any woman marrying in church agreed to obey her husband – but Edith cannot bear it. Rather than obey Dombey she will blacken her name, live in exile, and give up her only affectionate relationship. At a time when numbers of well-meaning women writers were telling wives that it was right to submit to their husbands, Dickens had no doubt that it was evil.

Dombey cannot change until he has suffered a series of blows – his son, wife and business all fail him. He begins to be redeemed when he acknowledges that he had two children, instead of pretending in his heart that he had only one – 'He would count his children – one – two – stop, and go back, and begin again in the same way'. (Chapter 61) By the end of the novel he is able to love both grandchildren and to realise that 'his rejected daughter . . . will come out better than any son at last'.[1]

The 'message', surely, is that both sexes have equal worth, and that men will perish if they reject the 'feminine' values of sympathy and love. This does not mean that Dickens supported the infant movement for women's rights. On the contrary, he believed that a woman's job was to care for her family (it is Walter who begins to rebuild the firm Dombey and Son, not Florence) and that she should be loved and respected precisely for that reason.

Dickens lays great stress on Florence's 'firmness and self-reliance', which has been caused by her 'sad experience'. (Chapter 6) In *David Copperfield* he studies a very different type of woman, the babyish spoiled darling who goes to pieces as soon as things become difficult. Like Scott, he believed that over-protecting a girl leads to trouble, and Clara Copperfield shows what might have happened to Lucy Ashton if she had been a widow with a child. Lucy has 'a soft flexible character . . . susceptible of being moulded to any form by those with whom she lived' (*The Bride of Lammermoor*, Chapter 21). Clara's husband can 'mould her pliant nature into any form he chose'. (Chapter 4) She is pretty, weak and vain, a 'wax doll' who cannot live without admiration, and this makes her a natural victim of the Murdstone pair who make a habit of bullying young women. Dickens contemplates the destruction of Clara with deep and painful feelings and David, although he is the chief sufferer, never blames her. But her weakness does mean that she hands over her child to two cruel adults and thereafter does nothing to help him. Like many other people in his century, Dickens disliked the remarriage of widows because he felt it would make the children suffer.[2]

When David falls in love with Dora, a girl exactly like his mother, she too is guarded by Miss Murdstone and cannot do battle with her. Like Clara, she dies after failing to have a healthy baby. Nineteenth-century novelists often made women die in childbirth simply because this was happening all the time. But it is symbolic that these weak women fade away, together with their children, while the strong Agnes is last seen as the mother of a large family.

The third weak woman in the story is Little Em'ly, who exists partly to rouse sympathy for fallen women. Dickens wrote in a letter of 12 December 1849 that he hoped 'in the history of Little Em'ly . . . to put it before the thoughts of people in a new and pathetic way, and perhaps to do some good'. He was particularly concerned that prostitutes and other fallen women who wanted to make a fresh start were not getting the chance, and this was why he put Em'ly in danger of becoming a white slave or professional prostitute and had her saved by another female sinner, Martha. Here, as elsewhere, he showed a definite dislike for those who hunted fallen women down. He believed that women ought to show sympathy for each other, and the self-righteous Rosa Dartle is inferior to the fallen Em'ly – a judgement which was to become more and more acceptable.

Throughout the novel Dickens stresses that charm and beauty do not last, and that the quality which men really need is 'earnestness'. And this is personified in the 'calm, good, self-denying' Agnes, already a woman while she is still a child. From her earliest years Agnes has looked after her father's house, not going to school because 'Papa couldn't spare me'. (Chapter 16) Mr Wickfield, who admits near the end that his feelings for her were neurotic, is the main object of her life, and David even fears that she might marry Uriah for his sake. (Surprisingly Wickfield simply fades out at the end of the novel and does not present a problem when Agnes marries David.) Traddles' Sophy is in essentially the same situation: 'You see, Sophy being of so much use in the family, none of them could endure the thought of her ever being married'. (Chapter 41) Dickens raises – but does not answer – the question of how far an unselfish person should let herself be exploited by her family.

Although he wrote so memorably about the cruelty of depriving children of affection, Dickens evidently felt that a certain amount of pain and discipline could have a good effect on a child's or young person's character. We are told that Steerforth turns out badly because his mother spoiled him, and Agnes, like Florence, emerges from her sad childhood a stronger person than those who have never had to think or plan. We understand that she has no 'feminine' weaknesses because she immediately sees Steerforth for what he is, and does not resent Dora. She is always an adult, never a fascinating girl, and her marriage is a reward for years of unhappiness and struggle.

Yet Agnes always seems unreal, like an angel in a stained glass window. We may note her pious, flat and lifeless expressions when she is talking about Uriah's schemes to ruin her father:

> But if any fraud or treachery is practising against him, I hope that simple love and truth will be strong in the end. I hope that real love and truth are stronger in the end than any evil or misfortune in the world. (Chapter 35)

In fact her 'love and truth' achieve precisely nothing; she stands by passively while Uriah weaves his web and other people have to get rid of him. Compare her speech with Miss Trotwood's in the same chapter:

> 'Deuce take the man!' said my aunt, sternly, 'what's he about? . . . If you're an eel, sir, conduct yourself like one. If you're a man, control your limbs, sir! Good God!' said my aunt, with great indignation, 'I am not going to be serpentined and corkscrewed out of my senses!'

It is possible to argue that Betsey Trotwood is the real heroine of this novel. David is saved from the Murdstones (he actually, like Florence, saves himself by running away) because his great-aunt is a tough and independent woman who has no intention of being pushed around. She is an 'eccentric and somewhat masculine lady' (Chapter 41) who walked out on a bad husband (a most un-Victorian action) and is used to looking after herself. Miss Trotwood is something of a feminist, as she tries to stop the maids getting married, has a rule of 'No boys here', and has originally rejected David for not being a girl. Unlike Dombey, though, she cannot reject a child who appeals to her directly, even though it is a child of the 'wrong' sex, and she quickly and efficiently gets rid of the Murdstones, who paralyse so many other women with fear. Of course it helps that she has money and her own home; without them Peggotty, who is also a courageous woman, can do nothing.

One is left feeling that these two splendid older women are much more interesting, and have a much more useful role, than the pretty, youthful, middle-class heroines. But a heroine at that time could not be a servant with red arms or say things like 'Deuce take the man'. In his next two major novels, Dickens began to look more critically at the conventional Victorian girl.

Bleak House notes the existence of a phenomenon which Dickens did not want to take seriously; the increasing involvement of women in public life. 'They were the Women of England, the Daughters of Britain, the Sisters of all the Cardinal Virtues separately, the Females of America, the Ladies of a hundred denominations.' (Chapter 8) We are told that 'their objects were as various as their demands', and not all of them are feminists, but they include one lady, Miss Wisk, who believes that 'the idea of woman's mission lying chiefly in the narrow sphere of Home was an outrageous slander on the part of her Tyrant, Man'. (Chapter 30)

Dickens felt strongly that a woman's mission was indeed to make her home happy and that the large numbers of women who were beginning to become active outside the home did more harm than good. This novel is full of haunting images of ruined, unfinished, decaying and forsaken houses, symbols of a society whose members do not adequately care for one another. Esther's great quality is that she is a thoroughly good housekeeper, bringing harmony and order wherever she goes, while Mrs Jellyby, who neglects her 'natural duties and obligations' to work for Africa, has a miserable husband and an uncomfortable home. Dickens widens his argument by reference to the neglected Jo, the little girl Charley who is the sole support of her baby brother and sister, and the working-class women whose husbands ('masters') batter them. Women like the Jellybys, Wisks and Pardiggles seemed to him misguided because they took no interest in working-class women and children or in serious problems.

In this novel Dickens continues to study the selfishness of fathers and mothers. Caddy feels that Mrs Jellyby has cheated her because her home is sordid and because she does not know how to keep house or look 'neat and pretty' like Esther and Ada. The only escape, she believes, is into a traditional family where the father is the undisputed head, so she spends the rest of her life waiting on old Mr Turveydrop. There is no saying which set-up is the worse, and Dickens expresses his ambivalent feelings by giving her a deaf and dumb child.

Esther is another child who is made to suffer for the faults of her parents. Many Dickens heroines have guilt feelings[3] but they are particularly strong in Esther because she is illegitimate and has been rejected by her aunt. Because her mother's secret might be betrayed through her, she feels that perhaps she ought to have died. She loses her looks, a cruel calamity for a Victorian woman, but she comes to feel grateful for this because now 'I never could disgrace her by any trace of likeness'. (Chapter 36) In the same way she is so grateful to Mr Jarndyce for being kind to her that she agrees to marry him when she does not really want to. It is as if, like Florence, she has to atone for the crime of being herself.

Ada is a much more conventional heroine – young, pretty, blushing, accomplished and inexperienced. While Esther immediately takes over the housekeeping, Ada is not expected to do anything. 'I had never known any trouble or anxiety, so loved and cared for,' she says. (Chapter 50) Esther is determined to shield her from the 'east wind' which means suffering; when she catches smallpox it is Ada (more than anyone else in the house) who has to be protected. But of course this cannot last for ever. Ada sacrifices herself (uselessly) for Richard and is left a widow at twenty-one, forbidden by the conventions of the novel ever to marry again. Dickens never criticises her (although he shows her to be less shrewd and sensible than Esther) but he does suggest that her qualities do not make for survival. Apart from Lucie Manette, Ada was the last of his angelic golden-haired heroines, and he seems to have felt increasingly that this type was of limited interest. Older and less glamorous women, like Mrs Rouncewell and Mrs Bagnet, begin to come to the fore in *Bleak House*.

Amy Dorrit, a more convincing Madeline Bray, is a very traditional Dickens heroine. Like Esther, her life is 'all consumed in care of others', primarily her father, who loves but does not appreciate her. Her self-sacrifice is thrown into relief by a large number of selfish women – Fanny, Mrs Clennam, Miss Wade, Mrs Merdle, Mrs Gowan and Mr F's aunt. She is also contrasted with a much more conventionally attractive girl, Pet Meagles, with whom Clennam predictably falls in love. But, like Ada, Pet is not destined to be happy, and for the same reasons.

The Meagleses have always protected and 'petted' her, which means that she cannot judge men. At the same time they have taken a friendless illegitimate girl into their home, not as a daughter but as a maid. Tattycoram, not surprisingly, can't bear 'to see *her* always held up as the only creature who was young and interesting, and to be cherished and loved'. (Chapter 27) It seems that Dickens was reworking the Charley episode in *Bleak House*, when the little girl is given to Esther by her guardian as 'a present'.[4] In the earlier novel, Charley is happy and thankful to be Esther's maid, and does not resent being told that she has been rescued from a life of hard work only for the love of Esther. On second thoughts, though, Dickens suspected that most people would object to being used in this way. When Tattycoram runs off with Miss Wade his feelings are divided. He understands that both women have a real grievance, but he is repelled by Miss Wade's 'unwomanly' qualities, her coldness, self-sufficiency and indifference to the claims of others. Mr Meagles is so shocked by the unnatural spectacle of two women running away together that he obliquely accuses Miss Wade of being a lesbian (Volume 1, Chapter 27). But what the two actually have in common is their illegitimacy, plus the consciousness that no-one will ever want to pet or spoil them.

Dickens solves the problem by saying explicitly that Miss Wade is cruel and by having Meagles tell Tattycoram to imitate Little Dorrit's life of 'active resignation, goodness and noble service' (Volume 2, Chapter 33). In the same vein, Little Dorrit herself advises Mrs Clennam to forget her wrongs and try to follow Christ.

There is no doubt that Dickens meant what he said, yet he cannot help asking, how effective is Little Dorrit's goodness? It would seem that the effect is minimal. The worst character in the book, Merdle, is universally praised, while the best, Amy, is almost universally slighted. Dickens knows that people will go on taking advantage of her; indeed he makes it clear in the last paragraph that her future life will be one of caring for her shiftless family and getting no praise or rewards. And while he feels that there is a desperate need for this kind of devotion, it cannot solve all the world's problems. For example, Little Dorrit can only shrink in horror from Rigaud-Blandois, who is too bad to be redeemed. There is no suggestion that she would ever be strong enough to get rid of him, as Miss Trotwood does with the Murdstones, or Sissy Jupe with Mr Harthouse. People like Rigaud, says the French landlady, 'must be dealt with as enemies of the human race' (Volume 1, Chapter 11), and it is noted that women are particularly keen to have his blood. The total effect of the novel is to suggest that, although Little Dorrit's goodness is precious, she cannot change the evil system under which all the characters live.

The women in *Great Expectations* (except Biddy) are completely different from their predecessors. In this novel it is the man whose heart is wrung by the coldness and cruelty of women, not the other way round. Pip is brought up by his sister, who ill-treats him, physically and emotionally, with the result that he becomes 'morally timid and very sensitive'. He falls in love with Estella, who torments him in a more refined way, and Estella has been coached by yet another woman, Miss Havisham, who wants to see her punish men. Biddy's failure to make a deep impression on Pip suggests that he is unprepared for and cannot accept kindness from a woman, although he can accept it from men (Joe, Herbert, Wemmick and finally Magwitch). At the same time, Dickens realised that cruelty by men to women was more usual and took pains to account for his characters' behaviour. Joe allows his wife to bully him and Pip because his mother had been seriously ill-treated by his father and he does not want to make the same mistake. Miss Havisham hates men because one of them has jilted her (although Dickens makes it clear that she over-reacted). Estella is an example of how a young girl can be corrupted if she grows up in a bad environment, something Dickens was reluctant to admit when he created heroines like Florence, Esther and Little Dorrit. But Estella cannot escape from the realities of the man–woman relationship; once she is married to Drummle he beats her and this is what eventually makes her realise that she underestimated Pip.

In his last two novels, *Our Mutual Friend* and the unfinished *Edwin Drood*, Dickens seems to be feeling towards a new conception of what a woman should be like. Each novel has two heroines, who belong to very different types. Lizzie Hexam and Helena Landless are both strong, responsible women (each has to care for a wayward brother) with no charm or playfulness. Bella and Rosa are delightful, Dora-like girls who eventually grow up without ceasing to be charming. Rosa turns out to be a stronger character than she appears because she has the sense to break off the marriage which has been arranged for her; Dickens calls her 'that pretty sympathetic nature which . . . could so quietly find itself alone in a new world to weave fresh wreaths of such flowers as it might prove to bear'. (Chapter 13) Although she will certainly marry someone, Rosa is not a girl who must be married at all costs. Bella Wilfer gives up her scheme to marry for money and becomes a perfect wife and mother – a 'Home Goddess'. (Volume 2, Chapter 13) She is not quite as unreal as Dickens' earlier heroines, but her creator emphatically approves of her pouring all her energy into the making of a happy home.

7   The Brontës

The Brontë sisters were attacked by many Victorian readers because their 'mode of writing and thinking was not what is called "feminine" '.[1] (The names Currer, Ellis and Acton Bell deceived no one for long.) If we compare their women characters with those of Dickens, or glance at Mrs Ellis's handbooks for women published a few years earlier,[2] we can easily see why. Women were not supposed to feel or show violent emotions, or to fall in love without encouragement, or to defy men, and Brontë heroines do all these things. Even in Charlotte's unimpassioned first novel, *The Professor*, there is a flicker of female resistance:

> Frances was then, a good and dear wife to me, because I was to her a good, just and faithful husband. What she would have been had she married a hard, envious, careless man – a profligate, a prodigal, a drunkard, or a tyrant – is another question, and one which I once propounded to her. Her answer, given after some reflection, was:
> 'I should have tried to endure the evil or cure it for awhile; and when I found it intolerable and incurable, I should have left my torturer suddenly and silently.'
> 'And if law or might had forced you back again?' . . .
> I would have an answer, because I saw a strange kind of spirit in her eye, whose voice I determined to waken.
> 'Monsieur, if a wife's nature loathes that of the man she is wedded to, marriage must be slavery. . . . I would resist as far as my strength permitted; when that strength failed I should be sure of a refuge. Death would certainly sever me both from bad laws and their consequences.' (Chapter 25)

This passage sticks out awkwardly in this particular novel, but a central image for all the Brontës is that of a woman running away. We have Jane Eyre escaping from Rochester, Helen from Arthur Huntingdon, Isabella and Cathy Linton from Heathcliff. Lucy Snowe could be said to be escaping from her past when she plunges without friends or money into an alien country. Another persistent image is of a woman becoming dangerously depressed or ill because she is trapped by her circumstances (Catherine threatening to jump out of the window, Caroline Helstone, Agnes Grey in her employer's house, Lucy at Madame Beck's school).

Another thing all three Brontës have in common – and this made them unusual at the time – is their sympathy with women who worked. Helen, who had dabbled at painting as a girl, takes it up seriously to earn her living as a single parent. Frances Henri is a lace-mender; Jane, Lucy and Agnes are all teachers; Nelly Dean is a servant. They shared a contempt for fine ladies who did nothing, and for mindless women. We often see older, plainer women (Nelly, Agnes, Lucy) giving good advice to a giddy young girl (Catherine, Isabella, Rosalie, Ginevra), which is not taken. In the same way they liked a man to have a strong character and despised effeminate men; the most extreme example being Linton Heathcliff.

The only Brontë who lived long enough to comment on feminism was Charlotte, who had mixed feelings about it (see page 18). It is possible that Emily, and particularly Anne, would not have reacted in quite the same way. Certainly Emily and Anne have more in common with each other than they had with their elder sister. Charlotte's women are always lonely, and yearn for a man who can be their 'master', but in *Wuthering Heights* and *The Tenant of Wildfell Hall* rebellious women are trapped by an all-powerful man.

CHARLOTTE BRONTË

To understand the patterns of feeling in Charlotte's later work, it is helpful to read one of her Angrian stories, *Mina Laury*, written in 1838.[3] The heroine, a beautiful and intelligent woman, is the mistress of the faithless Zamorna:

> Miss Laury belonged to the Duke of Zamorna. She was indisputably his property . . . She had but one idea – Zamorna!

Zamorna! It had grown up with her, become a part of her nature. Absence, coldness, total neglect for long periods together went for nothing.

She explains her feelings for her 'master', as she calls him, in great detail.

I lost the power . . . of discerning the difference between right and wrong. I have never in my life contradicted Zamorna, never delayed obedience to his commands. I could not. He was something more to me than a human being. He superseded all things – all affections, all interests, all fears or hopes or principles.

The story leaves her trapped in this situation. She will always love Zamorna, and he will never love her. When his wife turns up unexpectedly, Mina pretends to be the housekeeper, but she knows that the other woman does not believe her because she is wearing diamonds:

Miss Laury could have torn the dazzling pendants from her ears. She was bitterly stung. 'Everybody knows me,' she said to herself. ' ''Mistress'', I suppose, is branded on my brow.'

This throws a new light on some parts of *Jane Eyre* which seem puzzling or irrelevant on the first reading. Rochester wants to put a diamond chain round Jane's neck, clasp bracelets on her wrists, and load her fingers with rings. He suggests that he should 'attach you to a chain like this (touching his watch-guard)'. Jane becomes more and more irritated at being 'dressed like a doll' by him, and compares him to a sultan or the Grand Turk. (Chapter 24) Rather than be like an Eastern woman she writes to her uncle, hoping he will leave her enough money to be independent, and this is what ruins Rochester's plans. Between *Mina Laury* and *Jane Eyre*, Charlotte had come to feel that it was degrading to be a kept woman, married or not; gold and jewels, heaped by rich men on their favourites, could be forged into chains. When the crisis comes, Jane senses that if she agreed to live with Rochester he would grow tired of her as he did of other women. After she has escaped, found work as a schoolmistress, and done some real good to her pupils, she has no doubt that she acted wisely.

Keeping one's own school is a cherished dream for Charlotte's working heroines. Jane hopes to do it, Lucy actually does and Frances, in *The Professor*, insists on going on teaching although her husband is able to support her. She is both a good wife and a competent headmistress (very unusually for that time, she has only one child). It is suggested that a woman should not be totally dependent on her husband, if she can possibly avoid it.

For it now seemed to Charlotte very dangerous to give up one's whole soul into a man's keeping. Jane sees, in retrospect, that she has made an idol of Rochester; he 'stood between me and every thought of religion'. (Chapter 24) Ultimately she has to act according to her own sense of right and wrong – 'I can live alone, if self-respect and circumstances require me to do so. I need not sell my soul to buy bliss'. (Chapter 19) She has to struggle quite hard to live in the way that seems right to her. Rochester is tempted to kill her when she does not submit and she knows that if she agreed to marry St. John she would soon die. St. John is another man who demands absolute obedience – 'I want a wife; the sole helpmeet I can influence efficiently in life, and retain absolutely till death'. (Chapter 34) Jane resists both men, although both of them mean much to her, and marries Rochester only when they have a more equal relationship – 'I love you better now, when I can really be useful to you, than I did in your state of proud independence, when you disdained every part but that of the giver and protector'. (Chapter 37)

To make this possible, Rochester must turn out to be what Emily Brontë called, ironically, a rough diamond (*Wuthering Heights*, Chapter 10). He risks his life trying to save his mad wife and tells Jane that 'he would never have forced me to be his mistress. Violent as he had seemed in his despair, he, in truth, loved me far too well and too tenderly to constitute himself my tyrant.' (Chapter 37) He has certainly seemed very like a tyrant at earlier points in the novel, but it was important for Charlotte that her hero should be a good person. She was repelled by a really violent man, like Heathcliff. The urge to love a man had to be controlled by reason and self-respect precisely because it was, for her, so frighteningly strong.

There are several calm, scholarly women in *Jane Eyre* – Helen, Miss Temple, Diana and Mary Rivers – and Jane realises that they are much freer from passion than she is and wishes to be like them. At the other extreme are Georgina, Blanche Ingram and

Bertha Mason, who all are or were sexually attractive (Bertha was a nymphomaniac before going mad) but have nothing else to offer. Charlotte takes an emphatically feminist viewpoint in denying that a woman's first duty is to be beautiful. Jane does not want to be Blanche, any more than Lucy wants to be Ginevra Fanshawe, although she assumes that a Blanche will win most of the prizes in life. She tries to be fair to other women, disliking Rochester's attitude to his wife and worrying about Blanche's feelings – 'Seriously: may I enjoy the great good that has been vouchsafed to me, without fearing that anyone else is suffering the bitter pain I myself felt a while ago?'. (Chapter 24) She also feels that she needs other women, like Diana and Mary, as 'sisters', quite apart from her need for a man.

On the other hand, children, although they have their claims, are not very important for Charlotte Brontë's women; Jane sends Adèle away to school because Rochester takes up all her time. Anne Brontë in *The Tenant of Wildfell Hall* takes a different attitude, for Helen is intensely interested in the welfare of her child and comes to feel that he is more important than her husband.

Jane, in the end, is 'supremely blest . . . because I am my husband's life as fully as he is mine'. While Charlotte did not want a woman to become a Mina Laury, she still felt that the man–woman relationship was enormously important. And it was not quite an equal relationship, for all her heroines want not just a husband but a 'master'.[4] First found in the Angrian stories, this is a key word in all her novels. Her women normally call their lovers or husbands 'my master', 'sir', 'monsieur'. Charlotte spelled out the precise meaning of the word in her next novel, *Shirley*. The heroine is a strong-willed girl who has a man's name, holds a man's position (she is a landowner with no immediate family), and fantasises about being male. But it turns out that what she really wants is a traditional womanly role. Explaining why she will not marry an eligible suitor, she says:

'He is very amiable – very excellent – truly estimable, but *not my master* . . . I will accept no hand which cannot hold me in check. . . . When I promise to obey, it shall be under the conviction that I can keep that promise: I could not obey a youth like Sir Philip . . . Any man who wishes to live in decent comfort with me as a husband must be able to control me.'
   'I wish you had a real tyrant.'

'A tyrant would not hold me for a day – not for an hour. I
would rebel – break from him – defy him . . . Did I not say I
prefer a *master?* . . . A man whose approbation can reward –
whose displeasure punish me. A man I shall feel it impossible
not to love, and very possible to fear.' (Chapter 31)

There is a distinction between a master and a tyrant. Shirley
shows no respect to men when she does not feel it, and she
reserves the right to break away from a bad husband, but she does
not find the promise to obey offensive in itself. It is worth
remembering Mrs Gaskell's comment that Charlotte 'would
never have been happy but with an exacting, rigid, law-giving,
passionate man'.[5]

Caroline, the alternative heroine, appears to be a pattern
Victorian girl, but her secret thoughts are most subversive. She is
quiet, ladylike, fond of animals, plants and children, and the type
to make a perfect wife. But when the man she loves ignores her
she is forced to rethink her assumption that she will get married.
She becomes more sympathetic to old maids (see page 37) and
decides that women ought to have a profession to stop them
brooding endlessly and hopelessly about love. For she is
compelled to see that Robert's thoughts are not with her but in
the mysterious world of 'business' – 'far away, not merely from
her, but from all which she could comprehend, or in which she
could sympathise'. (Chapter 10)

Caroline is the only Charlotte Brontë heroine who lives with
her family; in this case an uncle who despises women and will
only allow her to talk about 'slight topics'. But he has absolute
power over her; when he forbids her to be a governess, that is
final. She is less free than Jane or Lucy because she cannot even
find 'a new servitude'. Many girls in this position are 'dropping
off in consumption or decline' (Chapter 22) – actually dying of
depression – and Caroline nearly dies after suffering in silence for
months. 'Do you wish to live?' Mrs Pryor asks, and Caroline
replies 'I have no object in life'. (Chapter 24) This forces Mrs
Pryor (another patient and submissive woman who has been both
an ill-used governess and an ill-used wife) to reveal that she is
Caroline's mother, and the loving relationship which develops
between them is a great source of strength to them both. But
Charlotte did not show Caroline forgetting Robert and going off
to live with her mother; such an ending would have been very

hard for her readers to take. Instead he reforms, promising to be less selfish, and Caroline is left in the traditional role of the wife who has a good moral influence on her husband.

Most readers of *Shirley* feel that both heroines make an unsatisfactory marriage, yet Charlotte was aware that women might have other alternatives. 'I am resolved that my life should be a life,' says the twelve-year-old Rose, 'not . . . a long, slow death like yours.' (Chapter 23) But the present generation is trapped:

> Nobody in particular is to blame [thinks Caroline] . . . for the state in which things are; and I cannot tell, however much I puzzle over it, how they are to be altered for the better; but I feel there is something wrong somewhere. I believe single women should have more to do – better chances of interesting and profitable occupation than they possess now . . . People hate to be reminded of ills they are unable or unwilling to remedy . . . Old maids, like the houseless and unemployed poor, should not ask for a place and an occupation in the world: the demand disturbs the happy and rich. (Chapter 22)

The novel is confusing because Charlotte gives it a conventional ending and sympathises with Shirley's desire for a 'master', yet can also appreciate the feminist point of view. Both Shirley and Caroline are annoyed when Joe Scott says that 'women is to take their husbands' opinion, both in politics and religion'. (Chapter 18) But they cannot explain away what St Paul said, and Charlotte cannot believe that not all women want to be dominated when they meet the right man.

Villette is one of the few nineteenth-century novels (Mrs Oliphant's *Kirsteen* is another example) where the heroine ends as a career woman rather than a bride. Some years earlier Charlotte had written:

> I speculate much on the existence of unmarried and never-to-be-married women nowadays; and I have already got to the point of considering that there is no more respectable character on this earth than an unmarried woman, who makes her own way through life quietly, perseveringly, without support of husband or brother; and who, having attained the age of forty-five or upwards, retains in her possession a well-regulated

mind, a disposition to enjoy simple pleasures and fortitude to support inevitable pains, sympathy with the sufferings of others, and willingness to relieve want as far as her means extend.[6]

The early chapter, 'Miss Marchmont', which seems superfluous, is actually firmly integrated into the novel. Miss Marchmont is elderly, sick, and irritable, but nevertheless a good woman who has helped many people. Her fiancé died and she has paid for her brief happiness with 'thirty years of sorrow'. As we eventually know, the same thing happens to Lucy, who writes as an elderly woman looking back on her unconsummated love for M. Paul. In the last chapter, when we have almost forgotten Miss Marchmont, Lucy inherits a legacy from her which helps her to build up her school. This school is all she will ever get, for she is to be one of the millions of women who do not marry.

We learn at an early stage that women with strong feelings are likely to suffer, when Lucy warns Paulina not to bother Graham and not to mind because he cares less for her than she does for him – 'it must be so'. (Chapter 3) Lucy is especially vulnerable because she is not attractive and is 'born only to work for a piece of bread'. (Chapter 21) She is well aware of how much she is missing; at times she sinks into nightmarish depression and her contact with Madame Beck's child 'made me almost cry with a tender pain'. (Chapter 13) But she tells herself that 'a great many men and more women hold their span of life on conditions of denial and privation. I find no reason why I should be one of the few favoured.' (Chapter 31)

In Belgium Lucy is plunged into a mass of girls who repel her by their stupid and selfish behaviour. 'Then first did I begin rightly to see the wide difference that lies between the novelists' and poets' ideal *jeune fille*, and the said *jeune fille* as she really is.' (Chapter 8) Men's concept of a heroine is cleverly satirised in Dr John's raptures about Ginevra, 'So spotless, so good, so unspeakably beautiful . . . such a simple, innocent, girlish fairy'. (Chapters 13 and 14) This exasperates Lucy, who sees her from a woman's point of view.

Lucy is invited to look at several pictures which express stock images of women – Cleopatra, the sex goddess; *'La Vie d'une Femme,'* the conventional wife and mother; and Justine Marie, the nun. Of these three, becoming a nun is the only real possibility, but it is a temptation which Lucy resists. There is yet another way of life which she finally chooses, that of the independent teacher. Her happiest years are over but she is self-respecting, her own mistress, and unlikely to become a victim of depression again.

In all Charlotte Brontë's books we sense that the heroine is not suited to, and will not get, a conventionally attractive husband. Lucy is drawn to Dr John but realises that he (and his mother, a cheerful, stable woman) have little in common with her. Besides, she is obviously not a good match, and although Jane Eyre took Mr Rochester from the more 'suitable' Blanche this does not happen here. Dr John wants his wife to be a lady and would not have married Paulina if she had been 'a dependent worker' – 'to satisfy himself did not suffice; society must approve'. (Chapter 32) Charlotte Brontë was aware that she had not been able to make Paulina convincing. She is charming and good, but very ignorant, as we see when she asks Lucy why she should go out to work. Lucy is not jealous, but Paulina's good fortune makes her acutely conscious of her own unprotected condition. She refuses to be her companion (although she had been Miss Marchmont's) because the contrast would be too painful.

Her real affinity, she finds, is with a man who is ugly, middle-aged, full of faults and bullies her (although, of course, like Rochester, he has a heart of gold). But she cannot marry M. Paul because she is not fated to be lucky. Outside events control her destiny. There is an awareness in all Charlotte Brontë's novels that women live in a small enclosed world and men in a much wider, more mysterious and dangerous one:

How often, while women and girls sit warm at snug firesides, their hearts and imaginations are doomed to divorce from the comfort surrounding their persons, forced out by night to wander through dark ways, to dare stress of weather, to contend with the snow-blast, to wait at lonely gates and stiles in wildest storms, watching and listening to see and hear the father, the son, the husband coming home. (Chapter 25)

We see this in *Jane Eyre*, where the house suddenly becomes an exciting place when Rochester arrives, and in Caroline's realisation that 'women have so few things to think about – men so many'. (Chapter 12) Miss Marchmont's lover is killed, then

Lucy's, and they go on living useful, but not happy lives. 'We should accept our own lot,' says the older woman, 'whatever it be.' (Chapter 4)

'I often wish to say something about the "condition of women" question', Charlotte had written in 1848, but she found this difficult because she could not suggest any solutions.

> One can see where the evil lies, but who can point out the remedy? When a woman has a little family to rear . . . her vocation is evident; when her destiny isolates her, I suppose she must do what she can, live as she can, complain as little, bear as much, work as well as possible . . . At the same time, I conceive that when patience has done its utmost and industry its best, whether in the case of women or operatives, and when both are baffled, and pain and want triumph, the sufferer is free, is entitled, to send up to Heaven any piercing cry for relief.'[7]

Villette, and the Caroline plot in *Shirley*, are a 'piercing cry' on behalf of 'unmarried and never-to-be-married women'.

EMILY BRONTË

Emily Brontë, arguably the greatest woman writer who ever lived, said nothing directly about 'the woman question'. Indeed *Wuthering Heights* offers no direct opinions on anything; the story is always told by an imaginary person and, unlike her sisters, the author never clearly states her views. But we do know from Charlotte that Emily had certain strong beliefs about the differences between the sexes. In the 1850 Preface to *Wuthering Heights*, after pointing out that Edgar's character is 'an example of constancy and tenderness' she adds:

> Some people will think these qualities do not shine so well incarnate in a man as they would do in a woman, but Ellis Bell could never be brought to comprehend this notion . . . She held that mercy and forgiveness are the divinest attributes of the Great Being who made both man and woman, and that what clothes the Godhead in glory can disgrace no form of feeble humanity.

We can feel fairly sure that Charlotte was not mistaken because in *Wuthering Heights* the violent characters are not all men and the gentle characters not all women. We also know that Anne, to whom Emily was very close, argued in *Wildfell Hall* that boys had to be protected from bad influences just as much as girls. *Wuthering Heights* assumes a moral equality between the sexes, for it demonstrates that all children (not just boys) benefit from education, and that young women (not just young men) deteriorate in a bad environment.

Emily Brontë shows a sound knowledge of the laws affecting women around 1800. Heathcliff can make Isabella a prisoner and after she leaves him (which everyone agrees is the wise thing to do), he can force her to come back. She is only allowed to live away from him because he cannot bear her, and he can at any time claim their child. Cathy Linton does not inherit her father's estate because she is a female and then loses her income by marrying Heathcliff's son. Heathcliff uses marriage, first his own and then the boy's, to get hold of all the Linton property. But he also wants to control and torment the Linton women, Isabella and Cathy, for being members of the family he hates.[8] He schemes to marry Cathy to his son, not in order to get Thrushcross Grange – he is sure to get it anyway – but in order to make her suffer. Once a woman has married into his family he is her 'legal protector', and as he keeps 'strictly within the limits of the law' she has no right to 'claim a separation'. (Chapter 14)

Wuthering Heights shows the enormous powers of the head of the household, and how they can be used against the weaker members of the family. When Lockwood blunders into the Heights he meets an unfamiliar type of woman, a beautiful girl who behaves in a 'singularly unnatural' way, treating him and everyone else with open hostility. It turns out that she is trapped in her enemy's house – 'they wouldn't let me go to the end of the garden wall'. In the next chapter Lockwood reads the older Catherine's diary and we hear of another girl protesting against her treatment by the master of Wuthering Heights. A major theme of this novel is the oppression of the young by a violent father-figure, first Hindley and then Heathcliff. (The only character for whom the author shows no sympathy at all is the man who persecutes two generations of children, Joseph.) Hindley's treatment of Heathcliff, which includes depriving him of education, is 'enough to make a fiend of a saint'. (Chapter 8) Heathcliff too becomes an oppressor when he grows up, doing his

best to make Hareton illiterate and destroying Cathy's books. It is
not enough for him to defeat his 'old enemies', Hindley and
Edgar, he also wants to 'revenge myself on their representatives',
that is, their children. In the beginning Heathcliff is 'a nameless
man', whom no young lady can marry without degrading herself.
But he is determined to found a dynasty of his own and assert its
power:

> I want the triumph of seeing *my* descendants fairly lord of their
> estates – my child hiring their children to till their father's land
> for wages. (Chapter 20)

This plan means that he has to treat people, not according to his
own instincts, but according to who their fathers were. He
despises Linton, but protects him (up to a point) because he is a
Heathcliff. He sympathises strongly with Hareton, but degrades
him because he is an Earnshaw. He hates Isabella and Cathy, but
insists on having them in his house to punish them for being
Lintons. No wonder he finds, in the end, that it is all too much of
an effort. In fact he has been making the same mistake as
Catherine when she married Edgar – smothering his own deepest
feelings about people and judging them by external factors. His
schemes are futile, and the Heathcliff line dies out.

All the young girls in the novel are seen through the shrewd
eyes of Nelly, a woman with no personal life but with a deep
devotion to *her* children, Hareton and Cathy, whom she has cared
for from birth. Being more practical than these girls, she always
gives them sound advice, as when she tells Catherine not to marry
Edgar and Isabella not to marry Heathcliff, and later when she
warns Cathy not to write off Hareton because he seems uncouth.
As in the other Brontë novels, the concept of 'young ladyhood'
comes under severe attack. Catherine Earnshaw is infected with it
when she stays at the Grange and becomes ashamed of Heathcliff.
But however hard she tries to be ladylike Catherine is actually a
girl with violent passions, attracting men by her sexual
magnetism but unable to behave as they wish. Edgar gets a
glimpse of her real character when she starts hitting out in all
directions, but pacifies her during the first year of their marriage
by doing exactly what she wants. When the crisis comes she
breaks down with horrifying speed; a single row with her husband
causes brain fever, hallucinations and death. Catherine is like

Lucy Ashton (we know that Scott was read and appreciated in Haworth Parsonage) in that she goes mad and dies because of the wrong marriage. She has sacrificed the real happiness of her life to a false idea of gentility.

Isabella is characterised as 'silly' and 'infantile' because she falls in love with Heathcliff, unasked, 'picturing in me a hero of romance'. Catherine tries to make it clear to her that this is no Mr Rochester:

> Pray don't imagine that he conceals depths of benevolence and affection beneath a stern exterior. He's not a rough diamond . . . he's a fierce, pitiless, wolfish man. (Chapter 10)

Isabella's marriage, which damages every member of her family, is made because she clings to her romantic dreams in the teeth of the evidence. Even after her marriage she finds it difficult to believe that Heathcliff hates her and evokes his contempt by forgiving his bad treatment. (Chapter 14) This is surely a comment on the folly of sheltering young girls from the realities of life.

Cathy is a more conventional heroine than her mother – 'she could be soft and mild as a dove, and she had a gentle voice, and pensive expression; her anger was never furious; her love never fierce; it was deep and tender'. (Chapter 18) But she too is sheltered and a recluse, 'conversant with no bad deeds' so it is easy for Heathcliff to make her fall in love with the first eligible man she meets. Emily Brontë is able to convince us of a fact which many novelists would not admit, that Cathy genuinely loves her father and yet needs to live her own life. Once she is trapped at the Heights her character changes dramatically; she stops being a charming girl and becomes bitter and sarcastic in self-defence. But eventually she is strong enough to overcome her snobbishness and to realise which cousin is her natural mate. Hareton, too, shakes off the 'clouds of ignorance and degradation' in which he has been bred. It is a hopeful ending, because although Cathy has been over-protected and both have been oppressed, they are still capable of refusing to be moulded by forces outside them.

Wuthering Heights represents 'masculine' qualities, like courage and toughness, but those who live there tend to become brutal. Thrushcross Grange is a stronghold of 'feminine' values – comfort, kindness, civilisation – but the Lintons tend to be over-soft. The novel implies that the extremely violent and the extremely weak cannot go on living. The two masters of the Heights, Hindley and Heathcliff, both die young and the place is closed down; their violent way of life has gone for good. Linton Heathcliff, who looks like a girl, dies of sheer weakness; his relationship with Cathy a failure because he has no manly qualities and she has to protect him, not the other way round. At best he can only be a 'pet', or a 'pretty little darling', not a husband for a normal girl. The survivors are Cathy and Hareton, who both have strong, even violent feelings, but are both intrinsically kind. We are left feeling that the two very different houses both represent something valuable, just as the dead both 'walk' and rest quietly in their graves.

ANNE BRONTË

Charlotte Brontë described her sister Anne, in the 'Biographical Notice of Ellis and Acton Bell', as a patient, mild, religious woman who should never have written a book like *The Tenant of Wildfell Hall*. If we accept this image of her, both her novels come as a surprise. They are realistic, often witty, in many ways unorthodox, and they are filled with quiet fury about the treatment of women in England. Anne Brontë was a Christian, but in her novels she was not meek and mild. She belonged, in fact, to the same tradition as the religious feminists like Josephine Butler who flourished in the 1870s.

Anne was 'feminist' in the sense of believing that women should work; Agnes Grey and Helen Huntingdon both choose to do so although their relations are willing to support them. More unusual still, she did not believe that a woman should always sacrifice herself for her husband. Possibly as a result of reading *Wuthering Heights*, she felt that a little boy could be corrupted if he was brought up by bad men. In *Agnes Grey* 'Uncle Robson' teaches his nephew Tom to torment animals and despise women, 'Curse me, if ever I saw a nobler little scoundrel than that. He's beyond petticoat government already: by God! he defies mother, granny, governess, and all!' (Chapter 5) Arthur Huntingdon and his friends try to 'make a man' of his little son – 'he was not going to have the little fellow moped to death between an old nurse and a cursed fool of a mother' (*Wildfell Hall*, Chapter 39). As a result of her experiences Helen argues that it is wrong to keep girls ignorant – 'tenderly and delicately nurtured like a hothouse plant; taught to cling to others for direction and support, and guarded, as much as possible, from the very knowledge of evil' (Chapter 3), while boys are exposed to all kinds of temptation. The conclusion seems to be that boys and girls are not particularly different and need much the same kind of upbringing. She also claims that a mother has the right to take a child away from his father if that is best for the child.

Agnes Grey is probably the best English novel based on the life of a governess (*Jane Eyre* only touches on the problems of these women, and compared to Agnes, Jane has a very easy job). Many people had pointed out that governesses were often more refined than their employers. Agnes certainly is; the Bloomfields and Murrays allow their children to torment her and the young men who pay attention to Rosalie Murray behave as if Agnes did not exist. She is too tough, though, to be humiliated by this treatment – 'in truth, I considered myself pretty nearly as good as the best of them'. (Chapter 13) Rosalie is punished when she marries for money and produces a 'little girl that should have been a boy' (Chapter 22) and this is contrasted with Agnes's own happy marriage.

Agnes breaks the rules by falling in love with Mr Weston and endures months of depression, like Caroline Helstone. The blank existence of a girl who can only wait and hope is compared to a man's freedom – 'He leads an active life, and a wide field for useful exertion lies before him. He can *make* friends, and he can make a home too, if he pleases.' (Chapter 13) It is an uneventful novel, but it shows that Anne Brontë had a more militant nature than has been supposed.

The Tenant of Wildfell Hall was attacked by some critics for being 'unwomanly', a term which Anne could not understand. In the Preface to the second edition she wrote:

> I am at a loss to conceive how a man should permit himself to write anything that would be really disgraceful for a woman, or why a woman should be censured for writing anything that would be proper and becoming for a man.

This novel strongly challenges the conventional view of a woman's duty. Helen has left home, illegally, partly because she can no longer stand her husband's behaviour and partly because she is sure that their child will be ruined if she stays. Most people, including the local clergyman, find this shocking:

> She had done wrong to leave her husband; it was a violation of her sacred duties as a wife . . . nothing short of bodily ill-usage (and that of no trifling nature) could excuse such a step. (Chapter 51)

Helen strikes Gilbert, on their first meeting, as being rather too hard and sharp, and Arthur often complains of her unkindness. He compares her unfavourably with her friend Millicent, who never stands up for herself, but Millicent's own husband says, 'How can I help teasing her when she's so invitingly meek?'. (Chapter 32) Helen is gradually forced to see that, however sweet and kind she tries to be, it will make no difference. Before she marries Arthur she believes that she can save him from his errors, but, as her aunt points out, there is no reason why he cannot save himself:

> Mr Huntingdon, I suppose, is not without the common faculties of men . . . his Maker has endowed him with reason and conscience as well as the rest of us; the Scriptures are open to him as to others. (Chapter 20)

This is a clear rejection of the idea that women can or should purify men. Helen finds that instead of her improving Arthur he is corrupting her; she is 'debased, contaminated by the union'. (Chapter 30) 'My misfortunes have soured and embittered me exceedingly: I was beginning insensibly to cherish very unamiable feelings against my fellow mortals – the male part of them especially'. (Chapter 41) If she wishes to remain a reasonably good person, her only chance is to get away.

Helen does not have the excuse of 'bodily ill-usage', the only one that might have been acceptable. Her husband does not beat her but he does subject her to other forms of degradation – 'his idea of a wife is a thing to love one devotedly and to stay at home – to wait upon her husband, and amuse him and minister to his comfort in every possible way, while he chooses to stay with her; and, when he is absent, to attend to his interests, domestic or otherwise, and patiently await his return'. (Chapter 28) She is alternately a 'household deity', who must never leave her home, and a sex object – 'I could do with less caressing and more rationality. I should like to be less of a pet and more of a friend.' Arthur demands that she should live only for him, will not let her see Rome and Paris 'as it proved that I could take delight in anything disconnected with himself', and objects to her religion, which is a source of great strength to her, because it 'ought not to lessen her devotion to her earthly lord'. (Chapter 23)

We get a brief glimpse of a circle where marriages are arranged, men are expected to sow their wild oats and extra-marital affairs are normal. It turns out that the only part of the marriage service which Arthur takes seriously is the wife's promise to 'honour and obey'. Conventionally enough, he tells her that a wife's infidelity is much worse than a husband's because 'it is a woman's nature to be constant – to love one and one only, blindly, tenderly, and for ever'. (Chapter 27) Helen does not believe this, and tells him bluntly that she will no longer endure his 'conjugal endearments' when she knows he is sleeping with someone else. It is important to remember that at this time, and for a long time afterwards, married women were expected to forgive their husbands' infidelity.

Anne Brontë also questions the assumption that mothers and sisters should sacrifice themselves for the son of the family. Mrs Hargreave forces her daughter Millicent to make a 'good match', and tries to make her other daughter do the same, so that there will be more money for her son Walter. Gilbert's mother also prefers her sons, and tells him that when he has a wife 'it's your business to please yourself, and hers to please you'. But Gilbert disagrees:

> I might sink into the grossest condition of self-indulgence and carelessness about the wants of others, from the mere habit of being constantly cared for myself . . . I should expect to find more pleasure in making my wife happy and comfortable, than in being made so by her: I would rather give than receive. (Chapter 6)

It is understandable that Charlotte Brontë did not like *Wildfell Hall*, for her feelings about men were very different from her sister's. Anne did not expect a reformed rake to become a good husband, and had not the faintest wish for a 'master'. None of the men she admires is violent to women. Gilbert does not, like Rochester, try to force Helen into a sexual relationship, and she is always the dominant partner; at the end *she* proposes to *him*. Moreover, Gilbert accepts her child – which is unusual in a nineteenth-century novel[9] – because 'he was my own Helen's son, and therefore mine'. (Chapter 53)

Anne Brontë, then, had much in common with the early feminists. She might well have reacted more favourably than Charlotte to 'The Enfranchisement of Women', which appeared two years after her death. Like her elder sister, she believed in 'self-sacrificing love and disinterested devotion', but *Wildfell Hall* argues that self-sacrifice should not undermine self-respect.

8   Elizabeth Gaskell

'The outstanding fact about Mrs Gaskell,' writes a twentieth-century critic, 'is her femininity.'[1] Her first readers had much the same opinion. Mrs Gaskell was only once (at the time of *Ruth*) attacked for writing an 'unwomanly' novel. Because she was known to be happily married with children, she did not, like Charlotte Brontë, have to face private and public sneers.[2] Her novels express many feelings which are more acceptable in women than in men. 'I know nothing of Political Economy, or the theories of trade', she wrote in the Introduction to *Mary Barton*. She had tried to give a true picture of the condition of workers in Manchester, but 'whether the bitter complaints made by them . . . were well-founded or no, it is not for me to judge'. This was her way of saying that of course the problems must be solved by men who understand them, but that they should not forget the 'womanly' virtues of compassion and goodwill. The elderly Maria Edgeworth realised that this was a weakness – *'Emigration* is the only resource pointed out at the end of this work, and this is only an escape from the evils not a remedy'.[3]

Nevertheless, Mrs Gaskell was a more independent thinker than she admitted. She wrote three novels (*Mary Barton, Ruth, North and South*) which strongly challenged accepted ideas, and as she grew older her views on 'the woman question' became more liberal. In 1856 she signed a petition for a Married Women's Property Act, though with reservations – 'A husband can coax, wheedle, beat or tyrannise his wife out of something and no law whatever will help this . . . However our sex is badly enough used and legislated *against*, there's no doubt of *that* – so though I don't see the definite end proposed by these petitions I'll sign.'[4]

The women in her novels are usually better than the men. John Barton's wife has a good influence on him until she dies – 'One of the ties which bound him down to the gentle humanities of earth was loosened, and henceforward . . . he was a changed man'. (Chapter 3) But in the same novel she shows men helping children and sick people (George Wilson with his wife, Job Legh with the baby, John Barton with the Davenport family) and this is thoroughly suitable work for them. She emphatically did not believe that there should be one moral code for women and another for men.

Mrs Gaskell wrote novels of several different kinds, and these included studies of various groups of women who had not previously had much attention. It is easiest to look at her work under several different headings.

WORKING WOMEN

In *Mary Barton* Mrs Gaskell focused on a body of people whom most novelists ignored – the working class. Jane Austen became almost tongue-tied with embarrassment when she mentioned Emma's visit to 'a poor sick family', and many other novelists who did describe the poor used them as comic relief. One of Mrs Gaskell's great achievements was to give a clear, sympathetic and convincing picture of working-class life in Manchester, and this is what makes the first half of the novel so impressive. She firmly believed in the value of these obscure people, and she was particularly interested in the forgotten members of the working class, women and children:

> But remember! we only miss those who do men's work in their humble sphere; the aged, the feeble, the children, when they die, are hardly noted by the world; and yet to many hearts, their deaths make a blank which long years will never fill up. (Chapter 10)

Nearly all the women in *Mary Barton* work outside the home. Mary is a dressmaker because her father 'considered domestic servitude as a species of slavery'. (Chapter 3) The widowed Mrs Davenport minds the children of working mothers 'who brought their daily food with them, which she cooked for them, without wronging their helplessness of a crumb'. (Chapter 7) (This strongly suggests that other minders were less scrupulous.) Alice works as a servant, washerwoman and unpaid nurse. Margaret is a needlewoman, who gradually goes blind because she feels she cannot deprive her grandfather of her earnings – 'I'm so loath to think he should be stinted of what gives him such pleasure!'.

(Chapter 5) Bessy Higgins is another girl who allows her health to be destroyed at work rather than inconvenience her family – 'Father he were always liking to buy books, and go to lectures of one kind or another – all which took money – so I just worked on till I shall ne'er get the whirr out o' my ears or the fluff out o' my throat.' *(North and South,* Chapter 13)

Resignation and self-sacrifice come naturally to these women. Unlike the men, they do not join unions or take much interest in politics, and they are more likely to be influenced by religion, which John Barton thinks 'a sham put upon poor ignorant folk, women, and such-like'. (Chapter 35) Bessy is a Christian, and worries because her father isn't. Alice Wilson (written off as a 'canting old maid') leads an utterly unselfish life, helping anybody who needs her and never going home to the longed-for north country because 'first one wanted me, and then another'. (Chapter 4)

Mary, who reads silly romances and dreams of being a lady, is a completely different type. She is an attractive girl who enjoys her power over men, and such a girl, in Mrs Gaskell's work, is sure to come to grief. The well-behaved Margaret cannot sympathise with her because 'she had no idea of the strength of the conflict between will and principle in some who were differently constituted from herself'. (Chapter 22) 'Principle' wins eventually, but Mary's aunt Esther is not so lucky. Working away from home ruins her life:

> That's the worst of factory work, for girls. They can earn so much when work's plenty, that they can maintain themselves any how . . . You see Esther spent her money in dress, thinking to set off her pretty face, and got to come home so late at night . . . (Chapter 1)

Mrs Gaskell, like many other people, felt that industrial work destroyed the 'womanly' qualities. The girls in *North and South* have a 'boisterous independence of temper and behaviour' (Chapter 17) and do not want to be servants, preferring 'the better wages and greater independence of working in a mill'. (Chapter 8) Jane Wilson, who has worked in a factory since childhood, cannot boil a potato, and the married women workers in *Mary Barton* put their children out to nurse, let their homes get dirty, and drive their husbands to drink. (Chapter 10) In the last scene Mary is in her proper place, waiting with her baby for her husband to come home. Mrs Gaskell did not believe that women's only talents were for home-making; in fact she stresses that Margaret has a singing voice which could have made her famous. But she did believe that all women had to fulfil their natural responsibilities. The working men in *Mary Barton* and *North and South* become enraged because they cannot support their wives and children as men should. Women take no part in this struggle; their task is to keep the home together, and to remind men of 'the gentle humanities of earth'.

OLD MAIDS

Like Charlotte Brontë, Mrs Gaskell was interested in the problems of the single woman. 'I think an unmarried life may be to the full as happy, *in process of time*,' she wrote, 'but I think there is a time of trial to be gone through with *women*, who naturally yearn after children.'[5]

Her interest dates from her first published work, 'Libbie Marsh's Three Eras' (1847). Libbie, who knows she is plain, resolves, 'I must not lose time in fretting and fidgetting after marriage, but just look about me for somewhat else to do'. She helps another woman nurse her dying child and then goes to live with her. The same thing happens in her Welsh story 'The Well of Pen-Morfa' (1850). A pretty young woman loses her fiancé when she is lamed in an accident; after considerable suffering she takes a mentally handicapped girl into her home and cares for her for the rest of her life. Both these stories suggest that women can expect more kindness from each other than from men.

Cranford is a small town 'in possession of the Amazons'; the householders are all women and are often fiercely anti-male. Miss Jenkyns 'would have despised the modern idea of women being equal to men. Equal, indeed! she knew they were superior.' (Chapter 2) Miss Jessie Brown, at thirty, is the youngest of the old maids and the only one who still has time to change her condition. She has given up her lover because 'there was no one but herself to nurse her poor Mary, or cheer and comfort her father during the time of illness'. (Chapter 2) He comes back after her father and sister have died, illustrating the fact that a good woman cannot get married while inconvenient members of her family exist. But Miss Matty Jenkyns, who is in her fifties, gets no second chance.

Miss Matty has sent away the man she wanted to marry because her family objected to him. She does not complain or resent their behaviour, although she admits that she would have liked to have children. Having been denied the only kind of work she could have done well, she is helpless when she loses her income, and this illustrates the dreadful dilemma of the untrained woman 'past middle age, and with the education common to ladies fifty years ago'. (Chapter 14) She has only a ragbag of accomplishments with which she cannot possibly support herself.

Cranford is not a tragic novel, and Miss Matty survives because her brother comes home and the other ladies rally round. The moral seems to be that truly good people will come to no serious harm. But in fact Mrs Gaskell did not believe this; in 'Lois the Witch' (1859) she shows a thoroughly good, unselfish girl who perishes in the Salem witch hunts. This happens because she feels it right to go to an unfriendly community in America, rather than cause trouble for the man who wants to marry her. The same conviction that goodness is important for its own sake can be seen in a very fine story about an old maid, 'Half a Life-Time Ago' (1855).

Susan Dixon is a 'stateswoman' (an independent farmer in Cumberland) and is first seen as a 'tall, gaunt, hard-featured woman, who never smiled, and hardly ever spoke an unnecessary word'. We discover that she had been an attractive girl who would have got married if her young brother had not been mentally handicapped. Her lover, Michael, wants her to send the boy to an institution, but Susan is sure he will be cruelly treated and refuses. Michael decides she is a 'termagant' and marries a more tractable girl. There are many Victorian stories about sacrifice, but few which are so painful and realistic. Mrs Gaskell convinces us that it is both necessary, and terribly difficult:

> Then she would wonder how she could have had strength, the cruel, self-piercing strength, to say what she had done; to stab herself with that stern resolution, of which the scar would remain till her dying day. It might have been right; but, as she sickened, she wished she had not instinctively chosen the right. How luxurious a life haunted by no stern sense of duty must be! And many led this kind of life, why could not she?

Dickens apparently disliked this story, and it is not hard to see why. Susan is not miraculously rescued from the consequences of her actions, and unselfishness does not beautify her character. She becomes a tough, competent, solitary, middle-aged woman – 'her manner curt, her wits keen'. When Michael dies and she breaks the news to his wife she realises exactly what self-sacrifice has done to her:

> The pretty Nelly Hebthwaite was pretty still; her delicate face had never suffered from any long-enduring feeling . . . Susan felt the contrast even at that moment. She knew that her own skin was weather-beaten, furrowed, brown – that her teeth were gone, and her hair grey and ragged. And yet she was not two years older than Nelly.

The surprise ending returns to the theme of women consoling one another; Susan provides a home for Michael's widow and children – 'and so it fell out that the latter days of Susan Dixon's life were better than the former'.[6]

Most Gaskell heroines do get married, but marriage, in her scheme of things, is never simply a good-conduct prize. In *Wives and Daughters*, Cynthia and her mother both find eligible husbands, but both are clearly seen to be selfish women. By contrast, many of her altruistic women – Susan, Miss Matty, Faith Benson, Hester Rose – have to go through life alone. But Mrs Gaskell did not feel that they were either comic or failures, and in her attitude to the single woman she was far ahead of her time.

FALLEN WOMEN

In an early story, 'Lizzie Leigh' (1850) Mrs Gaskell made a plea for the fallen woman, and in *Mary Barton* she gave a compassionate account of the life and death of the prostitute, Esther. In *Ruth* (1853), the central figure is a young girl who has been seduced and had a child, and the novel was sharply attacked.

Mrs Gaskell, like many other writers, pointed out indignantly that fallen women were treated very differently from the men who had ruined them. 'Indeed, and young men will be young men,' says the landlady in *Ruth*. Harry Carson says, 'My father would have forgiven any temporary connection, far sooner than my marrying one so far beneath me in rank.' (*Mary Barton*, Chapter 11) 'Pure' women were supposed to have no sympathy with those who had not been so fortunate. Hester, the virtuous wife in Trollope's *John Caldigate*, believes that 'crafty women . . . get hold of innocent men, and drive them sometimes into perdition'.[7] Thackeray's Mrs Pendennis is brutal to the girl whom she finds nursing her sick son – a scene which Mrs Gaskell adapted for her own purpose in *Ruth*. In this scene, Ruth is denounced as 'artful' and 'vicious', and is accused of corrupting young men. She shares this judgement of herself, feeling much more guilty than Bellingham although, unlike him, she never really knew what was going on.

In 'Lizzie Leigh' the women are much more compassionate than the men and manage to rescue the girl from prostitution. In *Ruth* the author's spokesman is Mr Benson, who is set apart from ordinary men by being a clergyman and a cripple. His positive attitude to Ruth and to her baby is something quite new. Novelists usually felt that the best thing to do with an illegitimate child was to kill it; Mrs Gaskell herself had done so in *Mary Barton* and 'Lizzie Leigh'. In *The Head of the Family*, by Dinah Mulock Craik, published the year before *Ruth*, the heroine is tricked into a false marriage, and although she eventually recovers her child dies:

> In one sense there was mercy in the death of the babe, taken in his innocence from evil to come. . . . The mother, amidst all her affliction, seemed dimly to comprehend this . . . 'Now, nobody will ever taunt my boy with having no father.' (Chapter 38)

Often this attitude extended to the fallen woman herself. David Copperfield thinks that perhaps Little Em'ly ought to have died as a child, while she was still innocent. 'It would be better for (Ruth) to die at once,' says Miss Benson. But her brother not only prevents Ruth from committing suicide but also protests against her baby being called the 'miserable offspring of sin':

> The world has, indeed, made such children miserable, innocent as they are . . . the world's way of treatment is too apt to harden the mother's natural love into something like hatred. Shame, and the terror of friends' displeasure, turn her mad –

defile her holiest instincts, and, as for the fathers – God forgive them! I cannot – at least, not just now. (Chapter 11)

He argues that if Ruth is given a chance motherhood will make her a responsible adult and the child will become a blessing. Motherhood does alter her so much that when she meets Bellingham again she refuses to marry him on the grounds that he would be bad for her child. Once again, Mrs Gaskell's attitude is unconventional; most people took it for granted that a fallen woman's only chance was to marry her seducer. In *The Vicar of Wakefield,*, for instance, we are expected to be pleased when Olivia's marriage to the Squire turns out to be legal, even though he is a villain. But Ruth has progressed from a willing sex object ('Her beauty was all that Mr. Bellingham cared for') to a mature woman who works hard to support her child, and will not allow any man to spoil his life.

Ruth is not a particularly good book, but like another novel of the 1850s, *Uncle Tom's Cabin*, it is important for its effect on public opinion. Charlotte Brontë thought that it might 'restore hope and energy to many who thought they had forfeited their right to both'.[8] Margaret Oliphant wrote two years later that it did 'not seem to have lessened the estimation in which her audience hold her'.[9] In the middle years of the century more and more novelists took up the theme seriously and expressed the same views as Mrs Gaskell – that good women cannot afford to be ignorant, that fallen women can lead useful lives, that marrying the man is not always the best solution and that the illegitimate child has a right to exist. Ruth dies; given the conventions of the novel at that time, this was almost inevitable. But this does not happen until she has won the respect of her community, and Leonard, although he will have to face some prejudice, is likely to do well.

'THE ONLY DUTY OF WOMEN': THE LATER NOVELS

'I long (weakly) for the old times when right and wrong did not seem such complicated matters, and I am sometimes coward enough to wish that we were back in the darkness where obedience was the only seen duty of women,'[10] Mrs Gaskell wrote, probably in 1850. In her later novels, from *Ruth* onwards, we constantly see a woman struggling to find her own moral bearings. Obedience is at best irrelevant and often conflicts with her sense of what is right. These novels show her growing conviction that the traditional role of women had to be rethought.

Jemima Bradshaw, in *Ruth*, has not at first 'overcome her awe of her father sufficiently to act independently of him, and according to her own sense of right'. (Chapter 19) She feels that her marriage is being arranged 'like an Oriental daughter' (Chapter 21), and finally rebels against her father's cruel treatment of Ruth. Her mother, who has always submitted to her husband, rebels too when she has to choose between him and their son. Both of them are behaving unconventionally, but they are also being traditional women because they are compassionate.

Margaret, in *North and South*, comes close to being Mrs Gaskell's ideal heroine. Essentially a strong character, she is contrasted with her London cousins and with Thornton's sister – 'nothing could strengthen Fanny to endure hardships patiently, or face difficulties bravely'. (Chapter 12) She feels out of place at parties because after moving North she works hard in the house and because she is interested in serious matters like the industrial war. She does not hesitate to argue with the two men who represent the opposing sides, Thornton and Higgins, in favour of the solutions which Mrs Gaskell herself thought right. This is stepping right out of a woman's proper place and, as Mrs Oliphant noted, Margaret's relationship with the man she marries is characteristic of a new type of heroine, whose 'furious love-making was but a wild declaration of the "Rights of Woman" '.[11]

But Margaret is still 'womanly', caring for those weaker than herself, and pleading against violence, 'If I saved one blow, one cruel, angry action that might otherwise have been committed, I did a woman's work' (Chapter 23), she says. This is after she has intervened between Thornton and the workers and exposed herself to unpleasant remarks. The same thing happens when she is put in a compromising position with Frederick. In both cases, however, she has 'weighty reasons, which may and ought to make her overlook any seeming impropriety in her conduct' (Chapter 38). In the same speech, Thornton states that, while other people must guard Fanny, 'I believe Miss Hale to be a guardian to herself'.

For much of the novel Margaret also has to be a guardian to others. Her parents are weaker characters than she is and she has to 'act the part of a Roman daughter, and give strength out of her own scanty stock to her father'. (Chapter 30) Like Jessie Brown, she is only free to marry when the dependent members of her family have died. By this time, left alone except for a few cousins, she asserts her 'right to follow her own ideas of duty':

> But she had learnt, in those solemn hours of thought, that she herself must one day answer for her own life, and what she had done with it; and she tried to settle that most difficult problem for women, how much was to be utterly merged in obedience to authority, and how much might be set apart for freedom in working. (Chapter 49)

The question of how a woman is to act continued to preoccupy her in her greatest novel, *Sylvia's Lovers*. She takes what looks like a slight story – which of two men a flighty girl will marry – and uses it to illustrate universal issues. The vulnerability of women is a constant theme in this novel. Men, like Coulson and Kinraid, usually get over their first love; women usually don't. We hear about a girl who died when Kinraid left her and another girl who became insane for the same reason, unable to say anything except 'He once was here'. (Chapter 15) Sylvia and Hester, although they are as different as Hetty Sorrel and Dinah Morris, never really recover from their first attachment. Sylvia, who begins as every man's ideal woman, becomes 'a pale, sad woman, always dressed in black', and dies young. Hester remains unmarried and devotes herself to others.

Sylvia is not a wicked person; she is simply unaware of the great realities outside herself until it is too late. She gets her first hint of this at the sailor's funeral, when she goes into church thinking about her new cloak and comes out 'with life and death suddenly become real to her mind'. (Chapter 7) Hester is 'ignorant of the strange mystery of Sylvia's heart, as those who are guided by obedience to principle must ever be of the clue to the actions of those who are led by the passionate ebb and flow of impulse'. (Chapter 44) This is the same contrast as that between Mary and Margaret in *Mary Barton*, and again Mrs Gaskell sympathises with both girls. But she is certain that they should act on 'principle' rather than 'impulse', however difficult this may be. Philip, who is governed by principle in every other action of his life, abandons it for the sake of Sylvia – 'the desire of his eyes and the lust of his heart'. (Chapter 15) And because his feeling for Sylvia is lust, not concern for her as a person, he comes to see that it has harmed them both, 'If I could live my life o'er again I would love my God more, and thee less, and then I shouldn't have sinned this sin against thee'. (Chapter 45)

'Principle' is not the same thing as automatic obedience. Sylvia grows up in a household where her father is the undisputed lord and her mother thinks that women should 'go through life in the shadow of obscurity – never named except in connection with good housewifery, husband, or children'. (Chapter 11) When Sylvia is married to Philip she makes 'absolute obedience' her 'rule of life' because she has been taught to consider this a wife's duty and has nothing else to give. Of course this does not lead to a good relationship, any more than Philip's efforts to give her what he thinks she wants. Sylvia finds herself surrounded with 'silk gowns' and 'creature comforts', and, for the first time, has no work to do. Her life soon becomes a 'comfortable imprisonment' which she can only endure by escaping occasionally to 'the freedom and solitude of the sea-shore'. (Chapter 31) 'She missed the free open air, the great dome of sky above the fields; she rebelled against the necessity of "dressing" (as she called it) to go out.' (Chapter 30) Particularly after her mother has made her promise never to leave the house without Philip's permission, she bitterly resents her bondage:

> 'I'm glad enough I've getten a baby;' said Sylvia, 'but for ought else I wish I had niver been married, I do!' (Chapter 32)

Unlike some captive wives, Sylvia never feels oppressed by her child; in fact she likes to get her away from the nurse and escape with her to the sea. It is the child who stops her running away with Kinraid and the child who finally brings her back to Philip. Motherhood and suffering are the two great forces which make her morally aware. For most of the novel she is 'too much a child, too entirely unaccustomed to any independence of action' (Chapter 37) She finds that romantic love is not an absolute and that it is sometimes necessary to accept an imperfect relationship. Mrs Gaskell, like many of her contemporaries, was concerned about the problems of unhappy marriages, but she felt that reconciliation should be possible. 'You and me have done wrong to each other,' Philip says, 'yet we can see now how we were led to it; we can pity and forgive one another.' (Chapter 45)

Wives and Daughters, set in an old-fashioned community in the 1820s, shows, more subtly than *Ruth,* the intense pressures on a girl to conform. 'Women should mind what they're about, and never be talked of,' says Mrs Goodenough (Chapter 47), and Dr Gibson warns his daughter, 'You don't know, Molly, how slight a thing may blacken a girl's reputation for life'. (Chapter 48) Molly very nearly loses her reputation, ironically because she is trying to save Cynthia's. An engagement is such a serious commitment – it 'cannot be broken off except by mutual consent' – that Cynthia will be degraded in everyone's eyes if they find out about her teenage romance with Mr Preston. Molly's father decides to remarry because he thinks she needs a chaperone – ironically, because Molly has quite enough sense to do without one.

The book builds up an extended moral contrast between the kind, responsible Molly, and Mrs Gibson and Cynthia. Mrs Gibson, before her marriage, is forced to work without enjoying it, and Mrs Gaskell stresses the unpleasant aspects of a lone woman's life. Her only way out is to find a husband – 'some one who would work while she sat at her elegant ease in a prettily-furnished drawing room'. (Chapter 10) She is also preoccupied with her looks in a way which Mrs Gaskell, and her generation, found quite inappropriate for older women. When Molly visits the bedroom where her mother died, and finds it re-decorated for her father's new wife, we get an inkling that Mrs Gibson is unaware of deep emotions. She is ultra-feminine, but she is not womanly; she unashamedly hopes that Osborne's son will die. Indifference to a child was the most serious of all sins for Mrs Gaskell, and Cynthia's faults are blamed on her mother's neglect.

Cynthia, too, is extremely feminine, 'tickling the vanity of men' by her 'unspoken deference' (Chapter 37), when she pretends that they know much more than she does. She is 'one of those natural coquettes, who, from their cradle to their grave, instinctively bring out all their prettiest airs and graces in order to stand well with any man, young or old, who may happen to be present'. (Chapter 42) Mrs Gaskell says cautiously of Cynthia's charm that 'perhaps it is incompatible with very high principle'. (Chapter 19) 'Molly, you see, devotes herself to the useful,'

Cynthia says, 'and I to the ornamental.' (Chapter 29) So while men fall helplessly in love with Cynthia, Molly is the person who is needed whenever anyone is in trouble. And although Molly, unlike Cynthia, dislikes any kind of deception, she is forced to keep two important secrets. Several writers, like Charlotte Yonge, considered that keeping secrets from one's parents was a grave fault, but for Molly, as for Jane Austen's heroines, knowing when and when not to speak is a part of adult responsibility.

Molly cannot 'transfer her love to the next comer' (Chapter 60) (this is more excusable in Roger, being a man) whereas Cynthia constantly changes her mind. Mrs Gaskell does not believe that she should be held to an unsuitable engagement. But she does feel that Roger will think less of her when he knows about her past, and will be happier with a more stable wife.

While much of the novel is about the contrast between Roger, a future Darwin, and the dilettante Osborne, it is clear that women are not expected to be academically gifted. Molly has to struggle to get even a basic education. Cynthia is aware that women are more attractive if they seem ignorant (a problem explored in 'Cousin Phillis', where the heroine is 'more like a man than a woman – she knows Latin and Greek', and fails to hold a lover). Mrs Gibson, though a teacher, can only join in conversations 'if the subject spoken about did not refer to serious solid literature, or science, or politics, or social economy'. (Chapter 9) She says approvingly that 'Cynthia's talents are not for science and the severer studies', and that Molly 'reads such deep books – all about facts and figures; she'll be quite a blue-stocking' (Chapter 24) – a word which annoys Molly very much. The implication is that the most a woman can do is take an intelligent interest in her husband's work.

Intelligence, though, is never the most important quality for Mrs Gaskell. 'Goodness', in *Wives and Daughters* as in her other works, is 'the only enduring thing in this world'. (Chapter 19) Firmly believing as she did in objective standards of good and evil, she judged both men and women on a moral basis. 'The only duty of women' is not obedience, or good housekeeping, and certainly not to catch a husband, it is to struggle seriously in all circumstances to do right.

9 The Male Image of Women

Women novelists were often accused of being unable to draw a man successfully. Men had precisely the same difficulty with women; 'Their good woman is a queer thing, half-angel, half-doll,' Charlotte Brontë complained.[1] R. D. Blackmore's *Lorna Doone* (1869) embodies many male fantasies about women. It is fashionable for men and boys to despise them – 'creatures of a lower order, only good enough to run errands for us, and to nurse boy-babies'. (Chapter 9) The novel is full of such remarks, often dragged in for no reason, for instance, 'a horse (like a woman) lacks, and is better without, self-reliance'. (Chapter 3)

But although the other women in the novel are ordinary faulty human beings, Lorna (though anything but self-reliant) belongs to another sphere. She is 'purer than the morning dew, than the sun more bright and clear'. (Chapter 33) She is too good to be allowed to do housework, and the suggestion that she eats sausages (Chapter 34) fills John with contempt. She has somehow managed to grow up pure in mind and body among a group of violent men (who call her 'the queen'), and the thought that one of them might get her so upsets John that he would rather see her die:

> One thing was quite certain – if Lorna could not have John Ridd, no one else should have her. And my mother . . . agreed that this was comfort. (Chapter 37)

All the hard and dangerous work has to be done by John; Lorna, who faints four times in the course of the novel, can do nothing whatsoever to help herself. John is so determined to shield her from reality that he will not answer her questions – 'which I rather had answered upon her lips, than troubled her pretty ears with them' – when the Doones are coming to carry her off. 'I always think that women, of whatever mind, are best when least they meddle with the things that appertain to men.' (Chapter 48)

When Lorna turns out to be an earl's daughter and far above him, John has to perform still greater deeds of strength and daring to prove that he deserves her. Only a superman could win a woman so lovely and perfect as this very typical mid-Victorian heroine. And the enormous success of *Lorna Doone* showed that this was what the public wanted to read.

At the other extreme were 'crafty women' who 'get hold of innocent men, and drive them sometimes into perdition'. The hero often has to escape from a woman who is older and more experienced than himself, and is not worthy of him. This is always happening in the novels of Thackeray, Trollope and Collins, who give a comprehensive picture of what mid-Victorian men thought of the opposite sex.

THACKERAY

'He never can have known a good and sensible woman', Harriet Martineau wrote of Thackeray,[2] and Charlotte Brontë, too, thought he was 'unjust to women, quite unjust'.[3] If intelligent women living at the time resented Thackeray, this is not very surprising. His heroines may be good, or may be sensible, but hardly ever both at once. Even when he is drawing what is supposed to be a good woman she is jealous, intolerant, or simply silly. When she has political views they are based on emotion, not reason. 'The book of female logic is blotted all over with tears.' (*The Virginians*, Chapter 4) He does not seriously think that a woman can embrace any career except marriage; Chapter 12 of *Vanity Fair* laughs at 'a ladylike knowledge of botany and geology', and says bluntly that men prefer a pretty face.

Yet Thackeray was a man of unusually liberal attitudes for the mid-nineteenth century. He did not believe (see page 26) that parents had a right to spoil their children's lives. As they grew up, he argued, they would want to leave home, the sons to see the world and the daughters to get married. And he was well aware that most women had a harder lot than most men. Again and again he shows a woman trapped in a cruel marriage, or loving a child (that is, a son) who does not love her back.

We should go mad had we to endure the hundredth part of those daily pains which are meekly borne by many women. Ceaseless slavery meeting with no reward; constant gentleness and kindness met by cruelty as constant, love, labour, patience, watchfulness . . . all this, how many of them have to bear in quiet, and appear abroad with cheerful faces as if they felt nothing. (*Vanity Fair*, Chapter 56)

'In our society,' Thackeray wrote, 'there's no law to control the King of the Fireside . . . He may kill a wife gradually, and be no more questioned than the Grand Seignior who drowns a slave at midnight.' (*Esmond*, Volume 1, Chapter 13) The good women in his novels sometimes find an exceptional man, an Esmond or a Dobbin, who protects them and puts up with their weaknesses. But more often they realise that the husbands and sons whom they adore are discontented at home. On the other side are the bad women, who love nobody, and marry for purely selfish reasons. It is difficult to say who is happier in the end, and the moral in Thackeray's novels is seldom simple.

Vanity Fair is full of ill-used women – Sir Pitt's wife, the women in the Steyne household, Jane Osborne and, for much of the story, Amelia. Thackeray's attitude to her, as every reader knows, is ambiguous. At times, as when she is nursing her dying parents or being made to give up her child, it is thoroughly sympathetic. She is certainly better than the hard-boiled young women who marry for money and this is why her own sex dislike her. On the other hand, she is popular with men, who sense that she is capable of sincere devotion. But the author's final judgement is that she is 'no more fit to live in the world than a baby in arms'. (Chapter 67) Until the very end, Amelia is a victim of sentimental ideas about the nature of women. Dobbin makes George marry her because he is convinced she is dying. In fact Thackeray feels that no one ever dies of love, and it would have been kinder to have let her be miserable. Afterwards Dobbin tells himself not to be 'hurt that such a heart as Amelia's can love only once and for ever' (Chapter 58), and most readers probably took this quite seriously. Only in the last chapter do we see that Thackeray does not believe that a good woman only falls in love once, and that Amelia's sentimentality is thoroughly destructive.

Becky is not at all sentimental (although she can produce a devastating parody of the sentimental style when she wants to, which is why we never quite believe Thackeray when he asks us to take such stuff seriously). Having been overworked and underpaid as a girl, she is determined 'to get free from the prison in which she found herself'. (Chapter 2) Another woman who does not see why she should have to suffer is Miss Crawley, a female rake who belongs to a more liberal age. Like Becky, she has connections with France (in Thackeray's novels, as in Miss Edgeworth's, France is a country of loose women with advanced, even feminist, views). Miss Crawley has read Voltaire and Rousseau, and 'talked very lightly about divorce, and most energetically of the rights of women'. (Chapter 10) But, like Becky, she has to be discredited so that the good women can triumph. Her 'daring liberal opinions' are not sincerely held – she is, in fact, a snob – and she recants as soon as she begins to be ill. She is an ugly, selfish, religionless old woman who should 'learn to love and pray'. (Chapter 14)

Yet his next major novel, *Pendennis,* shows how a woman who does love and pray can bully and damage those around her. Helen, like Amelia, has spoiled her son by worshipping him, and like Amelia's son Pen doesn't fully return his mother's love. Although she and Laura can make him feel guilty, they cannot make him stay at home. Thackeray stresses that young men lead a life which would horrify their female relations if they knew about it. They drink, get into debt and run after unsuitable women, but they still need to feel that there are good women in the background to pray for them. 'How weak and wicked we are' says Pen, 'how spotless and full of love and truth Heaven made you.' (Chapter 71) Laura, when she recoils from Blanche's selfishness, is aware that Pen is selfish too, but she convinces herself that the two cases are not the same:

> Pen was different. Pen was a man. It seemed natural, somehow, that he should be self-willed and should have his own way. (Chapter 24)

Helen, we are asked to believe, is a saintly woman; Thackeray says so emphatically more than once. Yet he also uses the astonishing phrase 'sexual jealousy' to describe her feelings for Pen. She loves Laura, her adopted daughter, much less than her son (but significantly Laura is the more upset when Helen dies) and turns on her viciously when she refuses to be manipulated.

Helen is firmly convinced that men are not morally responsible. If Pen has sinned, it is not his fault; it is Fanny's fault for seducing him and Laura's for not having married him. Her 'cruel and ruthless' treatment of Fanny provokes an ironic comment on woman's inhumanity to woman:

> What could Fanny expect when suddenly brought up for sentence before a couple of such judges? Nothing but swift condemnation, awful punishment, merciless dismissal. Women are cruel critics in cases such as that . . . and we like them to be so. (Chapter 53)

Thackeray makes the same point in *Vanity Fair*; the one time Lady Jane defies her husband is when she insists that Becky is a bad woman and must leave her house. A good woman is naturally devoted to her menfolk, but it was very difficult for Thackeray to believe that she could have any kindly feelings for a member of her own sex.

In *Pendennis*, as in *Dombey*, a lot of attention is paid to the brother–sister relationship and the assumption that the boy child is the one who really matters. While Laura accepts that she is less important than her 'brother' and gives up everything for him, including money, Blanche Amory resents the small brother who has 'deprived' her 'of her mamma's affection'. (Chapter 24) The arrangement is that she should have only a fraction of their mother's money while all the rest goes to little Frank. Because Blanche thinks this unfair, and tries to get the money divided equally, her mother – a vulgar but good woman – brands her as evil and warns her fiancé not to marry her:

> Lady Clavering shrank from her with a sort of terror. 'Don't touch me', she said, 'you've no heart; you never had. I see . . . why you threatened that you would make me give you half Frank's fortune. And when Arthur offered to marry you without a shilling, because he wouldn't rob my boy, you left him, and you took poor Harry. Have nothing to do with her, Harry.' (Chapter 75)

It is not surprising to hear that Blanche gives herself French airs (while Laura is an English rose) and has 'settled the divorce question, and the rights of women' (Chapter 23) after reading

George Sand. Thackeray makes it clear what we are to think of her when he tells us that she is prepared to marry for money and is cruel to servants and children. Helen's faults are forgivable, but not Blanche's. She is that worst of all women in the nineteenth-century novel – one who does not care about her family and cannot feel disinterested love.

In *Henry Esmond* there is the same contrast between good and bad women, and again the 'good' heroine has some radical faults. Lady Castlewood genuinely loves the men in her family, but she competes against both her daughters for their attention.[4] 'With the other sex perfectly tolerant and kindly, of her own she was invariably jealous.' (Volume 1, Chapter 7) Beatrix is not content to 'love and pray', but wants greatness, asking rebelliously, 'Why am I not a man?' (Volume 3, Chapter 3). Of course Beatrix is a hard-hearted woman who ends up losing her virtue (predictably in France). But both here and in *The Virginians* Thackeray stresses that if Beatrix has faults she has a grievance too, because her mother has never loved her. And in the latter novel his attitude to Beatrix has become fairly sympathetic.

In *The Newcomes* he creates a rather different pattern. Here the contrast is not so much between good and bad women as between weak and strong ones, and Thackeray suggests that the worst thing a young woman can do is meekly to marry the husband her parents choose. 'You men,' Ethel says correctly, 'like dolls for your wives.' (Chapter 52) The doll-like Rosey, being 'of a very obedient and ductile nature, had acquiesced gladly enough in her mamma's opinion, that she was in love with the rich and handsome young Clive'. (Chapter 73) The result is that everyone around her is made miserable and that she dies. Lady Clara also marries on her mother's orders and is also wretched. But Thackeray's verdict is that she should not have eloped with another man, hateful though her husband is, because this separates her from decent people and from her own children. Ethel, who had been about to make yet another arranged marriage, is sufficiently shocked to reform and devote herself to Clara's children. Eventually, Thackeray suggests, she may be able to marry for love.

In this novel – the last which we need consider seriously – Thackeray tried, with Laura and the reformed Ethel, to create women who are pure, religious and home-loving, and who have no serious faults. Neither of them, however, is at all convincing.

The good women whom the reader does believe in are Amelia, who is weak, Helen, who is possessive, and Lady Castlewood, who is neurotically jealous. All of them are unhappy because they have to live vicariously through their men. Although he paid lip-service to the ideal of the Angel in the House, Thackeray made it clear that these good, passive wives and mothers had a bitter and empty existence. And in Becky Sharp he created one of the most memorable bad, active women in literature.

TROLLOPE

Anthony Trollope was the son of a tough, energetic woman who supported her family, including her husband and grown-up sons, by writing, and who for some time was a better-known novelist than himself. He had every reason to be aware that not all women were clinging creatures who needed male support. Yet that is the impression he gives in his fiction, and of all the male nineteenth-century novelists, his attitude to women is the most conventional.[5]

'That women should have their rights,' he wrote (after seeing something of the American feminist movement) 'no man will deny. To my thinking neither increase of work nor increase of political influence are among them. The best right a woman has is the right to a husband.'[6] 'A desire to get married is the natural state of a woman,' he said in *Miss Mackenzie*. 'Many of the most worthy women of the day' were trying to teach spinsters to enjoy their lives, but they were going against human nature, 'The truth in the matter is too clear. A woman's life is not perfect or whole till she has added herself to a husband.' (Chapter 11)

All the heroines in the Barsetshire novels are passive, long-suffering, and intensely devoted to a man. Eleanor, in *Barchester Towers*, 'had once declared that whatever her father did should in her eyes be right. She then transferred her allegiance, and became ever ready to defend the worst failings of her lord and master.' (Chapter 2) ('Lord' and 'master', in Trollope, are interchangeable with 'husband'.) Mary Thorne has the same feelings about Frank – 'master of her spirit, her bosom's lord, the man whom she had been born to worship' (*Doctor Thorne*, Chapter 42). Grace Crawley practically worships Major Grantly – 'you ought to go down on your knees before him, and kiss his highness's shoebuckle'. (*Last Chronicle of Barset*, Chapter 29)

Trollope's women are constantly going down on their knees or falling at somebody's feet.

But although a girl naturally wants a husband, she must not be a husband-hunter. The woman who schemes for a man or who marries for an establishment is always a target for Trollope's wit. A heroine, in his novels, is very anxious to behave correctly. She will not marry into a family which does not want her (Lucy, in *Framley Parsonage*, will not accept Lord Lufton until his mother asks her) or offend or disobey her own relations. Trollope believed that a woman's duty to her parents was less important than her duty to her husband, but she was still bound to obey them before marriage. And she must be ready to give up the man she loves rather than be a nuisance to him in any way. Suffering in silence while her man is away from her, like Mary Thorne, or Lucy Morris, or the 'modern Griselda', Miss Mackenzie, is an especially noble quality in a Trollope heroine. At the time he wrote these heroines were very much admired.

But Trollope created other women who were not dependent and feminine. In the Barsetshire novels we have Charlotte Stanhope, a free-thinker with no 'feminine delicacy', and Miss Dunstable, who has some masculine qualities but is a womanly woman at heart. Above all there is Mrs Proudie, Trollope's most famous comic character. She is funny, not because she is too worldly for a bishop's wife – many of Trollope's clergymen are worldly too – but because she doesn't 'confine herself to her wardrobes, still-rooms and laundries' (*Barchester Towers*, Chapter 43) and wants to run her husband's diocese herself. In an age when women were supposed to keep quiet in public, she interrupts and contradicts a male lecturer, 'I never knew a lady do such a brazen-faced thing before . . . in a public place, too!'. (*Framley Parsonage*, Chapter 7) Few men are bold enough to reprove her, except Mr Crawley, who believes strongly in a traditional role for women:

'Madam,' said Mr Crawley, 'you should not interfere in these matters. You simply debase your husband's high office. The distaff were more fitting for you.' (*Last Chronicle of Barset*, Chapter 18)

But in the end Mrs Proudie ceases to be comic. She realises that her husband hates her, and that, since all her importance comes from him, she will lose 'her income, and her palace, and her position' if she makes him unfit to do his work. She cannot endure this, and the shock kills her. When a woman refused to stay in her proper place, Trollope thought, this could lead to tragic results.

Lily Dale was the other female character who made a deep impression on the reading public. 'It was because she could not get over her troubles that they loved her', Trollope wrote.[7] Most unusually, she remains a single woman all her life because she is faithful to the memory of her only love affair. 'It is to me almost as though I had married him' (*The Small House at Allington*, Chapter 54). Trollope – and his readers – undoubtedly felt that a woman lost some of her feminine delicacy if she fell in love more than once. He did let a few heroines recover from an unfortunate first engagement, but never without serious feelings of guilt.

Lily is a sacrifice to middle-class man's inability to marry before he can support a household. This situation comes up again and again in Trollope. Women who have money are a prey for fortune-hunters; women who have not find it hard to get married at all. When a couple do not possess a reasonable income – like Mr and Mrs Crawley – they are likely to suffer terribly. Trollope often had to devise an unconvincing ending, as in *Doctor Thorne* and *The Vicar of Bullhampton*, to make his young lovers both happy and rich. This does not happen in *The Small House at Allington*, but we are made to see that Crosbie would have been happier if he had chosen true love and 'a small house full of babies' instead of a larger income and a bossy, unfeminine wife.

Apart from her poverty, Lily is everything a man can want. Crosbie muses on his miserable honeymoon journey, 'She would have knelt at his feet on the floor of the carriage, and . . . promised him to do her best – her best – her very best'. (Chapter 45) Lily trips across the garden to hand him his coffee, agrees to everything he asks and forgives him for leaving her, 'These things are different with a man'. (Chapter 54) To crown it all, after having been in love with him she can never love anyone else. Any man would feel flattered by so much devotion, and Crosbie soon finds that it is one of the things he has forfeited when he marries for money. To Alexandrina he is merely 'her senior attendant' (Chapter 40); he has to run errands for his mother-in-law and the de Courcys take away his money and freedom. He is beaten up, and shunned by all good men, but his real punishment is to be dominated by his wife's family when he could have had a proper husband/wife relationship with Lily Dale.

We are left in no doubt that it was a crime for a Victorian man to break off his engagement (Lily could have sued him for breach of promise). The reason why it seemed so monstrous was that a girl's whole future happiness depended on marriage, and if she was a nice girl she was not expected to recover quickly. Crosbie has 'in one sense murdered' Lily. (*Last Chronicle of Barset*, Chapter 23) But not all women deserve to be treated with so much respect. Johnny Eames, though deeply in love with Lily, gets mixed up with two disreputable women who want to marry him, and Trollope does not blame him seriously. 'Love is one thing and amusement is another,' Johnny explains (*Last Chronicle of Barset*, Chapter 46). There is a great gulf between women who are ladies and women who are nobody in particular. Trollope frankly defends the double standard in *John Caldigate* where the hero has an affair with one woman and flirts with two others but eventually marries a pure young girl, 'He has sown his wild oats, and he's none the worse for that.' (Chapter 58) But Lily feels that to fall in love again would be to commit 'a great sin – the sin against which women should be more guarded than against any other'. (*The Small House at Allington*, Chapter 57)

The fate of women who do commit this sin is studied in *Can You Forgive Her?* Alice is foolish enough to jilt a 'worthy man', John Grey, for a 'wild man', George Vavasor, and the title of the whole novel could be 'Showing how Alice was punished'. (Chapter 54) Her real crime (see page 18) is to have picked up mildly feminist notions:

> What should a woman do with her life? There had arisen round her a flock of learned ladies asking that question, to whom it seems that the proper answer has never yet occurred. Fall in love, marry the man, have two children and live happy ever afterwards. (Chapter 11)

Her fiancé, though an almost perfect character, 'always spoke and acted as though there could be no question that his manner of life was to be adopted, without a word or thought of doubting, by his wife'. (Chapter 3) 'Had he deigned to discuss it with me!' Alice so often said, 'But no . . . I am to go there to fetch him his slippers, and make his tea for him.' (Chapter 63) So she becomes the victim of George who is, we gradually learn, a potential murderer. Once she has put herself in his power Alice is much too frightened to act independently. He bullies, abuses and robs her, but she keeps on giving him money and feels she will have to commit suicide to get out of marrying him. His sister Kate, who has brought them together, is also punished, when George breaks her arm. There is a distinct undertone of sadism here, and at the end when Alice, totally humiliated, is taken back by Grey. She is a 'fallen creature', she says, who has no right to be happy, and 'ought to stand before him always as a penitent – in a white sheet'. (Chapter 75) The moral is that women who want independence will be attacked by violent men, and the best thing they can do is to find a good man to protect them. 'It's a very fine theory,' says Grey, 'that of women being able to get along without men . . . but . . . it will be found very troublesome by those who first put it in practice.' (Chapter 3) Alice finally admits that she has 'found her master' and in future must let him make the decisions.

Parallel to this plot runs the story of Lady Glencora Palliser, who has been married off 'exactly as they make nuns of girls in Roman Catholic countries'. (Chapter 48) This gives her some excuse for wanting to elope with another man. But if she does, nothing awaits her but ruin; she will be 'a thing to be hated and despised' (Chapter 62) and even her lover will not respect her. Trollope does not let this happen because Glencora is basically a good woman – that is, one who puts a man's interests before her own. She has been made to feel a failure because she has not yet produced a son, so she tells her husband:

> What matters it whether I drown myself, or throw myself away by going with such a one as him, so that you might marry again and have a child? I'd die – I'd die willingly. (Chapter 58)

Palliser, like Grey, forgives her erratic behaviour – 'killing her by his goodness' is Trollope's ambiguous phrase. Glencora does get a son, but not before she has had to 'lie awake trembling' in case 'one of the vile weaker sex should come to disturb the hopes of your lords and masters'. (Chapter 80) The human cost of this 'happy ending' is a high one. Glencora and Alice are both 'jumped on' by their great relations who dislike nonconformity, and Alice acknowledges 'that she deserved all the lashes she received. She had made a fool of herself in her vain attempt to be greater and grander than other girls, and it was only fair that her folly should be in some sort punished before it was fully pardoned.' (Chapter 79) This is because Trollope feels that a woman who breaks off her engagement has 'behaved in a manner which the world will call unfeminine' (Chapter 32), betrayed the idea of 'feminine constancy' (Chapter 74), 'sinned against her sex'. (Chapter 37) While she is not exactly a fallen woman, she has certainly been contaminated. And all her 'troubles and sorrows' come from 'an overfed craving for independence'. (Chapter 43)[8]

A later Palliser novel, *The Prime Minister*, has a rather similar theme. Emily insists on marrying a bad man against her father's wishes and is humbled to the dust. As a widow she feels 'disgraced and shamed' (Chapter 74) and believes herself unfit to remarry, although she is persuaded to change her mind. Once again the clear message is that girls do not know how to run their lives, and make good men suffer through their folly. In the same novel Glencora breaks her husband's orders by interfering in politics and seriously embarrasses him. While Palliser does not want his wife to have 'any duties unconnected with our joint family and home' (Chapter 7), Glencora craves to be a person in her own right. She is treated with more sympathy and insight than Mrs Proudie, but her conduct is just as blameworthy.

Trollope's later novels show an increasing interest in women who suffer because they do not conform. *The Vicar of Bullhampton* makes a plea for fallen women. Carry Brattle is weak, but she is a pleasant girl whom men like and is much to be preferred to women who are chaste but not charitable. Many of the novels written after *Can You Forgive Her?* refer to the women's rights issue, and in *The Way We Live Now* he gives a cross-section of the types of women of whom he disapproved.

By this time, Trollope recognised, things were changing. Young women 'in these days did have, and would have, and must have more liberty'. (Chapter 43) The three girls who misbehave – Ruby, who runs away from her fiancé, and the husband-hunters Marie and Georgiana – are all humiliated, though in a comic context. So is Lady Carbury, who is one of Trollope's few attempts to draw a working woman. Most of his heroines have no job (Lucy in *The Eustace Diamonds* is a governess, but this is an acceptably ladylike occupation) and Trollope considered this natural and proper. However much they need money, his young women hardly ever think of trying to earn it.

Lady Carbury is a writer, and although this was considered quite respectable for a Victorian woman Trollope did not like it. He tells us that her work is shoddy, and is sold only because she exploits her friendships with literary men. It is understandable that she tries to earn money for her son, but she has a less worthy motive – to 'make some career for herself . . . become somebody' (Chapter 2), and she is being coarsened by the life she leads. She finally marries an editor who makes her give up writing novels, and decides to sink her personality in his, 'Was it not a career enough for any woman to be the wife of such a man, to receive his friends, to shine with his reflected glory?'. (Chapter 99) She is last seen kneeling at his feet.

In a sub-plot, Paul Montague has rashly promised to marry Mrs Hurtle, a solitary woman whom he met while travelling (Mrs Smith in *John Caldigate* is a similar type). When he meets Hetta, the only pure woman in the novel, he breaks off the engagement, and although he is apparently doing exactly the same thing as the despicable Crosbie, Trollope has no doubt that it is necessary. What matters, it seems, is not the act of jilting a woman, but who the woman is.

Hetta is young, has a proper family background, and has not 'undergone the cruel roughness of the world'. (Chapter 91) Mrs Hurtle is an American ('America is certainly the country for women', we are told in Chapter 98), and American women have the reputation of being 'loud, masculine and atheistical'. (Chapter 87) Paul's friends urge him to give her up because he knows hardly anything about her. When he does know he becomes even more determined, for she is something of a 'wild cat', has defended herself against her violent husband and shot a man who tried to rape her. 'She had seen so much of drunkenness, had become so handy with pistols, and had done so much of a man's work, that any ordinary man might well hesitate before he assumed to be her master.' (Chapter 47) When Hetta hears the full story she has not much more sympathy than Alexandrina de Courcy for Lily Dale. 'What was it to Hetta that her lover had been false to this American stranger?'(Chapter 91) The idea of solidarity between women was entirely alien to Trollope.

Yet in many ways Mrs Hurtle has the best of the argument. 'He could change his love as often as he pleased,' she reflects, 'and be as good a lover at the end as ever – whereas she was ruined by his defection.' (Chapter 97) She also points out that it is not fair to blame her for being unfeminine when she has not had much chance to be anything else, 'When a woman has no one to help her, is she to bear everything without turning upon those who ill-use her? Shall a woman be flayed alive because it is unfeminine in her to fight for her own skin?' (Chapter 51) Her fate is a very sad one, because she would like to forget the past and live the life of an English lady, but knows it is too late. 'I would dream of fair, feminine women,' she says, 'of women who would be scared by seeing what I saw, who would die rather than do what I did.' (Chapter 97) This was perhaps the nearest Trollope could come to acknowledging that the 'fair, feminine women' whom he created were of little practical use, and were possibly a dream.

WILKIE COLLINS

Wilkie Collins' attitudes to women were unusual for his time. He was quite capable of drawing a conventional heroine when he wanted to, but his real interest was in women who broke the rules. Unlike some men, he admired intelligence in a woman; he is said to have created the first female detective in a short story, 'The Diary of Anne Rodway'.[9] He criticised the idea that a woman's place was in the home when he showed 'ladies' coming to gape at mental patients in *Armadale*:

> In the miserable monotony of the lives led by a large section of the middle classes of England, anything is welcome to the women which offers them any sort of harmless refuge from the established tyranny of the principle that all human happiness begins and ends at home. (Book the Last, Chapter 3)

Rachel, the heroine of *The Moonstone*, is unusual because she always takes her own decisions, 'This absolute self-dependence is a great virtue in a man. In a woman it has the serious drawback of morally separating her from the mass of her sex, and so exposing her to misconstruction by the general opinion.' (Second Period, Second Narrative, Chapter 1) While continuing to pay lip-service to convention, Collins became increasingly interested in independent women cut off from the respectable members of their sex.

In *The Woman in White* he shows us a 'fair' and a 'dark' heroine – Laura, the helpless girl whom men want to marry, and Marian, fated to be a maiden aunt, who has 'the foresight and resolution of a man'. Walter cannot marry Laura at first because, like most novelists, Collins assumed that a decent man cannot reverse the natural order of things by marrying a woman who is 'above' him.[10] He has to wait until she is poor and friendless and then prove himself by doing a succession of brave deeds to win her, like John Ridd. Laura is the same type of heroine as Lorna Doone because she too has nothing to offer but beauty and can do nothing for herself.

Her fatal marriage to Percival is one of those pointless self-sacrifices which litter the pages of mid-nineteenth-century novels. There is no reason for it except that 'her father sanctioned it on his deathbed' and that 'she never broke a promise in her life'. This might have been good enough for most novel-readers but, as Margaret Oliphant pointed out, it was unpleasant and improbable:

> Mr Wilkie Collins drives his sensitive and delicate heroine, without any reason in the world for the sacrifice, into a marriage which she regards with horror; makes her drive away her lover, and half-kill herself in the attempt to give him up, and rather holds her up as the victim of an elevated sense of duty when, at the cost of all these agonies, she fulfils her engagement, and becomes the unhappy wife of Sir Percival Glyde. Bad morals under any explanation; but when no real reason exists, absolute folly as well.[11]

Of course there would have been no story if Laura had not married Percival, but the point is that Collins could only make this happen by appealing to a concept of womanly goodness which was already beginning to seem outdated.

Once married, Laura finds that her husband has almost unlimited powers to bully her. The one time she resists him, by refusing to sign a document she has not read (and she cannot do even that without Marian's support), he locks her up. When Marian protests

> There are laws in England to protect women from cruelty and outrage. If you hurt a hair of Laura's head, if you dare to

interfere with my freedom, come what may, to those laws I will appeal. (Story continued by Marian Halcombe, Chapter 7)

she is silently acknowledging that the law will not protect *Laura's* freedom. So long as he does not actually murder her, Sir Percival can do much as he likes.

Collins has no doubt that Laura is entitled to use her own judgement and ask her husband to 'treat me as a responsible being'. (Story continued by Marian Halcombe, Chapter 4) What happens when a woman gives up having opinions is shown in the character of Madame Fosco, who used to advocate women's rights but now waits for her husband to tell her what to think. As Fosco ironically points out, she cannot be blamed for her part in his crimes:

> I ask if a woman's marriage obligations in this country provide for her private opinion of her husband's principles? No! They charge her unreservedly to love, honour, and obey him. That is exactly what my wife has done. (Story continued by Count Fosco)

Apart from her one assertion of personal responsibility, Laura is, in the housekeeper's words, 'so dreadfully alarmed and distressed, that she was quite useless'. (Story continued by Eliza Michelson, Chapter 1) Marian, a highly intelligent woman, has to look after her, at first alone, and later with Walter's help. We know from Marian's first appearance that she is not going to marry the hero because she is ugly. Although by most standards she would make a better mate than Laura, Collins feels strongly (and it becomes obvious in his later work) that physical attractiveness is almost the most important womanly virtue.

At one point Marian is strongly tempted to murder Percival.

> They say we are either better than men, or worse. If the temptation that has fallen in some women's way, and made them worse, had fallen in mine at that moment – Thank God! my face betrayed nothing that his wife could read. The gentle, innocent, affectionate creature thought I was frightened for her and sorry for her, and thought no more. (Story continued by Marian Halcombe, Chapter 7)

In his next two novels Collins explores what happens when women are tempted to do evil. These novels are dominated by reckless, outcast, and criminal women, while the good, conventional heroine is pushed far into the background.

In *No Name* Magdalen and Norah Vanstone are left destitute when their parents die and they find out that they are illegitimate. The money intended for them goes to a cousin who refuses to give them anything. Collins attacks both the divorce laws and the way that illegitimate children are treated, but his main interest is in the story of a woman fighting society for her rights. Norah submits, and becomes an unsuccessful governess. Magdalen, a brave and talented girl, becomes a popular actress (a career she is forced to give up because it is harming her sister's reputation), and plots to get the money back by marrying her cousin under a false name. Although Magdalen is neither a fallen woman nor a criminal most people, including herself, think her a great sinner. Her misdeeds are running away from her natural protectors, scheming, lying and marrying a man she despises, which involves 'the profanation of myself'. (The Fourth Scene, Chapter 13) Collins shows, with great power, how this once carefully protected girl suffers when she cuts herself off from 'all home dependence . . . all home control' to lead a sordid life on the fringes of society. In the end she realises that her efforts have been futile; the family money comes back when the man who has inherited it marries Norah for love:

> Norah, who had patiently accepted her hard lot, who from the first to the last had meditated no vengeance, and stooped to no deceit – Norah had reached the end which all her sister's ingenuity, all her sister's resolution, and all her sister's daring had failed to achieve . . . The recovery of the lost fortune was her sister's triumph, not hers. (The Last Scene, Chapter 3)

In spite of this thoroughly conventional moral, many critics thought that Magdalen got off too lightly and should not have been allowed to reform and get married. 'Do I deserve my happiness?' she asks on the last page. 'Oh, I know how the poor narrow people who have never felt and never suffered would answer me . . . they would fasten on my sin, and pass all my suffering by.' In *Armadale* Collins studied a still more reckless woman and tried to balance her suffering against her sin.

In this novel women prey on men. By far the most powerful character is Lydia Gwilt, who overshadows the marriageable heroine, a schoolgirl of sixteen, and the two heroes, Allan Armadale and Midwinter. Lydia is cultured, intelligent (she would have made a great lawyer if she had been a man) and sexually magnetic, but she is also a murderess, a fallen woman, and thirty-five. In the past she has been directly or indirectly responsible for the deaths of several men and she is on the lookout for an establishment when the two heroes, both years younger than herself, fall in love with her. It takes another woman, Major Milroy's wife, to see through Lydia – '*Miss* Gwilt! *Miss*, with those eyes and that walk!'

Mrs Milroy has married an older man who had been a womaniser and now makes him miserable because her own looks have gone and she suspects him of having affairs. Driven by 'the most merciless of all human forms of contempt – the contempt of one woman for another' (Volume 3, Chapter 1) she encourages Allan (who, as a landowner, will not be allowed to marry a woman of obscure origins) to investigate Lydia's past. Allan traces her to a squalid beauty parlour/cum abortion clinic, draws the wrong conclusion and breaks with her. More sensitive men, like the Major and Midwinter, are repelled by 'the meanness of prying into a woman's secrets behind her back' (Volume 2, Chapter 13). Midwinter marries her without asking questions, but they are very quickly alienated:

> He has been noble and good in his past life [writes Lydia] and I have been wicked and disgraced. Who can tell what a gap that dreadful difference may make between us, unknown to him and unknown to me? . . . Oh me! is there no purifying power in such love as mine? Are there plague-spots of past wickedness on my heart which no after-repentance can wash out? (Volume 4, Chapter 1)

Lydia's love for Midwinter is real, but it has no future. The two men resent her for coming between them and she can only redeem herself by dying to save her husband's life. And it is not only her actual crimes which ruin her relationship with Midwinter; Lydia is haunted, too, by 'the ghosts of *those other men*' (Volume 3, Chapter 9).

Collins treats Lydia sympathetically and points out that many women would have done no better than she in the circumstances; she has had a very hard life. But he still seems to be influenced by the double standard. It is not wrong for Mrs Milroy to marry an older man, and if she had overlooked his past she would have been sensible. But a man cannot be happy with an older woman, or a woman with a past.

Rosanna Spearman in *The Moonstone* is another lost woman, a thief who wants to make a fresh start but who falls unhappily in love and drowns herself. 'The ugly women have a bad time of it in this world,' Sergeant Cuff says. (First Period, Chapter 14) Collins shows compassionately how she is forbidden to express her feelings; as a servant and an unattractive woman she cannot expect any fulfilment and might as well die.

Collins' later novels are much weaker than those written in the 1860s, but his interest in deviant women persisted to the end. *The New Magdalen* (1873) and *The Fallen Leaves* (1879) take up the cause of prostitutes. The heroine of the former novel finds that, although she wants to lead a good life, no one will accept her when they know about her past. She steals another woman's identity and proves that she is thoroughly superior to her rival. There is an important shift towards twentieth-century attitudes in this novel. The 'good' woman, Grace, is narrow-minded and unattractive, while the 'fallen' Mercy is noble and womanly. Collins does not quite say that the greatest virtue is sexuality, but we are moving in that direction.

10   George Eliot

Marian Evans published her work under the name of George
Eliot because, even in the 1850s, there was still some hostility to
women novelists.[1] G. H. Lewes wrote, after the great success of
Adam Bede, 'It is quite clear that people would have sniffed at it if
they had known the writer to be a woman but they can't now
unsay their admiration.'[2] She lived to be acclaimed as the greatest
woman of modern times. 'The female Shakespeare', 'She thinks
just like a man',[3] her admirers said. When she died she was called
'a woman whose achievements were without parallel in the
previous history of womankind'.[4]

'To her own sex,' wrote Henry James, 'her memory, her
example, will remain of the highest value; those of them for whom
the "development" of woman is the hope of the future ought to
erect a monument to George Eliot. She helped on the cause more
than any one, in proving how few limitations are of necessity
implied in the feminine organism.'[5] But George Eliot never
identified herself with this cause. In 1867, when Mill was trying to
get women the vote, she called it 'an extremely doubtful good'.[6]
She wrote that the fact that 'woman seems to me to have the
worse share in existence' should be the basis 'for a sublimer
resignation in women and a more regenerating tenderness in
man'.[7]

'Resignation' is a traditional womanly virtue. George Eliot
listed other qualities which she admired – 'that exquisite type of
gentleness, tenderness, possible maternity suffusing a woman's
being with affectionateness, which makes what we mean by the
feminine character'.[8] She told Edith Simcox that she 'cared for
the womanly ideal', but that she had never cared much for
women themselves.[9] Trivial women annoyed her, and she
supported higher education for girls because she felt they should
learn to rise above their small personal problems and take an
interest in serious matters.

George Eliot is very different from the 'lady novelists' whom she despised because she did not see things from an exclusively feminine angle. Although her women are more impressive than her men, she can write convincingly about men engaged in politics or business and can deal with the widest philosophical questions. This, no doubt, was why her earliest readers thought she had a 'masculine' brain.

She was always aware that there are more important questions than whom the heroine will marry. 'What were our little Tina and her trouble in this mighty torrent?' she asks in *Mr Gilfil's Love Story*, setting one girl's love problem in a universal context. In a famous passage in her last novel, *Daniel Deronda*, she asks the same question and suggests an answer:

Could there be a slenderer, more insignificant thread in human history than this consciousness of a girl, busy with her small inferences of the way in which she could make her life pleasant? – in a time, too, when ideas were with fresh vigour making armies of themselves, and the universal kinship was declaring itself fiercely; when women on the other side of the world would not mourn for the husbands and sons who died bravely in a common cause . . .

What in the midst of that mighty drama are girls and their blind visions? They are the Yea or Nay of that good for which men are enduring and fighting. In these delicate vessels is borne onward through the ages the treasure of human affections. (Chapter 11)

The three stories in *Scenes of Clerical Life*, none of which has a conventional happy ending, cover almost the whole range of her attitudes to women. Milly Barton, who represents 'the treasure of human affections', dies worn out with housework and childbearing, telling her husband that he has made her very happy. Patty, the eldest daughter, has to learn how to be a mother to the family, and is last seen as a spinster devotedly looking after her father, whose 'neat linen told of a woman's care'. There seems no doubt that the conclusion – 'Milly did not take all her love from the earth when she died. She had left some of it in Patty's heart' – is meant to be uplifting. *Amos Barton* was very popular with its first readers, including Dickens, partly because its attitude to women was reassuringly familiar. And it is worth noting that many of George Eliot's heroines after Patty – Maggie, Eppie, Romola, Esther, Mary Garth – follow tradition in being deeply devoted to their fathers.

Tina in *Mr Gilfil's Love Story* has been discussed already; she belongs to the tradition of weak women who die because they have fallen unhappily in love. Janet Dempster is a more interesting type; she is, in fact, the first of George Eliot's 'dark heroines'. In many ways her story is most unconventional. She is a woman of great potential, beautiful and intelligent in the 'grand' manner, but she is unhappily married and drinks.[10] George Eliot, like Anne Brontë, was breaking with tradition in showing a woman who did not remain perfectly pure and good in an unpleasant environment but allowed it to corrupt her. Janet recovers, but she does not marry again, feeling that she has 'lived through the great tragedy of woman's life'. She adopts a child and embraces a life of 'purity and helpful labour'.

The only 'fair heroine' in George Eliot is Eppie, a conventional golden-haired girl who has a happy life and no inner conflicts. In most of her novels the 'dark heroine' who tastes rejection and conflict dominates the scene. The 'fair' Lucy feels that the 'dark' Maggie is 'better than I am', because she has never had a great sorrow or been asked to make a sacrifice. Janet, Maggie, Romola, Dorothea, and Gwendolen are all 'dark' heroines because they struggle with evil, not just in the world but in themselves. Four of them have a miserable marriage and only one, Dorothea, gets married again; even then we are told that her action is 'not ideally beautiful'. The typical George Eliot heroine is a girl who wants life to be ideally beautiful but who cannot help letting it wound and damage her.

Before that, though, George Eliot wrote a novel deriving directly from Scott, whom she 'worshipped'.[11] *Adam Bede* is about two women, one good and the other bad, instead of one woman struggling against the evil in herself. As in *The Heart of Midlothian* one girl, the young and pretty one, is seduced, and is sentenced to death for child-murder. The older, stronger, more religious girl tries to save her, although eventually the younger girl has to bear the consequences of her actions and dies.

Dinah Morris, though perfectly gentle and womanly, scandalises many people because she is a preacher – that is, she has taken it upon herself to do a job which for eighteen centuries had been set aside for men. She deviates from the normal woman's role because she feels throughout most of the book that God probably does not want her to get married, and she warns Chad's Bess of the dangers in being an attractive young girl:

> You think of earrings and fine gowns and caps and you never think of the Saviour who died to save your precious soul. (Chapter 2)

Before this appeal, Bess had not listened to her arguments but merely wondered 'what pleasure and satisfaction there could be in life to a young woman who wore a cap like Dinah's'. Wiry Ben makes predictable jokes about Dinah's vocation – 'I'll stick up for the pretty women preachin', I know they'd persuade me over a deal sooner nor th' ugly men'. (Chapter 2) Any woman who ventures out of her proper womanly sphere must expect, at the very least, to be thought eccentric. But although George Eliot does not agree with Dinah's theology, she makes it clear that she has a real talent as a religious teacher and is a powerful influence for good.

Her unconventional and instinctive goodness is seen in her reaction to Hetty, a girl who could not be more different from herself. Hetty delights men because she is beautiful and wants to please them; it takes another woman, like Mrs Poyser, to see that she has none of the solid virtues. Unlike some of the fallen women in nineteenth-century novels (Effie, Little Em'ly, Ruth, Collins' New Magdalen, Hardy's Tess) Hetty is not romanticised in any way. George Eliot makes it clear that Hetty falls not because she loves Arthur but because she wants luxuries (like pearl earrings) and that she has almost no feeling for others. Effie Deans would never have hurt her baby but Hetty abandons hers; unlike Dinah, this very 'feminine' girl dislikes children. Only a really powerful appeal, like the memory of the child's crying, can make any impact on her self-absorption.

At the same time we are made to understand why Hetty wants her baby to go away. She knows that Adam will not marry her if he finds out the truth, that her relations will not have her back and that everybody in the village will despise her. 'She thought of a young woman who had been found against the church wall at Hayslope one Sunday, nearly dead with cold and hunger – a tiny infant in her arms.' (Chapter 37) The cruelty of respectable people is seen very clearly when the Poysers turn their backs on

Hetty and forget her as quickly as possible. The only people who actively help her are the Methodist woman who takes her in, and Dinah. It is made clear that Hetty would not have killed her baby 'if it had been only going to Dinah – if nobody besides Dinah would ever know'. (Chapter 37) To Dinah every human being is a sinner who at the same time has a 'precious soul'; like Mrs Gaskell's good women, she refuses to distance herself from social outcasts.

Yet at the end of *Adam Bede* George Eliot casts doubt on almost everything Dinah has been doing. We have constantly been told that 'she's cut out o' different stuff from most women'. (Chapter 50) Both the men who love her feel that they must leave her free to do her work, whether she gets married or not. She appears to have no need of a protector – 'her very walk was discouraging: it had that quiet elasticity that asks for no support'. (Chapter 3) In the last book, though, we find that Dinah has 'made great advances in household cleverness', and that she no longer feels able to manage alone. Having refused Seth, who seems the obvious husband for her, she feels 'an intense thrill' at Adam's 'deep strong voice'; like Maggie she is drawn not to the man who shares her mental life but to the man who is physically attractive. And it turns out to be just as well that she has Adam and the housework to fill her life, for soon afterwards the Methodists stop women preaching. Adam defends this decision in a smug little speech, which comes at the end of the novel and so has to be taken seriously, especially as Dinah is made to argue against herself:

> There's no rule so wise but what it's a pity for somebody or other. Most o' the women do more harm nor good with their preaching – they've not got Dinah's gift nor her sperrit; and she's seen that, and she thought it right to set the example of submitting . . . And I agree with her, and approve o' what she did.

Earlier Dinah has spoken of the many women preachers who are 'precious fellow-helpers', and at that time she would not have allowed herself to be praised at their expense. 'It isn't for men to make channels for God's Spirit . . . and say, "Flow here, but flow not there".' (Chapter 8) But now we are asked to believe that most women do harm when they leave their natural sphere, and that the few exceptional women should give up their own work to set a good example. It is rather like saying that Marian Evans should not have written novels because most women novelists wrote badly.

Dinah's collapse into conformity is paralleled in at least two other novels. Maggie and Dorothea both begin life as exceptional human beings but achieve little or nothing. Maggie is the best portrait in any English novel of a bright little girl suffering the inevitable frustrations of growing up with stupid people. To begin with, her looks are not acceptable, so her mother (whose life revolves around china and linen) is always tormenting her by curling her hair. The ideal woman is pretty, polite and passive, like little Lucy – 'you may set her on a stool, and there she'll sit for an hour together, and never offer to get off'. (*The Mill on the Floss*, Book 1, Chapter 6) Male supremacy is so much taken for granted ('We don't ask what a woman does – we ask whom she belongs to', Book 6, Chapter 8), that Tom automatically gets more pocket-money than Maggie, and an expensive education from which he cannot benefit, while she has to pick up odds and ends of information from books. Her father is torn between delight at her cleverness and his ingrained belief that 'an over-cute woman's no better nor a long-tailed sheep'. (Book 1, Chapter 2) This prejudice is shared by almost everybody; even an educated man like Mr Stelling dismisses girls as 'quick and shallow'. (Book 2, Chapter 1)

Maggie's problem is that the people she 'belongs to' think her brains are superfluous, and there is nothing obvious she can do with them as she grows up. She wants to be self-supporting (which seems an anachronism in the 1830s), but the only kinds of work she can do are plain sewing and teaching, neither of which gives her any satisfaction. Philip is the one person who fully appreciates her, because he too believes that 'poetry and art and knowledge' matter and because Maggie does not share the common prejudice against the handicapped. 'You were so full of life when you were a child,' he says. 'I thought you would be a brilliant woman, all wit and bright imagination.' (Book 5, Chapter 3) But the third volume of the book is a failure and we never see this brilliant woman; the witty speeches of the grown-up Maggie do not impress. We get a conventional plot about whom the heroine will marry. The lovable little girl of the first two books disappears, probably because there is no future for her in an environment like this.

We are made to feel just how oppressive it would be to live in Maggie's family – the 'narrow, ugly, grovelling existence' of the Dodsons and their friends. But Maggie cannot simply break away. She is devoted to her father and Tom (her mother hardly counts) and cannot defy them in cold blood. 'The need of being loved would always subdue her' (Book 6, Chapter 4), the author points out. However, she begins to think 'there can never come much happiness to me from loving . . . I wish I could make myself a world outside of it, as men do'. (Book 6, Chapter 7) Maggie is doomed, like the witch in the story-book, whatever course she takes. Neither of the men who wants to marry her is acceptable to her family. She cannot love Philip, who might have helped her to escape, and Stephen, whom she does love, is a commonplace man who likes women to be 'rather insipid'. (Book 6, Chapter 1) (He is blind to Lucy's 'rarest quality' – her ability to be 'loving and thoughtful for other women', and will console himself after Maggie dies.) So she can only turn to a gospel of renunciation based on duties towards the family, which is expounded by Dr Kenn:

> At present everything seems tending towards the relaxation of ties – towards the substitution of wayward choice for the adherence to obligation, which has its roots in the past. (Book 7, Chapter 2)

'All self-sacrifice is good', George Eliot wrote in another context, 'but one would like it to be in a somewhat nobler cause.'[12] We can understand why Maggie shrinks from hurting her father, or Lucy and Philip, who have all been kind to her. But we cannot understand why she should sacrifice herself for Tom, who has bullied her since birth. (She insists that she cannot marry Philip against his wishes – 'I can't divide myself from my brother for life'.) Throughout the novel we are made to feel that her deepest relationship is with Tom; when they are drowned it is not a tragedy but a triumph. They have to die because they could never have lived happily together, and Maggie evidently does not want to live without him. The relaxation of this particular tie might well have done her good.

Stephen offers Maggie a life of 'love, wealth, ease, refinement', which she senses would be wrong for her because there is 'something higher than mere personal enjoyment'. (Book 6, Chapter 13) In George Eliot's next long novel, *Romola*, Tito's desire for 'wealth' and 'ease' clashes with the high principles of his wife. When we first see Romola in her blind father's library she is obviously bored, but will not admit it. Her brother has left them to do the work alone and Bardo has never got over this, telling his daughter to her face that women cannot be serious scholars. This hurts her, but she does not rebel:

> I will try and be as useful to you as if I had been a boy, and then perhaps some great scholar will want to marry me . . . and he will like to come and live with you, and he will be to you in place of my brother . . . and you will not be sorry that I was a daughter. (Chapter 5)

Romola does marry a scholar who comes to live with them on the understanding that he will help his father-in-law, so Bardo is partly responsible for the great mistake of her life. We should note that, as he says, she has no particular gifts for scholarship, although she lives in a society which includes learned women like Cassandra Fedele. Both these assumptions are questioned in other novels (Maggie is more intelligent than her brother; Casaubon's life-work is clearly seen to be pointless). But Romola continues to feel, even after her father is dead, that his wishes are more important than anything else. When Tito finds that it is necessary for him to sell the library his arguments sound reasonable:

> I understand your feeling about the wishes of the dead; but wisdom puts a limit to these sentiments . . . You gave your life to your father while he lived; why should you demand more of yourself? (Chapter 32)

But Romola angrily rejects this in what is familiar language for George Eliot, arguing that 'faithfulness, and love, and sweet grateful memories' are the things which matter most. When she finds out that Tito has let the library go she turns against him for that reason alone, not yet knowing about his more serious crimes. From this point the book becomes George Eliot's first full-length study of a doomed marriage, a theme which preoccupied her more and more as the years went on. Romola decides not to leave Tito because, as Savonarola points out, she chose to marry him. But the damage is done; he knows that she has 'a nature that could judge him', and he gradually turns away from this inconveniently moral woman to the undemanding Tessa. In the end she has to tell Tito that she will denounce him if he causes other people to be killed. 'I too am a human being,' she says, 'I have a soul of my own that abhors your actions.' (Chapter 58) This was an extremely painful problem for George Eliot, who did not believe in 'light and easily broken ties'[13] but realised that marriage could be agonising, particularly when it was to someone who disliked the best part of your own nature. The end of this novel is very like *Janet's Repentance*. Romola is free at last, but she has suffered the 'supreme woman's sorrow' (Chapter 61) and there is no question of her marrying again. She finds her salvation in living for others, without a formal religion, and looking after Tessa and her children.

In her last two novels George Eliot took a very wide survey of the possibilities open to women in the late and early nineteenth century. In each of them we see several women making different choices about the kind of life they want to lead. Self-sacrifice, fulfilment, and the claims of others are central concepts in both.

If it were not for the first and last chapters of *Middlemarch*, it might not occur to us to call Dorothea a failure. Unlike many George Eliot heroines, she ends up happily married and a mother, and we already know that many other women have to make 'a far sadder sacrifice'. Her failure, if it is one, is of having been 'absorbed into the life of another' and living in obscurity when other women of her type had become famous. 'But no one stated exactly what else that was in her power she ought rather to have done.' (Finale)

It was not in Dorothea's power to change 'the society into which she was born', with its 'modes of education which make a woman's knowledge another name for motley ignorance'.[14] And George Eliot does not suggest that she could have worked quietly at home on her chosen subject – as she herself and other distinguished women had done. The only satisfying future which she can imagine is being the wife of a great man – 'a guide who would take her along the grandest path' (Chapter 3) – and helping him in his work. This is a much more generous mistake than Rosamond's, who only wants to marry a man with titled relations. But it is still a mistake, and both these disastrous marriages are caused by men's illusions about women.

While a girl is under pressure to marry as quickly as possible (Rosamond's aunt warns her that she is 'turned twenty-two') most men in Middlemarch expect to put it off until it is convenient. Farebrother cannot marry at all because he has to support three female relatives. Casaubon waits, and Lydgate intends to wait, until they have done a good deal of work and can afford to relax. These two men, who seem so different, have very similar ideas of what a wife should be. Casaubon decides to marry 'a blooming young lady – the younger the better, because more educable and submissive'. He assumes that 'a wife, a modest young lady, with the purely appreciative, unambitious abilities of her sex, is sure to think her husband's mind powerful' (Chapter 29), and is deeply hurt when she begins to ask awkward questions about his work. Lydgate, too, wants to marry an ornamental woman – 'an accomplished creature who venerated his high musings and momentous labours and would never interfere with them . . . instructed to the true womanly limit and not a hair's breadth beyond – docile, therefore, and ready to carry out behests which came from beyond that limit'. (Chapter 36) Both men, George Eliot suggests, are being unrealistic. In fact none of the young women in *Middlemarch* believes that her husband is always right, not even Celia – 'Of course, men know best about everything, except what women know better. . . . I should not give up to James when I knew he was wrong, as you used to do to Mr. Casaubon.' (Chapter 72)

Rosamond is condemned, not because she has a 'tendency to form opinions about her husband's conduct' (Chapter 37) but because she is selfish. She is compared unfavourably with her mother at the time of Fred's illness and with her aunt at the time of the Bulstrode scandal. Mrs Bulstrode, a very ordinary woman, wants to protect her husband, while Rosamond has no real feeling for hers. We have already realised that Lydgate is going to suffer for having a superficial view of women, although the perceptive Farebrother has told him that 'a good unworldly woman' 'may really help a man'. (Chapter 17) He has dismissed Dorothea for being 'too earnest' and not looking at things 'from the proper feminine angle', but Dorothea would have sympathised with his intellectual aims while Rosamond frustrates them. Whether Lydgate ever realises this is not clear; he comes to admire Dorothea simply because she stands by him when he is shunned by other people.

Dorothea, it is implied, is in some sense a genius, but hers is 'a genius for feeling nobly'. (Chapter 58) When George Eliot praises St Theresa it is not because she reformed a religious order but because she was willing to be martyred. Dorothea is far above the average woman because she cares for 'the destinies of mankind', not 'the solicitudes of feminine fashion' (Chapter 1), but she is thoroughly womanly nevertheless. She has 'powerful, feminine, maternal hands' (Chapter 4), and significantly the novel ends with her having a baby. She is seriously interested in theology (which is not quite the same thing as being pious) but her religion is much more vital than Casaubon's because it is concerned with real needs. While she builds cottages and starts infant schools, he is preoccupied with 'the Philistine God Dagon and other fish-deities'. (Chapter 20) Eventually she realises that he is not a great religious teacher but a pathetic failure, and that she no longer loves him. At this point a modern novelist might have suggested that she should simply go away.[15] But Dorothea decides, like Mrs Bulstrode, that she cannot 'in any sense forsake' her husband, and this is why, as Celia points out, she gives in to Casaubon knowing he is wrong. Her reason is that, like Romola, she has chosen this marriage:

> Was inheritance a question of liking, or of responsibility? All the energy of Dorothea's nature went on the side of responsibility – the fulfilment of claims founded on our own deeds, such as marriage and parentage. (Chapter 37)

But Dorothea, we should note, sacrifices herself for Casaubon only for as long as he is alive. She decides to do nothing which would hurt him (knowing that she has already hurt him by not being the 'elegant-minded canary-bird' he wanted) and to 'shut her best soul in prison, paying it only hidden visits, that she might be petty enough to please him'. (Chapter 42) But she feels that her responsibility is at an end once he is dead. Although he wanted her to complete his work, and did not want her to marry Will Ladislaw, she does what *she* wants in both cases. And, unlike Maggie, she is prepared to risk a break with her family. Apart from the Catherine Arrowpoint story in her next novel, this is the only time George Eliot suggests that a woman has a right to get married when her family objects.

In this novel, more than in any other, George Eliot tries to balance the claims of 'liking' and the claims of 'responsibility'. Like Maggie, Lydgate and Dorothea both decide that they must respect their commitments to a partner however painful this is. Mary Garth represents another possibility. She is tough-minded, having always had to work for her living, and does not agree to marry Fred until she is quite sure he will make a good husband. Unlike Dorothea, she will not carry out a dying man's last wishes when they are likely to harm her, telling Peter Featherstone, 'I will not let the close of your life soil the beginning of mine'. (Chapter 33) She is entitled to do this, though, because Featherstone is only her employer, not her husband. She lacks Dorothea's generous self-forgetfulness but she responds to real claims, giving up her savings to her parents without complaining. Unlike Rosamond (who patronises her for not being beautiful) Mary is a useful woman.

At the other extreme from Dorothea is the French actress Laure, who stabbed her husband because he bored her. 'I do not like husbands. I will never have another,' she says. (Chapter 15) In her next novel George Eliot looked more closely at women who did not want husbands. She also continued to examine the issue of 'liking' versus 'responsibility' and reached a more conservative conclusion than in *Middlemarch*.

In the upper-class world of *Daniel Deronda*, various things about sex and marriage are taken for granted. Catherine Arrowpoint is expected to take an 'eligible' husband whether or not she wants him. Grandcourt is expected to sow his wild oats and then 'make a suitable marriage with the fair young daughter of a noble house'. (Chapter 30) George Eliot shows, with a frankness which is new for her, that Grandcourt's past is fairly normal, that his male acquaintances know about it, and that Gwendolen would not have been allowed to know if it could have been prevented. When she does find out she feels indignant 'that she should have been expected to unite herself with an outworn life, full of backward secrets which must have been more keenly felt than any associations with *her*'. (Chapter 27) Charlotte Brontë had expressed precisely the same feelings:

And to think that such men take as wives, as second selves, women young, modest, sincere, pure in heart and life, with feeling all fresh, and emotions all unworn, and bind such virtue and vitality to their own withered existence.[16]

Grandcourt will 'put up with nothing less than the best in outward equipment, wife included' (Chapter 35), and Gwendolen is acceptable because she is young, attractive, a virgin, and can fill her position with style. But in this society a woman is valued only as what Daniel's mother calls 'a makeshift link'. Catherine is a 'misplaced daughter', who ought to have been a boy, and there are no less than ten little girls whose existence is vaguely felt to be a mistake. There are Grandcourt's three daughters, Gwendolen's 'superfluity of sisters', and the daughters of Sir Hugo Mallinger – 'little better than no children, poor dear things'. (Chapter 36) Their mother feels guilty about her failure to have a son and thinks that 'her husband might fairly regret his choice, and if he had not been very good might have treated her with some roughness'. (Chapter 25)

This brutality to women extends to illegitimate children, who are 'more rightfully to be looked shy on and deprived of social advantages than illegitimate fathers'. (Chapter 27) Gwendolen believes that Daniel is a son of Sir Hugo Mallinger's and that she is excluding him from his inheritance, as well as Mrs Glasher's boy. In the end both estates go back to the natural heirs, Sir Hugo's to his daughters and Grandcourt's to his illegitimate son. (His illegitimate daughters, being doubly disadvantaged, get nothing.)

Hundreds of nineteenth-century novels condemned mercenary marriages. *Daniel Deronda*, though, is the only one which shows exactly why a girl should make such a marriage, and without being particularly heartless or shallow. Gwendolen Harleth wants to control her life and not be a broken woman like her mother. 'Her observation of matrimony had inclined her to think it rather a dreary state, in which a woman could not do what she liked' (Chapter 4), but an 'unmarried woman who could not go about and had no command of anything' (Chapter 11) will have a dreary life too. Her best plan seems to be to marry a rich man who will let her have her own way. Her only alternative is to be a governess (which would be extremely unpleasant) and to ignore her mother's and sisters' needs. Grandcourt is so rich that he can leave his wife an income twenty times what she would have earned by teaching, although he is leaving the bulk of his property elsewhere. Everyone expects her to jump at his 'splendid offer'; Mr Gascoigne, though a clergyman, and although he knows something about Grandcourt's past, tells her that it is a religious duty. Against this she can only set her instinctive reluctance to marry (she dislikes men touching her), quite apart from her guilty feelings about Mrs Glasher:

> The inmost fold of her questioning now, was whether she need take a husband at all – whether she could not achieve substantiality for herself and know gratified ambition without bondage. (Chapter 23)

This is why she dreams of a career on the stage, but she has received a conventional education and is not qualified. And she has no idea that anything is wrong with society itself, feeling nothing in common with 'any sort of theoretical or practically reforming women'. (Chapter 6)

Since many readers think Gwendolen an evil person, it is worth pointing out that she has higher standards than most people in her circle. She sees at once that Mrs Glasher has a better claim on Grandcourt than she has, although she could have reasoned 'that her husband's marriage with her was his entrance on the path of virtue, while Mrs Glasher represented his forsaken sin'. (Chapter 36) She breaks her promise to the other woman only under intense pressure. Moreover, she cannot know what she is doing. She has always believed that charming girls get their own way, but, once married, she comes face to face with the terrifying power of the male. This power is so absolute that Grandcourt has no need to use violence; she has 'nothing that she could allege against him in judicious or judicial ears'. (Chapter 48) Another novelist who had realised that a tyrant does not actually have to do anything to a victim was Emily Brontë:

> I brought him down one evening [says Heathcliff] . . . and just sat him in a chair, and never touched him afterwards . . . In two hours I called Joseph to carry him up again, and since then my presence is as potent on his nerves as a ghost . . . he wakes and shrieks in the night by the hour together. (*Wuthering Heights*, Chapter 29)

Whether or not George Eliot had been impressed by this we cannot know (she had certainly read it) but she too understood the nature of mental cruelty. Gwendolen reaches the point where her husband gives her nightmares and where she cannot bear to be in his presence, particularly when they are alone. She does not want him to die; she wants to be allowed to leave him. 'When I was a child,' she says pathetically, 'I used to fancy sailing away into a world where people were not forced to live with anyone they did not like.' (Chapter 56) But if she runs away from Grandcourt there will be an appalling scandal (as there would have been if Hetty had had her baby at home) and he can in any case force her back. It is not surprising that she begins to dream about his death when that seems the only way out.

'Always among the images that drove her back to submission,' we are told, 'was Deronda.' (Chapter 48) She dreams that she escapes, and that he tells her to go back. Daniel is generally felt to be an unsatisfying character and his advice to Gwendolen, which is supposed to improve her, is highly conventional. Its general drift is that she must bear her lot and try to raise her mind above her own problems, and at one point this provokes the author into irony:

> Grandcourt put up his telescope and said 'There's a plantation of sugar-canes at the foot of that rock: should you like to look?'
> Gwendolen said, 'Yes, please', remembering that she must try and interest herself in sugar-canes as something outside her personal affairs. (Chapter 54)

This is the only time George Eliot acknowledges the futility of Daniel's good advice; how can Gwendolen take a deep interest in sugar-canes when she is in a state of deadly fear? What she needs is not platitudes but practical advice on how to get away from her husband, in which case she would not have been tempted to kill him. George Eliot makes it clear that she did not murder Grandcourt, yet we are still told that she has committed a serious crime and is unfit to marry Daniel: 'She was a banished soul – beholding a possible life which she had sinned herself away from.' (Chapter 57)

Granted that Gwendolen has faults, she has already made a moral breakthrough when she accepts her husband's will leaving his property to Lydia Glasher's son. She certainly has not deserved to be made to feel a criminal for doing what everyone around her expected and encouraged her to do. Daniel may think he is telling her to look outward, but he is really telling her to look inward at the state of her soul, rather than attempting to change the society which forces women into impossible situations.

George Eliot had no doubt that the majority of women have 'the worse share in existence'. Once Gwendolen is married she feels that 'her mother's dullness, which used to irritate her' is 'the ordinary result of woman's experience' (Chapter 35), and there are two moving passages where we see the suffering spreading down from mothers to daughters. One is where Gwendolen imagines herself 'sad and faded' like her mother, 'and their two faces meeting still with memory and love' (Chapter 26) and the other shows Mrs Glasher with her little girls:

The little faces beside her, almost exact reductions of her own, seemed to tell of the blooming curves which had once been where now was sunken pallor. But the children kissed the pale cheeks and never found them deficient. That love was now the one end of her life. (Chapter 30)

Given the powerlessness of women, what are they expected to do? One woman who does run away is Mirah, but she only feels justified in leaving her father, to whom she is always dutiful, because he tried to sell her to a man. She is a thoroughly traditional woman, sweet and uncomplaining, whose 'nature is not given to make great claims'. (Chapter 53) She is a good singer but dislikes the thought of women appearing on the stage and will presumably have to give up her career when Daniel takes her to the East.

Women 'artists', as Harriet Taylor noted, had a chance of finding satisfying work, and in *Daniel Deronda* we see several women who turn to the world of art. Mrs Arrowpoint writes about Tasso, Mirah and Catherine work seriously at their music, and the Meyrick girls, who are 'open to the highest things in music, painting, and poetry' (Chapter 18), have saved themselves from being governesses by drawing book illustrations at home. But the two chapters about Leonora, Daniel's mother, suggest that a woman may cease to be womanly if she lives for her career.

Leonora has done what Gwendolen wanted to do and become a great singer. Her talent was a real one, and she worked very hard to make the most of it. One might have expected George Eliot to admire such a woman, but in fact she does not; we are told that she has robbed her child and betrayed her father, who seems to have been much the same type of man as Mr Dombey. It is clear that his treatment of his daughter was cruel and insulting. He

wanted her to be a boy, he forced her to get married, and he tried
to stop her singing. He 'cared more about a grandson to come
than he did about me', an attitude which is explicitly compared
(Chapter 59) to that of the English upper class. 'Such men turn
their wives and daughters into slaves,' says Leonora:

> I had a right to be free. I had a right to seek my freedom from a
> bondage that I hated . . . You can never imagine what it is to
> have a man's force of genius in you, and yet to suffer the
> slavery of being a girl. (Chapter 51)

Daniel, as a good liberal, admits that she did have the right to be
an artist, but all his sympathy is with his grandfather, whom he
calls a man of 'ardent zeal and far-reaching hope'. (Chapter 55)
He is naturally thrilled to find that he is not, as he thought, a
superfluous child, but a long-awaited heir – both legitimate and
male. George Eliot directs our sympathy away from his mother by
having her tell Daniel that she did not want him and is not an
affectionate person. Although she is allowed to state her point of
view, we are surely meant to feel that she has sacrificed too much
to ambition; the family and the tribe are more important than one
woman's needs.

The message which finally comes across is that women like
Gwendolen and Leonora who struggle for personal fulfilment are
dangerously wrong. This might seem to be contradicted by
Catherine Arrowpoint, who says, 'I will not give up the happiness
of my life to ideas that I don't believe in and customs I have no
respect for'. (Chapter 22) But Catherine is only choosing a loving
marriage instead of an arranged one. Women who make more
ambitious claims – who want to live without a husband, or to have
free scope for their talents – are the losers. They have the right to
run away if they are in danger of committing murder or losing
their virtue, and they have the right to choose their own
husbands, but that is all. In the end George Eliot did not support
the feminist claims, partly because she could not really
sympathise with women who did not want a man. More
importantly, she clung to the idea that 'all self-sacrifice is good'.

In *Middlemarch*, and occasionally at other times, she argued
only that people should respect the ties which they had freely
chosen. But elsewhere she came close to saying that they should
be loyal to ties which they had not chosen, like a deeply bigoted

brother (Tom Tulliver), a dead father (Bardo), or an unknown grandfather (Daniel Charisi). Like Dickens, she felt that the highest type of woman was the one who did 'beautiful loving deeds' (*Romola*, Chapter 68), and she did not expect quite the same virtues from men. This idea could be, and was, used to keep women voteless and powerless. She could hardly help being deeply interested in 'the woman question', but in the end it was less important for her than 'the adherence to obligation, which has its roots in the past'.

11 Women Novelists of the Later Nineteenth Century

Women novelists writing after 1850 could hardly have been unaware of 'the woman question'. Most of them, right up to the end of the century, continued conservative. But more and more of them began to question the principles of complete submission to parents and husbands, and the idea that an unmarried girl should stay at home. By the last quarter of the century women's rights were a very topical issue, and feminist and anti-feminist writers appeared.

CHARLOTTE M. YONGE

'I have no hesitation in declaring my full belief in the inferiority of woman',[1] wrote Charlotte M. Yonge (1823–1901). She was a devout Anglican and her best novels are about the effect of religion on middle-class families. As the editor of a girls' magazine her ideas had a direct effect on thousands of young women. Feminism had some impact on her work; by the 1870s she had come to feel that spinsters, like herself, must think seriously about the purpose of their lives. 'While men kept them in subjection, they did not need to think it out, as the single ones must do now.' This is said by Geraldine, an artist who produces two drawings about the Rights of Women. In the first, they are arguing, in the second, working together in the shadow of the Church:

> While woman works merely for the sake of self-cultivation . . .
> it all gets absurd. But working for the Church makes all

harmonious, and sets each in her place. (*Pillars of the House*, Chapter 41)

Miss Yonge believed that unmarried women were not failures but 'pure creatures, free to devote themselves to the service of their Lord'.[2] There is not much conventional happiness for the women in her novels; the single and the widowed are often more contented than those who get a husband in the wrong circumstances.

The great principle which she taught her women readers was obedience – to God, their parents, and their husband if they had one. But her main interest was in the parent–daughter relationship. She believed that a child must not disobey her parents in any circumstances, even if this meant sacrificing her happiness. Amy and Laura in *The Heir of Redclyffe* illustrate this principle. Amy is sweet and dutiful, 'I don't think I could ever be a clever, strong-minded woman' (Chapter 26). She tells her mother before she even answers Guy's proposal, and submits when they are separated by her father (who is, as the author is well aware, a foolish man). She will not even send Guy a message, much as she loves him. 'It would not comfort him to think me disobedient.' (Chapter 17)

Amy, who is widowed at twenty and destined to remain a widow all her life, may seem to be in an unhappy situation, but Laura's fate is far worse. She and Philip conceal their engagement because her parents would separate them if they knew, and this is a serious sin. Although they are finally allowed to marry, they are broken down with remorse and 'must look to enduring the consequences all our lives'. (Chapter 43) Their young sister Charlotte is seen as a promising girl because she informs on a friend who plans to elope.

Miss Yonge's views are entirely – almost frighteningly – consistent. Parents have the right to condemn their children to celibacy; she believed that one daughter in each family should stay at home with her parents as long as they were alive.[3] *The Daisy Chain* centres on the self-sacrifice of an intelligent, high-principled girl, Ethel May. Ethel (see page 25) gives up her studies, her free time and her possible marriage to fill the place of a mother in her family. There are several growing children who have a serious claim on her, but her father's needs are more important still. It never occurs to Dr May that his daughters might wish to leave him; when Flora gets married his immediate reaction is self-pity and Ethel resolves 'that her father should never feel this pain on her account. Leave him who might, she would never forsake him.' (Volume 2, Chapter 6) But she is happier than Flora, who has sinned by being worldly, leaving home and marrying a man less intelligent than herself – 'there ought to be superiority on the man's side'. Flora gets a horrifying punishment when both her children die.[4]

The great strength of a Christian heroine like Amy is her 'spirit of yielding', which supports her through her troubles – 'struggling is fatal, when quietness saves'. (*The Heir of Redclyffe*, Chapter 37) Two other Yonge novels show a pure, inexperienced child-bride conquering evil through good. *Heartsease* (1854) may possibly have been written in response to *The Tenant of Wildfell Hall*. Violet Moss (whose name, like Lily Dale's, speaks of the quieter feminine virtues) marries a selfish man, called Arthur, who neglects her. But she tries patiently to do her best and eventually he reforms. Christina in *The Dove in the Eagle's Nest* (1866), a 'retiring lily of the valley', has a good influence on the rough fighting men around her because she is 'so strong yet so weak'.

But she did not always show women setting men a good example. On the contrary, she thought it false to say that 'the women are the religious part of the community' and believed that 'the man, if he chooses and seeks for grace, will attain the higher, nobler type'.[5] The really Christ-like characters in her novels are men, like Guy Morville, or Felix in *Pillars of the House*. Felix becomes the head of the family when his parents die, and his responsibility for a huge tribe of younger children eventually kills him. One sister leaves him to get married, another, Geraldine, refuses a proposal for his sake. Geraldine is a gifted artist whose water-colours are greatly admired – ' "I should not have thought it a woman's work" – the most ambitioned praise a woman can receive' (Chapter 29) – but she puts her home duties first.

Miss Yonge believed that girls should be educated – at home, not at school – and should cultivate their talents as far as possible. But they were not to be too proud of their achievements. Ethel May loves Greek, but is forced to cut down on it because she is needed in the house and anyway cannot hope to go to university like her brother. When she protests, 'I like Greek so much', her sister asks her:

And for that you would give up being a useful, steady daughter and sister at home? The sort of woman that dear mamma wished to make you, and a comfort to papa? (*The Daisy Chain*, Volume 1, Chapter 18)

This is unanswerable. Women might have real talents (though not equal to men's, of course) but they must never be so selfish as to put their personal development first.

MARGARET OLIPHANT

Few great writers are almost entirely forgotten, but that has been the fate of Margaret Oliphant (neé Wilson, 1828–97). Her name is known only to specialists; her work has long been out of print. But her best novels (she wrote over ninety, some of them very much better than others) are only a little below the level of Jane Austen and George Eliot, and she is indispensable reading for anyone interested in women in the nineteenth century. She had fresh and original things to say about self-sacrifice, the claims of a woman's family, work outside the home and the problems of marriage and parenthood. Her outlook is so much more sophisticated than that of her contemporaries that she often seems to belong to another age.

She wrote about an unusually wide range of women – widows, mothers and spinsters, working women in her native Scotland, teachers, artists, professionals, and older women who were supposed to have outlived the interesting time of their lives. Her attitude to women's rights, sceptical at first,[6] became steadily more sympathetic. 'I think I go in for everybody's rights,' says the heroine of *In Trust* (1882), 'I don't mind whether they are women or men.' (Chapter 14) Time and again she comments wryly on men's high opinion of themselves and contempt for women, seeing that 'a woman is, of course, twenty times the use a man is'. (*The Doctor's Family*, Chapter 16) Two types of men constantly reappear in her novels; the domestic tyrant – who is treated with no sympathy – and the weak man who cannot shoulder responsibilities and pushes them on to women.

Agnes, which is based on her own life, shows her dissatisfaction with the way in which most novelists wrote about women. A novel, she said in the preface, usually 'confines itself to the graceful task of conducting two virtuous young persons through a labyrinth of difficulties to a happy marriage'. Agnes's troubles only begin when she gets married, to a man who undervalues her, will not work and eventually dies. Mrs Oliphant hints again at the limitations of the novel when Agnes has to read to him on his deathbed about 'the agonies of a young girl who had quarrelled with her lover'. (Chapter 40) And although she is miserable she feels a kind of relief too – 'a feeling of freedom, though she had never desired to be free, a faint consciousness, unexpressed even to herself, that her plans would no longer be thwarted nor her wishes come to nothing'. (Chapter 46) (Margaret Oliphant's widows generally adjust to their circumstances, unlike, for instance, the wife of John Halifax, who survives him by only a few hours.) The death of her child is a far more painful and terrible blow.

The author stresses that Agnes is not a 'tragic exceptional case . . . she had only the common lot'. (Chapter 59) Women's suffering usually goes unrecognised; the 'sorrows of a young mother' – when her babies die – 'count for little in the estimation of the world, but are enough to cloud over an existence with unspeakable heaviness and discouragement'. (Chapter 30) Agnes, pregnant in a foreign country and drifting away from her husband, yearns for 'the tender sympathies of womankind'. (Chapter 21) All her life Margaret Oliphant believed that the husband–wife relationship was not everything, and that the novel must be widened to include basic female experiences.

The Doctor's Family, an impressive short novel, explores the contrast between those who give and those who take. Dr Rider wants to marry Nettie, the sister of his brother's wife, but she is committed to looking after this feckless couple (the husband is too lazy to work) and their children:

> It was not hard to work for the children – to support and domineer over Susan; but it was hard for such an alert uncompromising little soul to tolerate that useless hulk – that heavy encumbrance of a man, for whom hope and life were dead. She bit her lip as she discharged her sharp stinging arrow at him through the half-opened door, and then went down singing, to take her place at the table which her own hands had spread – which her own purse supplied with bread. Nobody there showed the least consciousness of that latter fact; nobody

fancied it was anything but natural to rely upon Nettie. (Chapter 5)

The doctor is not more selfish than other men, but he cannot face having to look after these people. Nettie is not a 'meek self-sacrificing heroine' – she is an Australian girl and extremely tough – but she cannot turn them out. There is no way they can get married until it suits Nettie's sister, for reasons of her own, to move on. Nettie is the first in a line of strong, responsible women who uncomplainingly carry other people's burdens, and who find that the weak people whom they care for are not in the least grateful.

Another bossy heroine is Lucilla in *Miss Marjoribanks*. When her mother dies she tells everyone that she means 'to devote herself to her father's comfort, and become the sunshine of his life, as so many young persons of her age have been known to become in literature'. (Chapter 1) What she really wants, though, is a power base in her father's house from which she can dominate her neighbours. She does this very successfully – 'It did her heart good to take the management of incapable people, and arrange all their affairs for them, and solve all their difficulties' (Chapter 23) – but the men are frightened of her, and Dr Marjoribanks, who knows that he must die, and leave her penniless, is worried about her future:

> How great a loss it was to society and herself that Lucilla was not 'the boy'. She could have continued, and perhaps extended, the practice, whereas just now it was quite possible that she might drop down into worsted-work and tea-parties like any other single woman. (Chapter 42)

Happily, Lucilla gets married at thirty and makes her husband buy an estate for her to run. Mrs Oliphant frequently said that women, if they had the chance, could be excellent administrators.

But the novel is not entirely comic. There is no happy ending for Rose, a young artist who has to give up her career to care for the children in her family. Several later Oliphant heroines are women who want to work, have a strong sense of responsibility, and end up single. *The Curate in Charge* recognises that work is extremely important, although there are still many people who think that 'no girl who works for her living is anything but looked down upon' (Volume 2, Chapter 9), and 'a good girl is always happy at home' (Volume 1, Chapter 6). Mab and Cicely are bright, active girls who have to provide for an unworldly father and two baby brothers. Mab becomes an artist and Cicely a schoolmistress (which is not considered genteel). It is not clear whether either of them will get married; Cicely's 'brave undertaking', the author says, 'ought to come to some great result in itself' (Volume 2, Chapter 9).

By contrast, *The Ladies Lindores*, one of her greatest novels, studies the problem of the woman who cannot look after herself, and the harm done when she meekly submits to what is called her 'duty'. It is one of the last marriage-market novels in England, and is a devastating assault on the power of husbands and fathers. Lord Lindores forces his daughter Caroline, a gentle cultured creature, to marry a man who terrifies her, and her mother acquiesces in order to save her own marriage. Edith, her sister, becomes convinced that women must learn to say no:

> The mother should not have permitted it, any more than the daughter should have done it . . . This was such obedience as no one of God's creatures had any right to render to another – neither wife to husband, nor to her parents any child. (Chapter 10)

Caroline's husband is a sadist, and also a male chauvinist who abuses women who want the vote or any life outside their homes. He treats his wife as a 'servant who could not throw up her situation', and when he dies she can feel nothing but relief because their marriage – the author hints – has been a form of rape:

> To think I shall never be subject to all *that* any more – that he can never come in here again – that I am free – that I can be alone. Oh, mother, how can you tell what it is? Never to be alone, never to have a corner in the world where – someone else has not a right to come, a better right than yourself . . . I have never had so many hours to myself for years. It is so sweet to sit still and know that no one will burst the door open and come in. (Chapter 29)

The marriage market (which is run by men, not women) cannot last much longer. Edith and her friends 'belonged to their period'

(Chapter 11) and are not convinced that wives and daughters must obey. Lord Lindores, in spite of his disapproval of modern notions which 'will ruin the tempers of girls if they are not checked' (Chapter 37), has to let all his children make unambitious marriages. Caroline, with a characteristic twist of irony, insists on marrying a weak man who is unlikely to do her much good, and at the end her mother has many fears for her. This ambiguous, very 'modern' ending suggests that a woman's life does not end when she gets married, and that ultimately each person is alone:

> Lady Lindores parted with the bridal pair afterwards with an anxious heart. She went home that night, travelling far in the dark through the unseen country, feeling the unknown all about her. Life had not been perfect to her any more than to others. She had known many disappointments, and seen through many illusions; but she had preserved through all the sweetness of a heart that can be deceived, that can forget today's griefs and hope again in tomorrow as if today had never been. As she drew near her home, her heart lightened without any reason at all. Her husband was not a perfect mate to her – her son had failed to her hopes. But she did not dwell on these disenchantments. After all, how dear they were! after all, there was tomorrow to come, which perhaps, most likely, would yet be the perfect day.

Margaret Oliphant admitted, towards the end of her life, that she had often been bored by the 'monotonous demand for a love story' and had wanted to 'kill or part' her lovers, although the public usually would not let her.[7] *Joyce* (1888) and her masterpiece, *Kirsteen,* focus on the achievements of the single woman. Joyce (a teacher who wants to go on working after marriage) is in a Maggie Tulliver-like situation, hesitating between the man she wants to marry and her 'duty' to keep her promise to someone else. In the end she runs away from both men to a remote Scottish island. 'The consequences of that self-sacrifice,' we are told, 'were disastrous all round.' Except, perhaps, for the 'primitive people' with whom Joyce hides, and whose lives she transforms. 'She taught them many things, among others what domestic comfort and cleanliness and

beneficent learning meant, and knew everything.' (Chapter 48)
Perhaps this is every bit as satisfying as wedding bells.

Kirsteen, a 'type of powerful and capable womanhood', is the
daughter of a Scottish laird, a violent man who cares only for his
sons and despises women. They are 'unlucky accidents, tares
among the wheat, handmaids who might be useful about the
house, but who had no future, no capabilities of advancing the
family, creatures altogether of no account'. (Chapter 5)
Throughout the novel people wonder whether Kirsteen will 'get a
man', but we soon realise that this is not the most important
question, 'She was one of those who make a story for themselves'.

When life becomes unbearable Kirsteen runs away to the
'unknown world' of London, where she becomes a partner in a
dressmaking business. She has an artist's feeling for her work and
realises that it is to be her life when the man she hoped to marry
dies. Her mother is eventually thankful that Kirsteen is single
because she will be 'the stand-by for the whole house':

> Oh, that I may make my fortune and help them all [Kirsteen
> prays] . . . They shall not be shamed as they think, they shall
> be thankful there was Kirsteen among the lassies, as well as
> seven sons to make Drumcarro great again. (Chapter 22)

Although she does make the fortune of her family, they
disapprove of her. 'Kirsteen was a rare and not very welcome
visitor in the house she had redeemed. They all deplored the
miserable way of life she had chosen, and that she had no man.'
(Chapter 46) The novel is full of images of Kirsteen walking
through the 'indecipherable dark', which doesn't frighten her as it
does weaker women. Her sisters all marry and take 'a higher
position than hers', but the author hints that a woman who is
over-dependent on her husband (one sister boasts that she 'never
goes a step without my man') is an incomplete person.

'I have learned to take perhaps more a man's view of mortal
affairs,' Margaret Oliphant wrote, ' – to feel that the love
between men and women, the marrying and giving in marriage,
occupy in fact so small a portion of either existence or thought.'[8]
Kirsteen has had her moment of sweetness, but her real
achievement has nothing to do with romance, and has been won
by her own unselfish efforts, celebrated on the last page:

In the times which are not ancient history . . . there lived in one of the most imposing houses, in one of the princeliest squares of Edinburgh, a lady, who was an old lady, yet still as may be said in the prime of life. Her eye was not dim nor her natural force abated; her beautiful head of hair was still red, her eyes still full of fire. . . . Her hospitality was almost boundless, her large house running over with hordes of nephews and nieces, her advice, which meant her help, continually demanded from one side or other of a large and widely extended family. No one could be more cheerful, more interested in all that went on . . . and she was well-known not only as the stand-by of her family, but as the friend of the poor and struggling everywhere . . . She was Miss Douglas of Moray Place . . . there was no one better thought of. And, so far as anybody ever knew, most people had entirely forgotten that in past times, not to disgrace her family, her name had appeared on a plate in conjunction with the name of Miss Jean Brown, Court Dressmaker and Mantau-Maker, as

MISS KIRSTEEN

BEST-SELLERS; FEMINISTS AND ANTI-FEMINISTS

Any woman novelist who became a best-seller in the mid-nineteenth century was likely to hold conventional views on the duties of women. One of the most popular of these novelists was Dinah Mulock (Mrs Craik, 1826–87), who, in *John Halifax, Gentleman* and elsewhere, created noble, upright heroes with a benevolent and protective attitude to their wives. The heroine of *Agatha's Husband* is a spirited girl who rebels against her husband 'when he acts outrageously, unjustly, insultingly – binds me hand and foot like a child'. (Chapter 17) But of course he turns out to be acting for the best and Agatha has to recognise 'the divine and unalterable law given with the first human marriage – *He shall rule over thee*'. The moral seems to be that women are full of weaknesses and can only rise 'above the ordinary standard of womanhood' by associating with a good man. 'If the noblest moral type of man and of woman were each placed side by side,' we are told, 'the man would be the greater of the two.' (Chapter 11) Just as some male writers obviously needed to believe that women were better than themselves, so some women needed to worship a man.

Another best-selling writer was Mrs Henry Wood (Ellen Price, 1814–87). She is best remembered for *East Lynne*, the story of a woman who runs away from her impossibly perfect husband, is abandoned by her seducer, and dies. All our sympathy is with her because she suffers so much, and because the double standard is so blatant. A fallen woman can never recover, but husbands can misbehave with impunity. 'Whatever trials may be the lot of your married life,' she advised her readers, ' . . . bear unto death.' (Volume 2, Chapter 10)

Mrs Wood was a staunch reactionary who warned women that if they rebelled they would meet a terrible fate. *Lord Oakburn's Daughters* (1864) shows the unhappy end of two girls who leave home 'in disobedience and defiance' because their father bullies them. Her appalled comment on one girl's behaviour – in running away to get married – shows that things were changing:

Reader! It has indeed come to this, grievous as it is to have to write it, at the present day, of a well-trained gentlewoman. (Volume 1, Chapter 18)

A more interesting and less conventional novelist was the thriller writer Mary Elizabeth Braddon (1835–1915). In *Lady Audley's Secret* she created a new type of woman, apparently normal but actually insane, who lives off men and murders them when it suits her. Miss Braddon, who as an old lady welcomed the twentieth century as a 'Golden Age of Womanhood',[9] herself admired women who were 'good-tempered, warm-hearted, frank, brave . . . those grander qualities which make the nobility of woman's character',[10] but she realised that men looked for sex appeal. Lady Audley is the baby-doll type who will marry anybody to get an easy life. She is like a mermaid, luring men to their destruction, and sometimes the hero blames her entire sex. Women are not 'merciful, or loving, or kind', he thinks; they 'riot in battle, and murder, and clamour, and desperation'. (Chapters 25 and 30) For the protection of society, such women must be confined in lunatic asylums as long as they live.

A later novel, *The Day Will Come*, also deals with an insane woman whose aggression is turned against men. Evelyn, a middle-aged lady 'of blameless character and reserved manners', says complacently:

Nobody here [in the asylum] would believe me if I were to tell them that I murdered a man who never offended me . . . They think it was only a couple of centuries ago in Southern Europe that women knew the meaning of revenge. (Chapter 37)

The Day Will Come is a powerful and disturbing attack on contemporary sexual morality. While Lady Audley kills for luxuries, Evelyn kills to avenge the wrongs of herself and her daughter, both victims of the double standard. The man she loves, a rising barrister, deserts her after ten years' union to make a conventional marriage. This is partly because he wants a younger and less demanding woman, but also because he knows she will harm his career:

How bitter a thing it would be for the fashionable Queen's Counsel to enter society with a wife of damaged character . . . People would insist upon finding out who Mr Dalbrook's wife was. It would not be enough to say, 'She is there – handsome, clever and a lady'. Society would peer and pry into the background of her life. Whose daughter was she? Had she been married before? And in that case who was her husband? . . . how was it that society had seen nothing of her? (Chapter 32)

Evelyn's daughter, unacknowledged by her father, is seduced by one of his friends. The fairy-tale wedding of his other, legitimate daughter finally pushes Evelyn into despair, madness and murder. The man's sin finds him out after twenty years of fame and success, 'wedded love and deadened conscience', and the shock kills him. Evelyn's revolt, obviously destructive though it is, is a passionate protest against the attitude that women must put up with whatever men do.

The Day Will Come is very much an end-of-the-century novel, full of divorced men and strong-minded women who smoke and read difficult books. Both the fallen woman, and the girl whose husband dies on their honeymoon, eventually get married, which could never have happened in novels of the 1850s. But the unloved, ageing woman, who has built her whole life around a faithless man, has no way out, and belongs to the twentieth as much as the nineteenth century.

Olive Schreiner (1855–1920), wrote one famous novel, *The Story of an African Farm*, which she described as 'a cry out against fate'.[11] Lyndall, like her creator, is a rebel and feminist who hopes for a future 'when each woman's life is filled with earnest, independent labour'. She wants women to be 'doctors, lawyers, law-makers, anything but ill-paid drudges' (Volume 2, Chapter 4), but she cannot escape from the fate of her sex. Like millions of women throughout history, she dies as a result of childbirth, but not before she has given voice to certain deep-rooted female emotions which had rarely found their way into literature:

'You will find a little grave at the foot of the tall blue gum-tree; the water drips off the long, pointed leaves; you must cover it up . . .'
It was the first time she had spoken of her child.
'It was so small,' she said, 'it lived such a little while – only three hours . . . Its feet were so cold; I took them in my hand to make them warm, and my hand closed right over them they were so little . . . It crept close to me; it wanted to drink, it wanted to be warm.' (Volume 2, Chapter 12)

Several anti-feminist women writers became best-sellers in the 1880s and 1890s. Mrs Humphrey Ward (Mary Arnold, 1851–1920) was an enormously influential novelist who combined liberal religious and social views with a horror of the women's rights movement; later she founded the Women's National Anti-Suffrage League. *Marcella* (1894) shows a wild young woman who takes up noble but wrong-headed causes and has to be saved by the love of a good man. Marie Corelli (1855–1924), who, like Mrs Ward, was hailed as a great thinker in some quarters, was also against women having the vote. The most violent attacks on feminists came from Eliza Lynn Linton (1822–98). Her *One Too Many* (1894) was dedicated to the 'sweet girls still left among us who have no part in the new revolt but are content to be dutiful, innocent and sheltered'. Young women who go to Girton are likely to be 'morally diseased' (one of them says, 'Let men die out') and to have lost their womanly charm.

Sarah Grand (Frances McFall, 1854–1943) was a feminist whose novel *The Heavenly Twins* (1893), followed by *The Beth Book* (1897), made her famous. Her heroines are active, purposeful women who behave unconventionally and insist on doing what they feel is right. Evadne in *The Heavenly Twins* leaves her husband because he has a past which disgusts her and she cannot see why purity should be demanded only from one sex. Beth leaves hers because 'no decent woman could associate with a man of his mind, habits and conversation without suffering injury' and becomes a public speaker – 'one of the first swallows of the woman's summer'. (Chapter 52) Both novels show unsuspecting girls being married off to older, all-too-experienced men, who sometimes infect them with venereal disease. Evadne cannot stomach the idea that women should accept their lot, or try to reform their husbands:

> So long as women like you will forgive anything, men will do anything . . . the world is not a bit the better for centuries of self-sacrifice on the woman's part. (Volume 1, Chapter 14)

In spite of showing much unhappiness between the sexes, Sarah Grand looked forward to a better future, 'No one can pretend that the old system of husband and master has answered well, and it has had a fair trial. Let us hope that the new method of partnership will be more successful.' (Volume 6, Chapter 8)

12   The Changing Image of Women

Between the death of George Eliot in 1880, and the turn of the century, a group of famous novelists, all men, looked sympathetically at the problems of the late-nineteenth-century woman. All of them except James went some of the way with the feminists, and all were more liberal than the mid-Victorians had been. They recognised that the past had gone for good; 'I am not an old-fashioned father in a novel,'[1] says Dr Sloper in *Washington Square* (although, of course, that is just what he is). Their female characters were more likely to support themselves or live away from home than they had been before 1880, and the question of free unions was often discussed. Their ideas about what was desirable in a woman were very different from those of Dickens and Trollope and, in some novels, the traditional heroine and anti-heroine change places.

GEORGE MEREDITH

Meredith, the oldest of these novelists (he began publishing in the 1850s and was still influential in the 1890s) was perhaps the most committed feminist. His later work ridicules men's complacent attitude to women and upholds their right to live as they want. 'My mind is my own, married or nor,' says Clara in *The Egoist*. (Chapter 8) But Clara also recognises that she faces great difficulties, saying sadly, 'We women are nailed to our sex'. (Chapter 21)

His mid-Victorian novel, *Richard Feverel*, seemed progressive at the time it was written. Like Thackeray, Meredith defended the young against the old and suggested (in Chapter 29) that a thrush was a better parent than a Victorian paterfamilias who refused to let his children go. Lucy is not blamed for running away to get married; as Meredith sees it, her first duty is to her husband, not her or his relations. But Lucy, though envisaged as a strong woman, actually comes over as a typical shrinking Victorian maiden:

> The fair young girl was sitting as her lover had left her; trying to recall her stunned senses. . . . Like a dutiful slave, she rose to him. . . . She dropped to her seat weeping, and hiding her shamed cheeks . . . She trembled from head to foot . . . She wept: 'O Richard, take me home! take me home!' (Chapter 27)

In this novel there is a great gulf between good women and bad ones (who smoke and wear men's clothes), and there is also a vast difference between women and men. Lucy is always pure and good while Richard is 'base and spotted'; she unhesitatingly forgives a sin which he could never have forgiven her, and she dies of brain fever while he has to go on living. (*Two* women die in this book because they are not allowed to be happy, so it seems their sex is very frail.)

Lucy would have been out of place in Meredith's later novels, which are concerned with 'women pushing out into the world for independence'. (*Lord Ormont*, Chapter 8) Some of his 1890s heroines, like Aminta and Carinthia, refuse to go on loving their husbands when they have treated them badly, and a constant theme in Meredith is of a woman becoming disillusioned with a man when she realises that he is totally selfish. The chief of these men is Sir Willoughby Patterne in *The Egoist* – a novel which incidentally shows how hard it was for a girl to break off her engagement – who is determined that his wife shall be 'utterly mine; every thought, every feeling'. (Chapter 7) He insists that she must not have been married before, or get married again if he dies. He despises Laetitia for being 'old' (she is actually younger than himself) and faded, but he still wants her to spend her life adoring him. 'She will live and die Laetitia Dale' (Chapter 34), 'To love like Laetitia Dale, was a current phrase' (Chapter 40), he says, and the echoes of Trollope's Lily Dale are not accidental. Meredith tells us, in Chapter 23, that Willoughby has read 'the imaginative composition of his time' – that is, Trollope and Mrs Henry Wood – and hopes Clara will end up 'a miserable spinster' for having snubbed him. He fantasises a scene where she begs his pardon 'on her knees'. Like Mrs Wood's Lady Isabel, or one of Trollope's erring women, she is to be humbled to the dust so he can graciously forgive her without having to take her back. But the real-life Clara sees his egotism for what it is, demands her freedom, and marries someone else.

The heroine of *Diana of the Crossways* is a brilliant, striking and unconventional woman who wants to be independent but can't. She is chaste, but respectable people disapprove of her because she has got herself talked about and because men have a 'horror of women with brains'. As a woman of the 1880s, she is protected by the Married Women's Property Act and can earn her living and sell her family home without her estranged husband's permission. But she cannot divorce him, and fears that he may force her out of the country by insisting on his right to live with her. Men assume she is 'accessible' because she has no male protector. All Meredith's sympathy is for the 'woman in the pillory', who is possibly one of the 'women of the future'.

The central incident of the novel is Diana's loss of her lover Dacier after she has sold his political secrets. Meredith admits that she did wrong (although she had excuses; Dacier put her under enormous pressures) but he insists that it was a 'trifling error, easily to be overlooked by a manful lover'. (Chapter 39) 'Does a man pretending to love a woman cut at one blow . . . the ties uniting her to him?' he asks. (Chapter 38) The answer is that a good many fictional heroes, from Edmund Bertram to Angel Clare, do cut these ties ruthlessly when they find out that the woman is not their ideal. Meredith insists, though, that such men are cruel and blinkered because they are straining after an impossible 'heroine of Romance' instead of the 'flecked heroine of Reality'. (Chapter 35) Diana is worthy to be loved, faults and all, because she is generous, honest, and 'a growing soul'. The woman Dacier marries instead, Constance Asper, a 'fair young creature undefiled by an interest in public affairs', is a savage caricature of the pure and pious Victorian girl.

Although Diana hopes for a time to do without a man, she finds herself unable to 'stand firmly alone'. (Chapter 43) She cannot survive as a freelance writer; her friendships with men damage her and she is lucky to find a husband who accepts her as she is. But perhaps the day will come 'when women will be encouraged to work at crafts and professions for their independence'. 'That is the secret of the opinion of us at present,' says Diana, '– our dependency. Give us the means of independence, and we will gain it, and have a turn at judging you, my lords! You shall behold a world reversed!' (Chapter 14)

THE EARLY JAMES

Trollope remarked, in 1862, that women's rights were 'a very favourite subject in America'.[2] Henry James, born in 1843, grew up in a climate where the position of women was being ardently discussed, and his earliest work shows that he knew the subject well. Time and again he compares the American woman – 'the fruit of a civilisation not old and complex, but new and simple' (*Roderick Hudson*, Chapter 17) – with the European woman, who is very much more 'civilised', but also much less free.

Daisy Miller shows exactly how many restrictions were imposed on young middle-class women. Daisy, an American girl in Europe – and emancipated even by American standards – is totally damned because of her innocent outings with men. Nobody has told her why it is wrong to flirt and she bluntly refuses to conform to European customs, 'The young ladies of this country have a dreadfully pokey time of it . . . I don't see why I should change my habits for *such* stupids'. (Chapter 4)

James sympathises with Daisy, who is certainly treated more harshly than she deserves, but at the same time he notes 'she lacked a certain indispensable fineness'. (Chapter 3) This is a key phrase. Genuine James heroines do have this 'indispensable fineness'; they do not flirt, and they are prepared if necessary to renounce their deepest desires. In *The American* James studies a European lady who is at the opposite extreme from Daisy Miller. Claire is an Anglo-French aristocrat, a Catholic, and a woman of exquisite refinement. Newman feels that she has 'passed through mysterious ceremonies and processes of culture in her youth' which 'made her seem rare and precious'. (Chapter 9) At first he is happy to accept her background, so different from his own, 'If such superb white flowers as that could bloom in Catholic soil, the soil was not insalubrious'. (Chapter 21) But he finds to his cost that Claire would not be the person she is if she had not been conditioned to obey. Her mother has already forced her into an unhappy marriage; now she forbids her, though a mature woman, to marry the man she wants. Like Scott's Catholic heroines (but they lived in the Middle Ages) she can only escape from intolerable pressures by becoming a nun.[3] Newman does not understand why she submits; and nor do we. She can only say, 'It's like a religion,' which Newman translates as 'the religion simply of the family laws'. (Chapter 21)

James was 'American' enough not to believe that wives and daughters should automatically submit to the head of the family. Catherine in *Washington Square* (a realistic Florence Dombey) feels she ought to obey her father for as long as she lives in his house, so she can only offer to leave it. Her lover is more important to her; she would have been, James says ironically, 'a dutiful and responsible wife'. (Chapter 20) At the same time this is a serious decision, and Catherine feels she has 'broken a sacred law'. (Chapter 22) There is no suggestion that a girl who defies her family to get married will be happy. In this situation no happy outcome is possible, and the most important virtue for the heroine is not obedience but integrity.

Questions of freedom and obedience are discussed again in *Portrait of a Lady*. In his treatment of Pansy Osmond, James returned to the Claire de Cintré theme and showed, more convincingly than in *The American*, why a young woman brought up 'in the old way' cannot simply take what she wants. Once again, submission to parents is associated with Catholicism. Pansy, whose father has had her educated to 'do what I prefer' (Chapter 37), really is the sweet, dutiful, obedient daughter who had been presented so superficially by lesser novelists than James, 'I obey very well', she says proudly. (Chapter 22) The idea of anyone defying Osmond disturbs her as much as if 'two of the saints in the great picture in the convent-chapel' had wagged their heads at each other, and therefore she cannot understand 'the secrets of larger lives than her own'. (Chapter 52) She is pathetic and good, but she is very limited.

James' real interest is in the American Isabel with her eager wish to see and experience as much as possible. Here, he suggests, is a woman who could really have achieved something interesting:

> It was a fine free nature, but what was she going to do with herself? . . . Most women did with themselves nothing at all; they waited, in attitudes more or less gracefully passive, for a man to come that way and furnish them with a destiny. Isabel's

originality was that she gave one an impression of having intentions of her own. (Chapter 7)

'I don't want to begin life by marrying,' Isabel says, after she has refused an eminently 'good' marriage. 'There are other things a woman can do.' (Chapter 15) When she does marry she realises with horror that Osmond hates and cannot tolerate her independence of mind. 'He would have liked her to have nothing of her own but her pretty appearance.' (Chapter 42) Nevertheless, she does not feel that she can simply leave him, as her friend Henrietta suggests. Like George Eliot, James felt strongly that a marriage or engagement was an enormously serious commitment, simply because it had been freely chosen. Isabel reflects that 'if ever a girl was a free agent, she had been . . . When a woman had made such a mistake, there was only one way to repair it, – to accept it'. (Chapter 40) Although she does eventually decide to disobey her husband, she cannot feel it is anything but dreadful to repudiate 'the most serious act – the single sacred act – of her life'. (Chapter 45) Her integrity and deep feeling of loyalty to an ideal mean that she is doomed to unhappiness. This is often the case with James' heroines. Fleda in *The Spoils of Poynton* loses her lover because she cannot let him break a promise. 'The great thing is to keep faith' (Chapter 16), she insists. The other girl, Mona, has no qualms about hanging on to her man and therefore has a shallow nature.

Isabel is halfway between the 'European' Pansy and the 'American' Mrs Touchett and Henrietta. Both these women globe-trot freely, are a law to themselves, and have no real need of a man. But Mrs Touchett is an unnatural mother and James does not take Henrietta seriously; the best thing she can be called is 'an excellent fellow'. (Chapter 47) She is incapable of Isabel's depths of feeling and it seems likely that the newspaper articles she writes for a living are not very profound.

James' dislike of emancipated women is made clear in an all-American novel, *The Bostonians*. Here he shows a group of 'advanced' women, one a doctor (the word he actually uses is 'doctress'), one an ageing spinster who has spent her life campaigning for liberal causes, and finally the redoubtable feminist Olive Chancellor. Into this group comes a charming girl with a superficial talent for public speaking; Olive takes her up and trains her to be a campaigner for women's rights. The novel is about Basil Ransom's struggle to get Verena away from the feminists and convince her that she is 'meant for something divinely different – for privacy, for him, for love'. (Chapter 28) 'For him' is the key phrase, of course, but the concept of privacy is important too. The idea that a woman should open her mouth in public or have anything to do with politics seems to have shocked Victorian men profoundly, and this explains Basil's determination to get her away from the public meeting at the end of the novel before she can say a word. James reassures us that Verena is not a particularly distinguished thinker, so nothing will be lost when she becomes a housewife. At no point does he bother to argue with the feminists; he simply assumes that they are bound to fail because all normal women want a husband.

James was well aware that women were living in a time of transition, and he did not want them to be slaves. His sympathy for women whose families trampled on their feelings was very great. But he wanted them to retain the traditional virtues – to be cultivated, refined, and unwilling to demand their rights. Isabel, and Claire, and Fleda Vetch would be unwomanly if they fought for their happiness as Basil unashamedly does. The James heroine, though more emancipated than her predecessors, is not really all that different.

GEORGE MOORE

A Drama in Muslin[4] discusses the new feminism and takes a last look at the marriage market, this time set in Ireland. Apart from the fact that Moore is franker – he says that some girls will get pregnant if they are kept waiting too long for a 'suitable' husband – it does not seem to have changed very much since the days of Mrs Gore. The 'poor muslin martyrs' of girls are taught by their mothers that their only duty is to amuse men:

> A woman is absolutely nothing without a husband; if she doesn't wish to pass for a failure she must get a husband, and upon this all her ideas should be set. Don't waste your time thinking of your books, your painting, your accomplishments; if you were Jane Austens, George Eliots and Rosa Bonheurs,[5] it would be of no use if you weren't married. (Chapter 14)

The plain heroine, Alice, written off as a 'gawk of a girl' because she likes reading and doesn't flirt, escapes by making an unfashionable marriage. At the end of the novel she is a happy mother who also writes books and articles, while her husband-hunting friends are likely to be unhappy spinsters. Another friend, Cecilia, hates and shuns men, and Moore notes that women like this are now coming out into the open:

> The gates of the harem are being broken down, and the gloom of the female mind clears . . . Beneath the great feminine tide there is an undercurrent of hatred and revolt. This is particularly observable in the leaders of the movement; women who . . . condemn love – that is to say, love in the sense of sexual intercourse – and proclaim a higher mission for women than to be the mother of men. (Chapter 19)

Esther Waters deals with the working-class women who were almost untouched by the feminist movement, and it breaks new ground in English fiction. To most novelists (including James and Meredith) servants are part of the furniture, not people to be taken seriously, and Gissing, in *The Odd Women*, denies that 'there can be any solidarity of ladies with servant girls'. (Chapter 6) Esther is 'the lowest of the low – the servant of servants'. (Chapter 20) It is made clear that working-class women can expect an extremely hard life, when their husbands gamble, drink or beat them, and when they get too old to find a job. Esther

> had to work from early morning till late at night, scrubbing grates, preparing bacon and eggs, cooking chops and making beds: she was one of the many London girls to whom rest, not to say pleasure, is unknown, and who, if they should sit down for a few moments, hear the mistress's voice crying: 'Now, Eliza, have you nothing to do, that you are sitting there idle?' (Chapter 3)

But Esther is pushed lower still by the fact that she has a child, and must protect him 'from the world which called him a bastard, and denied to him the right to live'. (Chapter 19) Although the women obviously have a worse time than the men – 'we poor women have more than our right to bear with' (Chapter 13) – Moore is not making a simple feminist point. Middle-class mothers who will not breast-feed are responsible for the death of the wet-nurses' children, who are given to baby-farmers and quietly killed. Esther has an easy way out, which she refuses to take. Mrs Spires assures her that the baby will ruin her life, that it is 'better out of the way', and that she can earn good money as a wet-nurse if she keeps on having babies and letting them die. The novel makes the familiar point that 'pure' women ought to show more compassion. But unlike most novels it also shows exactly how the ultra-respectable are driving 'unfortunate' women to murder. 'If they was all like you,' Esther tells the employer who sacks her, 'there would be more girls who'd do away with themselves and their babies.' (Chapter 20)

There is no conventional happy ending for Esther; her great achievement is to have brought up her child and remained a good person when everything was against her. The author is more perceptive than some greater novelists in that he does not feel a woman is interesting only when she is young and attractive. The story ends with Esther and the elderly Mrs Barfield tending the house and garden at Woodview, which would quickly be ruined – 'Nature does not take long – a few years, a very few years' – if they were not there. Mrs Barfield calls it 'keeping things together', and Esther does not 'want any more than that . . . she was no longer a young girl, she had her work to do'. (Chapter 45) Men come and go; children leave home, and sometimes die before their mothers, but there is still a great deal for women to do, struggling against nature and the inhumanity of society to keep some form of civilised life going. Religion is a help to them, as Moore notes, although he does not himself endorse their views. And, in Esther's relationships with her mother, Miss Rice, and Mrs Barfield, he shows how effectively women can support each other.

GEORGE GISSING

Gissing, who wrote one feminist classic, *The Odd Women*, had the reputation of being a woman-hater in his day. He constantly attacked stupid and vulgar women who make men's lives miserable. *Denzil Quarrier* and *In the Year of Jubilee* both seem hostile to the women's rights movement; in the latter novel the hero lives away from his wife and child because they interfere with his work. Gissing tried to explain the contradictions in his attitudes in a letter of 1893:

My demand for female 'equality' simply means that I am convinced there will be no social peace until women are intellectually trained very much as men are. More than half the misery of life is due to the ignorance and childishness of women.[6]

In *New Grub Street*, Amy Reardon causes the death of her husband and another hard-up writer, who are driven to despair because she cannot share their life. Amy is 'advanced', 'a typical woman of the new time' who can talk fluently about subjects which she does not understand in depth. The Married Women's Property Act has made her independent and she wants to liberalise the law of divorce. In some ways, Gissing says, she has a masculine nature. But she is also a traditional dependent woman who expects to be supported (in style) by her husband and withdraws her affection when he cannot do this. She has ruined him as an artist, because he has to write what he knows are bad novels to earn an income for her. Amy is not simply a consumer; she has a child whom she loves. But Gissing has little sympathy for her maternal feelings because they compete with her feelings for her husband. Reardon, who sometimes wishes he had married an uneducated girl who would have treated him with deference, tells her bluntly:

I begin to see how much right there is on the side of those who would keep women in subjection. You have been allowed to act with independence, and the result is that you have ruined my life and debased your own. (Chapter 25)

Amy, however, is contrasted with Marian, who is exploited by her father and her fiancé, both of them selfish men. Marian is a typical girl of the 1880s, who lives with her parents but works hard and conscientiously outside the home to supplement the family income. And she has 'modern' attitudes, in that she feels she can only take so much bullying from her father and has the right to leave home if she likes. But she still has the 'womanly' virtue of sacrificing herself for others; she feels that she must stand by her parents when they are destitute and cannot insist on marrying Jasper if it will harm his career. At the end of the novel she is a breadwinner, with no prospect of marriage, while Amy is the ornamental wife of a successful man. Selfish women, Gissing suggests, are those most likely to succeed.

Born in Exile also focuses on the man's dilemma. Godwin Peak feels his only chance of marrying a refined woman is to become a clergyman, although he is a secret atheist. He chooses the ladylike Sidwell, 'a woman of the highest type our civilisation can produce', who has 'never had her thoughts soiled by the vile contact of poverty' (Volume 2, Chapter 2). But Sidwell is a cold woman who lacks the courage to 'go forth into exile' with the man who loves her, and the result is that he dies. Gissing suggests that Peak made a great, though understandable, mistake in wanting a conventional woman. He assumes that a real lady will be incapable of supporting herself, and have religious beliefs which he does not share. Sidwell is contrasted, though, with Janet Moxey, a doctor who has 'that peculiar fragrance of modern womanhood, refreshing, inspiriting, which is so entirely different from the merely feminine perfume, however exquisite'. (Volume 6, Chapter 1)

Peak does not want to marry a 'truly emancipated woman', because he believes that they are 'almost always asexual' (Volume 3, Chapter 4). This type is studied in depth in *The Odd Women*, the novel in which Gissing looks most fully and sympathetically at women's problems. There were now (in 1893) so many 'superfluous females' that it was obviously absurd to tell women that they existed only to be wives and mothers. The old-fashioned, chivalrous Micklethwaite (who has had to put off his own marriage for seventeen years) says 'the life of unmarried women is a wretched one; every man who is able ought to save one of them from that fate' (Chapter 9), but Gissing seems to be saying that every woman ought to live as if she did not expect to marry.

Alice and Virginia Madden are 'English ladies of the familiar type' who have not been trained for a profession and are thrown defenceless on the labour market. They are both good women – they are devoted to their younger sister Monica and look after her child when she dies – but their employers take advantage of this goodness to pay them starvation wages. Alice consoles herself for the hardness of her life with religion, and Virginia with drink. Monica, an overworked shop assistant, is terrified of becoming an old maid like her sisters, so she gets married and soon finds that she has embraced a new kind of slavery. Her husband, Widdowson, is a conventional man who is always quoting

Ruskin, and who wants her to sit in the house all day and to obey him unquestioningly, 'I am no tyrant, but I shall rule you for your own good'. (Chapter 22)

Monica, who has sincerely tried to be a good wife, cannot bear his attitude; the marriage breaks down and she dies in childbirth. Yet this need not have happened if she had refused to be frightened by the bogey of old-maidenhood. The spinster heroine, Rhoda Nunn (see page 41), tells her:

Your mistake was in looking only at the weak women. You had other examples before you . . . who live bravely and work hard and are proud of their place in the world. (Chapter 29)

Rhoda and her friend Mary Barfoot work for the 'odd women' who do not marry. They believe that 'girls are to be brought up to a calling in life, just as men are' (Chapter 10), and teach them 'shorthand, book-keeping, commercial correspondence', 'to fit them for certain of the pursuits nowadays thrown open to their sex'. (Chapter 6) But Rhoda has to rethink her priorities when, like Monica, she is offered a match which most women would jump at. Her options are conventional marriage, a 'free union', and celibacy, and in the end she decides to be celibate, partly because she can best help single women by being single herself, and perhaps also because the Widdowson marriage has warned her that Everard, the man she loves, wants to dominate her. Like Gissing, Everard claims to hold advanced views on the status of women but is terrified of what uneducated women can do to men. It seems that good relations between the sexes are almost impossible in the present state of things.

The novel ends, not with the hero and heroine proudly producing a male baby, but with two spinsters looking at Monica's daughter, whose future is most uncertain. 'Make a brave woman of her,' says Rhoda, who believes that 'the world is moving' and that the feminists are flourishing 'like the green bay-tree'. (Chapter 31) It is possible that 'in far-off days' the world will change and 'equality between man and wife' (Chapter 16) will be the norm. 'When *all* women, high and low alike, are trained to self-respect, then men will regard them in a different light and marriage may be honourable to both.' (Chapter 10)

THOMAS HARDY

By the time Hardy began writing novels it had become quite normal for women to work or study, and this is what his women generally do. They are teachers, writers, art designers, land workers, even servants, and one, Bathsheba, surprises everyone by being an efficient farmer. Elizabeth-Jane, forbidden to do domestic work, uses her free time to learn Latin. 'The perfect woman, you see, was a working woman,' says Angel Clare's mother, 'not an idler; not a fine lady; but one who used her hands and her head and her heart for the good of others.' (*Tess of the d'Urbervilles*, Chapter 39) Idle women, like Eustacia (who realises that her problem is 'want of an object to live for'), Lucetta and Mrs Charmond are incapable of being anything but sex objects, and die.

Indeed, women are constantly dying in Hardy's novels. He believed, though reluctantly, that 'the woman mostly gets the worst of it in the long run'. (*Jude*, Part 6, Chapter 3) During the 1890s he expressed some sympathy with the feminist movement, but suggested that women might never be able to achieve equality because 'the unalterable laws of nature are based upon a wrong'.[7] The students at Melchester training school are modern young women preparing to go out into a man's world, but they are still intensely vulnerable:

> . . . their tender feminine faces upturned to the flaring gas-jets . . . every face bearing the legend 'The Weaker' upon it, as the penalty of the sex wherein they were moulded, which by no possible exertion of their willing hearts and abilities could be made strong while the inexorable laws of nature remain what they are. They formed a pretty, suggestive, pathetic sight, of whose pathos and beauty they were themselves unconscious, and would not discover till . . . the storms and strains of after-years, with their injustice, loneliness, child-bearing, and bereavement. (*Jude*, Part 3, Chapter 3)

Hardy felt it was very important to champion women because they were 'the Weaker'. It was women who bore children, who were sacrificed to the double standard, and who were most likely to go to pieces if anything went wrong. *Tess of the d'Urbervilles* and *Jude the Obscure*, which belonged to a whole cluster of unconventional novels that appeared in the 1890s, both end with a woman breaking down.

Tess was greatly admired, for by this time most readers were prepared to sympathise with the fallen woman. But few novelists (apart from Collins in *The New Magdalen*) had suggested that a man could know her history and still love her. Like Meredith, Hardy was interested in the theme of love 'which alters when it alteration finds'. In *The Trumpet-Major* (1880) he takes it for granted that Matilda cannot be allowed to marry Bob; his brother is doing him a kindness when he gets rid of her. But in *A Pair of Blue Eyes* he had looked closely at the male need for a perfect woman, and he returned to this theme in *Tess*.

Henry Knight and Angel both reject the woman they sincerely love because they cannot bear her to have made mistakes; the 'flecked heroine of Reality' is more than they can cope with. Tess is in an impossible position because she is trapped between men's lust and men's demand that she should be 'spotless'. In the beginning she is 'blank as snow', totally ignorant of the facts of life as every Victorian girl was expected to be. But all those around her know she is likely to get pregnant, and men molest her before and after her 'fall'. Both Angel (in Chapter 29) and Alec accuse her of provoking them past control, so that she is made to feel 'that in inhabiting the fleshly tabernacle with which Nature had endowed her she was somehow doing wrong'. (Chapter 45)

The irony is that Tess is in so many ways the Victorians' ideal woman. She accepts the sexual code of her time and feels that she 'could never conscientiously allow any man to marry her now'. (Chapter 21) She is no New Woman but 'a regular churchgoer of simple faith' who trustingly takes over her husband's opinions because 'what's good enough for him is good enough for me'. (Chapter 46) Her love and obedience to Angel, who is 'godlike in her eyes' (Chapter 29), are exactly what a good wife is expected to feel. It is impossible for her to stop loving him, however much he disappoints her – 'because you are yourself. I ask no more.' (Chapter 35)

Yet for all her wish to conform Tess is constantly punished, 'once victim, always victim'. She wants to be pure, and a faithful wife, but all the pressures on her are to be the opposite. In the end the contradictions are too much for her; when this essentially kindly girl drives a knife into Alec 'her mind had lost its balance'. (Chapter 57) Exactly the same thing happens in Hardy's next novel to a completely different type of woman, Sue.

None of the men in *Tess* is as good as the women. It is they who sacrifice themselves, who take responsibility for children, and who support each other under strain. But *Jude the Obscure* has a quite different pattern. Margaret Oliphant suggested that Hardy's 'object must be, having glorified women by the creation of Tess, to show after all what destructive and ruinous creatures they are'.[8]

'Yea, many there be that have run out of their wits for women . . . many also have perished, have erred, and sinned for women', runs the motto of Part One of *Jude*. This time it is the men who are victims. Jude, who assumes that he must marry Arabella if he gets her pregnant, is held up to ridicule and has his life blighted by her and her friends. As in Gissing, whose novels had considerable influence on Hardy, an unworldly man is dragged down and destroyed by a vulgar, selfish woman.[9]

Hardy believed, and had already hinted in *The Woodlanders*, that people should be able to get divorced if they wanted, and in *Jude* he makes several cynical remarks about the 'sacrament' of marriage. If this had been a simple anti-marriage novel, though, like *The Woman Who Did*, it would have had a very different type of heroine. Like Meredith, Gissing, James and Moore, Hardy was deeply interested in the 'new' woman who did not particularly want to marry anyone. Sue is 'a distinct type – a refined creature, intended by Nature to be left intact' (Part 6, Chapter 3), and 'impossible as a human wife to any average man' (Part 3, Chapter 9). A German reviewer told him that she

> was the first delineation in fiction of the woman who was coming into notice in her thousands every year – the woman of the feminist movement – the slight, pale, 'bachelor' girl – the intellectualised, emancipated bundle of nerves that modern conditions were producing, mainly in cities as yet, who does not recognise the necessity for most of her sex to follow marriage as a profession . . . The regret of this critic was that the portrait of the newcomer had been left to be drawn by a man, and was not done by one of her own sex, who would never have allowed her to break down at the end. (Postscript)

Apart from the fact that Sue was by no means the *first* such woman in fiction, this seems doubtful. Sue takes no part in the feminist movement, like Rhoda Nunn and Verena Tarrant; almost the only time she refers to the position of women is in some casual remarks about the giving-away of brides. Yet she is emancipated in the sense that she lives away from her family, works (she is anxious not to be a financial burden), reads seriously and is a daring and brilliant thinker. 'Her intellect sparkles like diamonds,' says Phillotson, 'while mine smoulders like brown paper' (Part 4, Chapter 4). Jude calls her 'a woman-poet, a woman-seer' (Part 6, Chapter 3). But she 'breaks down' and becomes conventional, and Hardy suggests that this is normal for her sex. 'Time and circumstance, which enlarge the views of most men, narrow the views of women almost invariably.' (Part 6, Chapter 10) So she goes back to Phillotson and the Church, and this is in effect the end of her.

Hardy argues, like Meredith in several novels, and Gissing in *The Odd Women*, that a man is not entitled to force any woman, even his wife, to live with him. Phillotson tries to behave in a civilised way ('it was a question for her own conscience – not for me. I was not her gaoler') but after her breakdown Sue doesn't want rational treatment. She insists that she is her husband's inferior – 'I shall try to learn to love him by obeying him' – and that he has total rights over her body, because he is the man 'to whom I belong, and whom I wish to honour and obey, as I vowed' (Part 6, Chapter 9). She is, of course, only echoing what most people then believed, for Phillotson faces strong disapproval when he sets her free, and Arabella tells him:

I shouldn't have let her go! I should have kept her chained on – her spirit for kicking would have been broke soon enough! There's nothing like bondage and a stone-deaf taskmaster for taming us women. Besides, you've got the laws on your side.

And she reminds him that the Church, too, discriminates against the weaker sex, ' "Then shall the man be guiltless; but the woman shall bear her iniquity". Damn rough on us women; but we must grin and put up wi' it!' (Part 5, Chapter 8)

Sue, a natural rebel, is to be broken like a horse at the end of this novel. Phillotson forsakes liberal for paternalist ideas, admitting his 'error in not restraining her with a wise and strong hand', and saying:

'Women are so strange in their influence, that they tempt you to misplaced kindness. However, I know myself better now. A little judicious severity, perhaps . . .'

Yes [says Gillingham] but you must tighten the reins by degrees only. Don't be too strenuous at first. She'll come to any terms in time. (Part 6, Chapter 5)

Although Sue is a type of woman whom novelists in 1800 could not have imagined, women's basic situation, on the eve of the twentieth century, has not changed – they are still 'the Weaker'. There are exceptions, but most New Women break down, die, or renounce love. The women in Hardy, Gissing, and Meredith are the great-granddaughters, not of Jane Austen's level-headed heroines, but of the tortured Bride of Lammermoor.

Notes and References

CHAPTER 1: WOMEN IN SOCIETY AND IN THE NOVEL

1. Clara E. Collet, 'Prospects of Marriage for Women', *Nineteenth Century*, April 1892.
2. Quoted in Elaine Showalter, *A Literature of Their Own* (Princeton, 1977), p.17.
3. 'Modern Novelists – Great and Small', *Blackwood's Edinburgh Magazine*, May 1855.
4. Ray Strachey, *The Cause* (London, 1928), Preface.
5. Alicia C. Percival, *The English Miss Today and Yesterday* (London, 1939), p. 27.
6. George Eliot, *Middlemarch* (1872), Finale.
7. W. R. Greg, *Literary and Social Judgments* (second edition, London, 1869), p. 282.
8. George Eliot, *Adam Bede* (1859), Ch. 5.
9. Anthony Trollope, *The Eustace Diamonds* (1872), Ch. 76.
10. W. M. Thackeray, *The Newcomes* (1855), Ch. 28.
11. Wilkie Collins, *The Woman in White* (1860), 'The Story Begun by Walter Hartright', Ch. 10.
12. T. J. Wise and J. A. Symington (eds), *The Brontës: Their Lives, Friendships and Correspondence* (Oxford, 1932), Vol. 2, p. 240.
13. W. M. Thackeray, *Vanity Fair* (1848), Ch. 65.
14. Florence Nightingale, *Cassandra*, published as Appendix 1 in Strachey, op. cit.
15. Olive Schreiner, *The Story of an African Farm* (1883), Vol. 1, Ch. 2.
16. Flora Thompson, 'Heatherley', quoted in *Observer Magazine*, 21 October 1979.
17. Mary Clive, *The Day of Reckoning* (London, 1964), pp. 68–9.
18. Sir William Blackstone, *Commentary on the Laws of England* (1765), quoted in Strachey, op. cit., p. 15.
19. George Eliot, *Daniel Deronda* (1876), Ch. 48.
20. Quoted in Strachey, op. cit., p. 109.
21. Anthony Trollope, *He Knew He Was Right* (1869), Ch. 59.
22. Thomas Hardy, *The Woodlanders* (1887), Ch. 39.
23. George Eliot, *Janet's Repentance*, Ch. 18, in *Scenes of Clerical Life* (1858).
24. Quoted in Gordon S. Haight, 'Male Chastity in the Nineteenth Century', *Contemporary Review*, November 1971.

25. Charlotte's death certificate gives the cause of death as 'phthisis', but a twentieth-century gynaecologist writes, 'The evidence is quite clear that she died of hyperemesis gravidarum, the pernicious vomiting of pregnancy' (Phillip Rhodes, 'A Medical Appraisal of the Brontës', *Brontë Society Transactions*, 16).

26. In M. E. Braddon's *Lady Audley's Secret* (1862) the heroine turns out to be mad, and we are told that her mother, too, became insane after having a baby. What is obviously post-natal psychosis is here described as a hereditary disease.

27. Grant Allen, 'Plain Words on the Woman Question', *Fortnightly Review*, October 1889.

28. Anthony Trollope described *(Autobiography* [1883] Ch. 2) how his mother had 'six children, four of whom died of consumption at different ages'.

29. Charlotte Brontë, *Villette* (1853), Ch. 37.

30. Wanda Neff, *Victorian Working Women* (second edition, London, 1960), p. 187.

31. George Eliot, *The Mill on the Floss* (1860), Book 4, Ch. 3.

32. Jane Austen, *Pride and Prejudice* (1813), Vol. 1, Ch. 8.

33. Sarah Stickney Ellis, *Daughters of England* (London, 1842), p. 183.

34. Florence Nightingale, *Cassandra*, op. cit.

35. John Ruskin, *Sesame and Lilies* (1865): Lecture Two, 'Of Queens' Gardens', paragraph 68.

36. Quoted in F. A. Hayek, *John Stuart Mill and Harriet Taylor* (London, 1951), p. 122.

37. Neff, op. cit., p. 182.

38. *'Vanity Fair, Jane Eyre*, and the Governesses' Benevolent Institute Report for 1847', *Quarterly Review*, December 1848.

39. Benjamin Disraeli, *Sybil* (1845), Book 3, Ch. 1.

40. 'A Woman's Thoughts about Women: Female Handicrafts', *Chambers's Journal*, 11 July 1857.

41. Charles Dickens, *Little Dorrit* (1857), Book 1, Ch. 5.

42. 'The Employment of Women', *North British Review*, February 1857.

43. Robert Blatchford, *Merrie England* (London, 1894), Ch. 23.

44. Elizabeth Gaskell, *North and South* (1855), Ch. 13.

45. Flora Thompson, *Lark Rise to Candleford* (Oxford, 1945), Ch. 10.

46. Dickens, *The Old Curiosity Shop* (1841), Ch. 34.

47. Greg, op. cit., p. 86.

48. E. Lynn Linton, *The Girl of the Period* (London, 1883), Vol. 2, p. 68.

49. See Showalter, op. cit., pp. 37–9, and J. A. Sutherland, *Victorian Novelists and Publishers* (London, 1976), p. 210.

50. Quoted in Elizabeth Gaskell, *The Life of Charlotte Brontë* (London, 1857), Vol. 2, Ch. 4.

51. Quoted in ibid., Vol. 1, Ch. 8.

52. Ibid., Vol. 2, Ch. 2.

53. Annette B. Hopkins, *Elizabeth Gaskell* (London, 1952), p. 318.

54. J. A. V. Chapple and Arthur Pollard (eds), *The Letters of Mrs Gaskell* (Manchester, 1966), Letter 68.

55. Ibid., Letter 515.

56. Mrs Harry Coghill (ed.), *The Autobiography and Letters of Mrs M. O. W. Oliphant* (London, 1899), Ch. 4.

57. R. W. Chapman (ed.), *Jane Austen's Letters* (second edition, Oxford, 1952), Letter 133.

58. Gaskell, *The Life of Charlotte Brontë*, op. cit., Vol. 2, Ch. 1.

59. 'The Employment of Women', *North British Review*, op. cit.

60. Charlotte M. Yonge, *Womankind* (London, 1876), p. 238.

61. Ruskin, op. cit., paragraph 74.

62. See George Gissing, *In the Year of Jubilee*, and E. Lynn Linton, *One Too Many*, both published in 1894.

63. Quoted in Gaskell, op. cit., Vol. 2, Ch. 10.

64. Quoted in Francoise Basch, *Relative Creatures* (London, 1974), p. 14.

65. Anthony Trollope, *Can You Forgive Her?* (1865), Ch. 11.

66. Quoted in Lytton Strachey, *Queen Victoria* (London, 1921), p. 238 in 1971 edition.

67. 'Appeal against Female Suffrage', *Nineteenth Century*, June 1889.

68. Quoted in C. Willett Cunnington, *Feminine Attitudes in the Nineteenth Century* (London, 1935), p. 294.

69. Yonge, op. cit., pp. 103, 105, 127, 128, 177.

70. M. M. Dilke, 'The Appeal against Female Suffrage: A Reply', *Nineteenth Century*, July 1889.

71. Sarah Grand, *The Heavenly Twins* (1893), Book 1, Ch. 19.

72. Quoted in Cunnington, op. cit., p. 291.

CHAPTER 2: IDEOLOGY AND THE NOVEL

1. Caroline Norton, 'A Letter to the Queen on Lord Chancellor Cranworth's Marriage and Divorce Bill' (London, 1855).

2. Mrs Jameson, *Shakespeare's Heroines* (London, 1897 edition), p. 37.

3. Henry Fielding, *Tom Jones* (1749), Book 17, Ch. 3.

4. Bulwer Lytton, *The Last Days of Pompeii* (1834), Ch. 6. Lytton's wife Rosina was the daughter of Anna Wheeler, one of the earliest feminists.

5. William Cobbett, *Advice to Young Men* (London, 1830), p. 159 in 1980 edition.

6. John Ruskin, *Sesame and Lilies*: Lecture Two, 'Of Queens' Gardens', paragraphs 68–9.

7. Walter Scott, *Waverley* (1814), Ch. 23.

8. J. A. V. Chapple and Arthur Pollard (eds), *The Letters of Mrs Gaskell* (Manchester, 1966), Letter 195.

9. Charles Dickens, *Nicholas Nickleby* (1839), Ch. 46.

10. Charlotte M. Yonge, *The Daisy Chain* (1856), Part 2, Ch. 9.

11. Fielding, op. cit., Book 18, Ch. 9.

12. Anthony Trollope, *The Small House at Allington* (1864), Ch. 13.

13. Susan Ferrier, *Marriage* (1818), Book 2, Ch. 16.

14. W. M. Thackeray, *The Newcomes* (1855), Ch. 21.

15. Mrs Humphry Ward, *Robert Elsmere* (1888), Ch. 7.

16. George Gissing, *Born in Exile* (1892), Part 7, Ch. 2.

17. Dinah Mulock (Craik), *John Halifax, Gentleman* (1857), Ch. 23.

18. Mrs Hugo Reid, *A Plea for Women* (Edinburgh, 1843), p. 28.
19. W. R. Greg, *Literary and Social Judgments* (second edition, London, 1869), p. 101.
20. 'Prostitution', *Westminster Review*, July 1850.
21. Anthony Trollope, *Autobiography*, Ch. 18.
22. W. E. H. Lecky, *History of European Morals* (London, 1869), Vol. 2, p. 299.
23. George Eliot, *Adam Bede* (1859), Ch. 45.
24. George W. and Lucy A. Johnson (eds), *Josephine E. Butler, an Autobiographical Memoir* (London, 1909), p. 31.
25. Raymond Blathwayt, 'A Chat with the Author of "Tess" ', *Black and White*, 27 August 1892.
26. Quoted in J. A. and Olive Banks, *Feminism and Family Planning in Victorian England* (Liverpool, 1964), p. 107.
27. Cobbett, op. cit., p. 199.
28. Sarah Stickney Ellis, *Wives of England* (London, 1843), p. 205.
29. George Meredith, *The Ordeal of Richard Feverel* (1859), Ch. 44.
30. Charlotte Brontë, *Jane Eyre* (1849), Ch. 27.
31. George Eliot, *Middlemarch* (1872), Ch. 81.
32. Wilkie Collins, *No Name* (1862), The First Scene, Ch. 13.
33. Percy Bysshe Shelley, Notes to *Queen Mab* (1813).
34. 'The Anti-Marriage League', *Blackwood's Edinburgh Magazine*, January 1896.
35. Blathwayt, op. cit.
36. Ruskin, op. cit., paragraph 73.
37. 'Silly Novels by Lady Novelists', *Westminster Review*, October 1856.
38. Charles Dickens, *Bleak House* (1853), Ch. 8.
39. See Charlotte M. Yonge, *Womankind* (London, 1876), Ch. 1.
40. Charles Kingsley, *Hypatia* (1853), Ch. 1.
41. Ibid., Ch. 27.
42. Josephine Butler (ed.), *Woman's Work and Woman's Culture* (London, 1869), p. 26.
43. Margaret Dalziel, *Popular Fiction 100 Years Ago* (London, 1957), p. 98.
44. Charles Dickens, *Oliver Twist* (1838), Ch. 29.
45. Dalziel, op. cit., p. 85.
46. Elizabeth Gaskell, *The Life of Charlotte Brontë* (London, 1857), Vol. 2, Ch. 1.
47. Charles Dickens, *Oliver Twist* (1838), Ch. 34.
48. Sarah Stickney Ellis, *Daughters of England* (London, 1852), p. 392.
49. Charlotte M. Yonge, *The Heir of Redclyffe* (1853), Ch. 10.
50. See Marilyn Butler, *Maria Edgeworth* (Oxford, 1972), Appendix C, 'The Post-Publication History of *Belinda* and *Patronage*'.
51. George Eliot, *Mr. Gilfil's Love Story*, Ch. 21, in *Scenes of Clerical Life* (1858).
52. Quoted in Margot Peters, *Unquiet Soul: A Biography of Charlotte Brontë* (London, 1975), p. 371 in 1977 edition.
53. Ellis, *Daughters of England*, op. cit., p. 406.
54. Jane Austen, *Emma* (1816), Ch. 10.
55. W. M. Thackeray, *Vanity Fair* (1848), Ch. 42.
56. Charlotte Brontë, *Shirley* (1849), Ch. 10.
57. Charles Dickens, *Nicholas Nickleby* (1839), Ch. 13.

58. Bumble's famous remark that 'the law is a ass' is provoked by his being told that 'the law supposes that your wife acts under your direction' *(Oliver Twist*, Ch. 51). When a married woman committed one of the smaller crimes in her husband's presence he was held responsible.
59. Anthony Trollope, *Barchester Towers* (1857), Ch. 25.
60. Wilkie Collins, *The New Magdalen* (1873), Ch. 19.
61. E. B. Harrison, 'Mothers and Daughters', *Nineteenth Century*, February 1894.
62. Charlotte M. Yonge, *The Clever Woman of the Family* (1865), Ch. 21.
63. Flora Thompson, *Heatherley*, op. cit.
64. Richard Jefferies, *Restless Human Hearts* (1875), Vol. 1, Ch. 16.
65. Ibid., Vol. 3, Ch. 13.
66. Grant Allen, *The Woman Who Did* (1895), Ch. 15.
67. Ibid., Ch. 24.
68. Ibid., Ch. 3.
69. Thomas Hardy, *Jude the Obscure* (1896), Part 4, Ch. 1.

CHAPTER 3: JANE AUSTEN

1. Margaret Drabble (ed.), *Jane Austen: Lady Susan, The Watsons, Sanditon* (London, 1974), p. 110.
2. R.W. Chapman (ed.), *Jane Austen's Letters* (second edition, Oxford, 1952), Letter 78.1.
3. See *Pride and Prejudice*, Vol. 2, Ch. 6. 'Upon my word', said her ladyship, 'you give your opinion very decidedly for so young a person.'
4. In *Northanger Abbey* (1818), Henry Tilney points out that the dance is 'an emblem of marriage' – 'in both man has the advantage of choice, woman only the power of refusal' (Ch. 10).

CHAPTER 4: SCOTT

1. John Ruskin, *Sesame and Lilies*: Lecture Two, 'Of Queens' Gardens', paragraph 59.
2. 'Men's Women in Fiction', *Westminster Review*, May 1898.
3. George Eliot, *The Mill on the Floss* (1860), Book 5, Ch. 4.

CHAPTER 5: WOMEN WRITERS OF THE EARLY NINETEENTH CENTURY

1. 'The Enfranchisement of Women', *Westminster Review*, July 1851.
2. Maria Edgeworth's date of birth was probably 1768 but is usually given as 1767.
3. Jane Austen, *Northanger Abbey* (1818), Ch. 5.
4. Maria Edgeworth, *Letters for Literary Ladies* (1795). See also her short story 'The Mimic' in *The Parent's Assistant* (1796).
5. James Kinsley and Gary Kelly (eds), 'Mary Wollstonecraft', *Mary and The Wrongs of Woman* (Oxford, 1980), p. 139.

6. Josephine Butler (ed.), *Woman's Work and Woman's Culture* (London, 1869), p. 187.
7. Margaret Sackville, Preface to *The Inheritance* (1929 edition).
8. See Harriet Martineau, *Autobiography* (London, 1877), Vol. 1, pp. 400–2. Despite her support for feminist aims, she disapproved of Mary Wollstonecraft as 'a poor victim of passion'.

CHAPTER 6: DICKENS

1. Kathleen Tillotson (ed.), *The Letters of Charles Dickens*, Vol. 4 (Oxford, 1977), p. 590.
2. Mrs Nickleby does not seriously consider getting married again because of her 'attachment to her children'. Kit in the *Old Curiosity Shop* is indignant at the suggestion that his mother might marry again – 'if the gentleman knew her he wouldn't think of such a thing' (Ch. 20).
3. Agnes feels she has been the 'innocent cause' of her father's deterioration (*David Copperfield* (1850), Ch. 25) and Lucie in *A Tale of Two Cities* (1859) also feels guilty for being happy while her father was in prison.
4. There are traces of the same idea in *Our Mutual Friend* (1865), when Mrs Boffin realises that if she adopts a child 'let it not be a pet or a plaything for me, but a creature to be helped for its own sake'.

CHAPTER 7: THE BRONTËS

1. Phyllis Bentley (ed.), *The Professor, Tales from Angria, etc.* (London, 1954), pp. 383–8.
2. Mrs Ellis reviewed *Jane Eyre* and *Shirley* and found both of them unwomanly. See 'The "Taste" of Charlotte Brontë', *Brontë Society Transactions*, 1962.
3. Bentley, op. cit., pp. 136–59.
4. On the other hand, when Dickens in *Bleak House* shows a wife calling her husband 'my master', he clearly indicates that this is wrong and that she is cruelly treated.
5. J. A. V. Chapple and Arthur Pollard (eds), *The Letters of Mrs Gaskell* (Manchester, 1966), Letter 191.
6. Elizabeth Gaskell, *The Life of Charlotte Brontë* (London, 1857), Vol. 1, Ch. 14.
7. T. J. Wise and J. A. Symington (eds), *The Brontës: Their Lives, Friendships and Correspondence* (Oxford, 1932), Vol. 2, pp. 215–16.
8. Heathcliff has another reason for hating Cathy; he tells her that her father 'cursed you, I dare say, for coming into the world – I did at least' (Ch. 27). This is franker than most nineteenth-century novels, which rarely admit that a father might resent a child whose mother died when it was born. In fact Edgar does not blame his daughter but, more conventionally, values her for being connected to the first Catherine. Heathcliff's attitude shows his habit of punishing women and children for things which they cannot help.

9. Most novelists believed that men would not accept a child who was not their own. *David Copperfield* is an example, and also two novels by Trollope, *The Prime Minister* and *He Knew He Was Right*. Emily Lopez loses her baby as well as her husband, and remarries, but Emily Trevelyan's child survives and she remains a widow. Most of the later nineteenth-century novels accepted that a widow could marry again, but not if she had a living child.

CHAPTER 8: ELIZABETH GASKELL

1. Lord David Cecil, *Early Victorian Novelists* (London, 1934), Ch. 6.
2. See G. H. Lewes's review of *Shirley* (*Edinburgh Review*, January 1850), which drew attention to Currer Bell's childlessness.
3. Quoted in Aina Rubenius, *The Woman Question in Mrs Gaskell's Life and Works* (Upsala, 1950), p. 152.
4. J. A. V. Chapple and Arthur Pollard (eds), *The Letters of Mrs Gaskell* (Manchester, 1966), Letter 276.
5. Ibid., Letter 453.
6. 'Half a Life-Time Ago' and 'Lois the Witch' are reprinted in *Cousin Phillis and Other Tales*, Angus Easson (ed.) (Oxford, 1981).
7. Anthony Trollope, *John Caldigate* (1879), Vol. 3, Ch. 8.
8. Elizabeth Gaskell, *The Life of Charlotte Brontë* (London, 1857), Vol. 2, Ch. 10.
9. 'Modern Novelists – Great and Small', *Blackwood's Edinburgh Magazine*, May 1855.
10. Chapple and Pollard, op. cit., Letter 69.
11. 'Modern Novelists – Great and Small', op. cit.

CHAPTER 9: THE MALE IMAGE OF WOMEN

1. Charlotte Brontë, *Shirley*, Ch. 20.
2. Harriet Martineau, *Autobiography* (London, 1877), Vol. 2, p. 376.
3. Quoted in Elizabeth Gaskell, *The Life of Charlotte Brontë* (London, 1857), Vol. 2, Ch. 10.
4. See Preface, 'The Esmonds of Virginia', in some editions of Thackeray's *Henry Esmond*.
5. Trollope's relationship with his mother is discussed in *The Trollopes: The Chronicle of a Writing Family*, by Lucy Poate Stebbins and Richard Poate Stebbins (London, 1946).
6. Anthony Trollope, *North America* (London, 1862), Vol. 1, Ch. 18.
7. Anthony Trollope, *Autobiography* (London, 1883), Ch. 10.
8. *Can You Forgive Her?* shows signs of having been influenced by a much cruder novel, Mrs Henry Wood's *East Lynne*. Lady Isabel has virtually the same experiences as Alice and Glencora. She leaves her worthy husband for the man she originally wanted to marry, who does not care for her and turns out to be a murderer. When it is too late she is overwhelmed with guilt and longs in vain to have her husband back.

9. In *The Queen of Hearts* (1859). See Robert Ashley, *Wilkie Collins* (London, 1952), p. 55.
10. In *The Tenant of Wildfell Hall* and *John Halifax, Gentleman* the woman actually has to propose to the man because her money prevents him from speaking.
11. 'Sensation Novels', *Blackwood's Edinburgh Magazine*, May 1862.

CHAPTER 10: GEORGE ELIOT

1. Her union with Lewes was another reason for concealing her identity.
2. Gordon S. Haight (ed.), *The George Eliot Letters* (Oxford, 1954–6), Vol. 3, p. 106.
3. Gordon S. Haight, *George Eliot: A Biography* (London, 1968), p. 468.
4. Ibid., p. 549.
5. Quoted in David Carroll (ed.), *George Eliot: The Critical Heritage* (London, 1971), p. 504.
6. *Letters*, op. cit., Vol. 4, p. 390.
7. Ibid., Vol. 4, p. 364. 'Resignation' is spelled 'recognition'.
8. Ibid., Vol. 4, p. 468.
9. Quoted in Haight, *Biography*, op. cit., p. 535.
10. Very few English novels have an alcoholic heroine, and George Eliot's publisher was rather worried about Janet. Flora in *Little Dorrit* drinks brandy, presumably out of frustration.
11. Haight, *Biography*, op. cit., p. 439.
12. *Letters*, op. cit., Vol. 1, p. 268. She was discussing *Jane Eyre*.
13. Ibid., Vol. 2, p. 214.
14. These words appeared in the Finale of the first edition of *Middlemarch* but were removed from subsequent editions.
15. A few novelists did suggest it towards the end of the century, for instance Thomas Hardy and Grant Allen.
16. T. J. Wise and J. A. Symington (eds), *The Brontës: Their Lives, Friendships and Correspondence* (Oxford, 1932), Vol. 3, p. 74.

CHAPTER 11: WOMEN NOVELISTS OF THE LATER NINETEENTH CENTURY

1. Charlotte M. Yonge, *Womankind* (London, 1876), p. 1.
2. Ibid., p. 5.
3. Ibid., Ch. 17.
4. See C. M. Yonge, *The Trial* (London, 1864) and *Pillars of the House* (London, 1873).
5. Yonge, *Womankind*, op. cit., pp. 139 and 234.
6. See three essays in *Blackwood's Edinburgh Magazine* – 'The Laws Concerning Women', April 1856; 'The Condition of Women', February 1858, and 'The Great Unrepresented', September 1866. In her later novels, though, it is very noticeable that only stupid or unpleasant characters attack women's rights.
7. Margaret Oliphant, 'On the Ebb Tide', Preface to *The Ways of Life* (London, 1897).

8.   Mrs Harry Coghill (ed.), *The Autobiography and Letters of Mrs M. O. W. Oliphant* (London, 1899), Ch. 4.
9.   Quoted in Robert Lee Wolff: *Sensational Victorian: The Life and Fiction of Mary Elizabeth Braddon* (New York, 1979), p. 380.
10.   M. E. Braddon, *Ishmael* (London, 1884), Ch. 3.
11.   Quoted in Richard Rive, introduction to Olive Schreiner, *The Story of an African Farm* (Johannesburg, 1975 edition).

CHAPTER 12: THE CHANGING IMAGE OF WOMEN

1.   Henry James, *Washington Square*, Ch. 12.
2.   Anthony Trollope, *North America* (London, 1862), Vol. 1, Ch. 18.
3.   Isabelle in Scott's *Quentin Durward* begs permission to become a nun when she is not allowed to choose her own husband (Ch. 35).
4.   References are to the revised edition, *Muslin* (1915), as the original *Drama in Muslin* is almost unobtainable.
5.   Rosa Bonheur (1822–99) was a famous French painter.
6.   Arthur C. Young (ed.), *The Letters of George Gissing to Eduard Bertz* (London, 1961), p. 171.
7.   Richard Little Purdy and Michael Millgate (eds), *The Collected Letters of Thomas Hardy* (Oxford, 1980), Vol. 2, p. 153.
8.   'The Anti-Marriage League', *Blackwood's Edinburgh Magazine*, January 1896.
9.   The sub-plot of Gissing's *The Unclassed* (1884), which Hardy admired, is very similar to the Arabella plot in *Jude*. For a fuller discussion of Gissing's influence on Hardy see M. Williams, 'Hardy and the Woman Question', Norman Page (ed.), in *Thomas Hardy Annual No. 1* (London, 1982).

Select Bibliography

NINETEENTH-CENTURY TEXTS

Butler, Josephine (ed.), *Woman's Work and Woman's Culture* (London, 1869).
Chapman, Elizabeth Rachel, *Marriage Questions in Modern Fiction* (London, 1897).
Cobbe, Frances Power, *The Duties of Women* (London, 1881).
Coghill, Mrs Harry (ed.), *The Autobiography and Letters of Mrs. M. O. W. Oliphant* (London, 1899). Reissued with an introduction by Q. D. Leavis (Leicester, 1974).
Ellis, Sarah Stickney, *Daughters of England* (London, 1842).
Ellis, Sarah Stickney, *Wives of England* (London, 1843).
Ellis, Sarah Stickney, *Mothers of England* (London, 1843).
Gaskell, Elizabeth Cleghorn, *The Life of Charlotte Brontë* (London, 1857). Reissued in Penguin English Library (1975) ed. Alan Shelston.
Greg, W. R., *Literary and Social Judgments* (London, 1869).
Linton, Eliza Lynn, *The Girl of the Period* (London, 1883).
Martineau, Harriet, *Autobiography* (London, 1877).
Mill, John Stuart, *The Subjection of Women* (London, 1869).
Mulock, Dinah (Mrs Craik), *A Woman's Thoughts about Women* (London, 1858).
Oliphant, Margaret, and others, *Women Novelists of Queen Victoria's Reign: A Book of Appreciations* (London, 1897).
Reid, Mrs Hugo, *A Plea for Women* (Edinburgh, 1843).
Ruskin, John, *Sesame and Lilies* (London, 1865).
Trollope, Anthony, *Autobiography* (London, 1883).
Yonge, Charlotte, *Womankind* (London, 1876).

TWENTIETH-CENTURY TEXTS

Banks, J. A. and Olive, *Feminism and Family Planning in Victorian England* (Liverpool, 1964).
Basch, Françoise, *Relative Creatures: Victorian Women in Society and the Novel, 1837–67* (London, 1974).
Béer, Patricia, *Reader, I Married Him: A Study of the Women Characters of Jane Austen, Charlotte Brontë, Elizabeth Gaskell and George Eliot* (London, 1974).
Bradbrook, F. W., *Jane Austen and her Predecessors* (Cambridge, 1966).
Calder, Jenni, *Women and Marriage in Victorian Fiction* (London, 1976).
Colby, Vineta, *The Singular Anomaly: Women Novelists of the Nineteenth Century* (Princeton, 1970).
Colby, Vineta, *Yesterday's Women: Domestic Realism in the English Novel* (Princeton, 1974).

Cruse, Amy, *The Victorians and their Books* (London, 1935).

Cunningham, Gail, *The New Woman and the Victorian Novel* (London, 1978).

Cunnington, C. Willett, *Feminine Attitudes in the Nineteenth Century* (London, 1935).

Dalziel, Margaret, *Popular Fiction 100 Years Ago* (London, 1957).

Dunbar, Janet, *The Early Victorian Woman (1837-57)* (London, 1953).

Ewbank, Inga-Stina, *Their Proper Sphere: A Study of the Brontë Sisters as Early Victorian Female Novelists* (London, 1966).

Fernando, Lloyd, *'New Women' in the Late Victorian Novel* (Pennsylvania, 1977).

Gilbert, Sandra M. and Gubar, Susan, *The Madwoman in the Attic – the Woman Writer and the Nineteenth-Century Literary Imagination* (Yale, 1979).

Hewitt, Margaret, *Wives and Mothers in Victorian Industry* (London, 1958).

Houghton, Walter, *The Victorian Frame of Mind* (Yale, 1957).

Millett, Kate, *Sexual Politics* (London, 1971).

Moore, Katharine, *Victorian Wives* (London, 1974).

Neff, Wanda F., *Victorian Working Women, A Historical and Literary Study of Women in British Industries and Professions, 1832-50* (London, 1929).

Pinchbeck, Ivy, *Women Workers and the Industrial Revolution, 1750-1850* (London, 1930).

Rees, Barbara, *The Victorian Lady* (London, 1977).

Reiss, Erna, *The Rights and Duties of Englishwomen* (Manchester, 1934).

Rosa, Matthew Whiting, *The Silver-Fork School: Novels of Fashion Preceding Vanity Fair* (New York, 1936).

Rubenius, Aina, *The Woman Question in Mrs Gaskell's Life and Works* (Upsala, 1950).

Showalter, Elaine, *A Literature of Their Own: British Woman Novelists from Brontë to Lessing* (Princeton, 1977).

Stebbins, Lucy Poate, *A Victorian Album: Some Lady Novelists of the Period* (London, 1946).

Strachey, Ray, *The Cause: A Short History of the Woman's Movement in Great Britain* (London, 1928).

Thomson, Patricia, *The Victorian Heroine, A Changing Ideal 1837-73* (London, 1956).

Tillotson, Kathleen, *Novels of the Eighteen-Forties* (Oxford, 1954).

Vicinus, Martha (ed.), *Suffer and be still: Women in the Victorian Age* (Indiana, 1972).

Index